Symphonic Metamorphoses

Subjectivity and Alienation
in Mahler's Re-Cycled Songs

RAYMOND KNAPP

Wesleyan University Press
Middletown, Connecticut

Published by Wesleyan University Press,
Middletown, CT 06459
© 2003 by Raymond Knapp
All rights reserved

Printed in the United States of America
Designed by Chris Crochetière
Set in Adobe Garamond type by B. Williams & Associates

The following works are used by generous permission:

Raymond Knapp, "Suffering Children: Perspectives on
Innocence and Vulnerablility in Mahler's Fourth Symphony,"
Nineteenth-Century Music 22, no. 3 (1999), by permission of
the University of California Press. © 1999 by The Regents of
the University of California. The article was substantially
revised for this book.

Raymond Knapp and Francesca Draughon, "Mahler and the
Crisis of Jewish Identity," *Echo: A Music-Centered Journal* 3,
no. 2 (2001). © University of California, Los Angeles. The
article drew on portions of the book, most prominently
chapters 3 and 7.

Arnold Böcklin, *Selbstbildnis mit fiedelndem Tod* (1872).
Reproduced by permission of the Staatliche Museen zu
Berlin—Preußischer Kulturbesitz. Nationalgalerie

Arnold Böcklin, *Der Heilige Antonius Predigt den Fischen*
(1892). © 2002 Kunsthaus Zurich. All rights reserved. Used
with permission.

CIP data appear at the end of the book

To Dashiell

Contents

List of Figures

preface

In this book I attempt to come to terms with one of the more puzzling features of Mahler's music: his extensive reuse of his own folklike songs in his early symphonies—a practice central to his first four symphonies, but which simply disappears thereafter. The project grew out of my earlier article on the first two movements of Mahler's Fourth Symphony, which I have appended here, Mahler-like (that is, with changed title and a somewhat more elaborate mounting), as a kind of finale or coda. It gives me some satisfaction to see that the resulting structure seems to mimic, even if fortuitously, some of the music it addresses, reproducing a trajectory that all Mahlerians will quickly recognize: a finale written earlier as a stand-alone piece, occupying the seventh position in a series that could have ended—albeit with much different effect—after the sixth.[1] Following this line a step further, I offer (but of course, following Mahler's practice, will eventually withdraw) the following "program" for the book: "Mahler marches in—What the Child told him—What the fishes told him—What the spirit of the forest told him—What the *fahrenden Gesellen* told him—What Music told him—What the World told him."

As in my article, my aim here is to help bridge a chasm that has opened up in Mahler studies between those who are concerned mainly to delineate Mahler's musical sophistication and the "advanced" logic of his musical discourse, and those who valorize its seemingly illogical twists and turns and its eclectic mixing of styles and forms, typically finding therein a suggestive but murky analog to either his life or his view of the world. These opposing poles are now deeply entrenched, with roots in both Mahler's own time and in the time of his American renaissance, beginning in the 1960s. The attempt to claim Mahler as a modernist, to see him as a sophisticated, high-art master of musical complexities, finds support both in Schoenberg's early tributes (offered in part out of gratitude for Mahler's sometimes theatrical support for his own pioneering work)[2] and in the esoteric musical modernism still in the ascendant during the 1960s, when Mahler was being "rediscovered" and placed before the public by Leonard Bernstein and others.[3] The extreme emphasis that this element has placed on Mahler's musical innovations has had at least one overt aim, which is to counter the long-standing discomfort occasioned by Mahler's stylistic eclecticism. Thus, the (mostly implicit) argument runs, we must not be misled by either Mahler's seeming affection for the banal or his apparent disregard for the traditional musical unities of form and style; if we look past the distracting surface discontinuities, Mahler's music is, after all and above all else, both extremely complex and tightly unified. On the other hand, those troubling surface discontinuities, along with sheer length and other tokens of extremity, are precisely what mattered to many who rushed to embrace Mahler's symphonies in the 1960s and later, taking them in with a generalized response of "Oh, wow!" and affecting a sense of mystified awe well in keeping with the variety of transcendentalisms and drug-based experiences, and the general veneration for epiphanous insight, that were then prevalent. And this kind of emphasis, too, had much historical grounding, not only in the chaotic turmoil of fin-de-siècle Vienna, with its unstable mix of high modernism and eventually catastrophic reactionary politics,[4] but also, and especially early on, in the mystifications offered up as explanations in his widow's memoirs.[5] Thus, the 1960s found, in Arnold Schoenberg and in Alma Mahler, precisely the poles that still dominate explications of Mahler's music.

Yet it is entirely possible to integrate these poles, to relate a detailed engagement with musical detail to a complex, historically situated expressive environment, and to establish Mahler's musical sophistication (if such is one's goal) through a grounded analysis of his music's expressive surface. For this, too, we may look to the Mahler renaissance of the 1960s for at least inspiration, and to the insightful interpretive readings of Theodor Adorno that have helped shape our collective understanding of Mahler's musical personality.[6] But because of the sometimes sketchy, even cryptic nature of Adorno's writings on Mahler, they have mainly fed the "oh, wow" component of Mahler research, so that if we are to extend his interpretive direction, we must begin by connecting his dots. If we take the trouble to do so, that is, if we take his insights, extending them and grounding them more elaborately in discussions of Mahler's music, we might achieve—as I hope this book demonstrates—a clearer sense of how Mahler operated as a composer than if we leave the musical detail largely unexamined, or construe either his principal agenda or his central contribution to music history as developing a progressively complex, essentially abstract musical language. The proliferation of Mahler studies over the past three decades has increased the difficulty of such an integration, but it must be attempted. One should not be led to feel, as one so often is by this growing body of work, that analytical treatments of Mahler and other, less technical discussions are confronting entirely different repertories, for which not only different, but actually incompatible notions of meaning and value hold sway.

In this book, I discuss the expressive import of both musical detail and larger organization and try to leave open, as much as possible, the ambiguities that Mahler himself left open. My approach, like Mahler's and partly in imitation thereof, departs deliberately from the conventions of both "elevated" musico-theoretical discourse and a more "accessible" engagement with what would conventionally be termed the programmatic dimension of Mahler's music. Some will find this disturbing and inadequate. Others will find that it offers far more than if I had hewed more closely to either side of the divide. If—like Mahler—I am able to provoke both types of response, I believe I will have succeeded in my larger project to produce a more suitably Mahlerian treatment of Mahler than what is currently available.

In the central chapters of the book, I consider several instances of Mahler's symphonic re-cycling of his songs, tracing in each case an ongoing process of refinement of the meanings he found within the particular musical constructs involved. I consider these instances in nearly reverse chronological order, since as it happens (and as will matter quite a bit to the larger discussion), Mahler's direct changes to and manipulations of his source material become progressively less extensive across the four symphonies. *Chapter 1* ("Mahler Marches In") details the problem presented by Mahler's odd self-dependence, discusses a number of promising yet inadequate explanations, and likens his procedures to his equally notorious (yet much more admired) approach to instrumentation. In *chapter 2* ("What the Child Told Him") I examine the case of "Das himmlische Leben," which eventually became the finale of his Fourth Symphony, but for which Mahler earlier envisioned at least three other settings, each appropriate, if in different ways, to his virtually unchanged musical setting of the *Wunderhorn* poem. I make an analogy here to the filmic technique of montage as theorized by Lev Kuleshov and others in the early twentieth century, in which an image is juxtaposed with other images to manipulate and bring out latent meanings. Within Mahler's similar manipulation of contexture, in which the particulars of form and setting interact to highlight specific meanings inherent in the song, "Das himmlische Leben" evolves from a fairly uncomplicated stand-alone lullaby through a consoling view of child-death by starvation and a childly (that is, child-oriented) projection of heaven that underscores our own inadequate view of heaven ("through a glass, darkly") even as it simultaneously queries our complicity in Christ's death, to a final, more complex setting in which new meanings combine with those of all three earlier settings.

Chapter 3 ("What the Fishes Told Him") traces Mahler's re-elaboration and extension of "Des Antonius von Padua Fischpredigt" in the scherzo of his Second Symphony. For the scherzo, Mahler refashions the song's narrative of alienation into a more devastating but similarly dysfunctional narrative. Here, Mahler treats "absolute music" as if it were a musical topic, imparting a sense of alienation through projecting a grotesquely self-contained, self-sustaining, and seemingly self-absorbed musical activity that registers as obsessively oblivious to an independently established vantage point. The discussion takes as its point of departure the related musical effects in the award-winning 1976 film *Sybil* and engages with a variety of discussions of the movement's program(s). *Chapter 4* ("What the spirit of the forest told him") discusses the parallel, yet substantially different adaptation for the scherzo of the Third Symphony, a movement that has two poetic sources: the *Wunderhorn* poem "Ablösung im Sommer" as set by Mahler, and Nikolaus Lenau's poem "Der Postillion." The subjectivities of the alienated parties in this case—the animating spirit of the forest and the intruding presence of man—are more equally balanced, so that the denouement is more richly ambivalent than in the "Fischpredigt" scherzo. In both scherzos, Mahler problematizes absolute music in two ways, in order to prepare for the introduction of the human voice at the beginning of the following movement: first, by enacting a "song without words" in which we perceive (whether we know the song source or not) that something is missing, and second, by treating "absolute music" negatively as a topic, as an emblem of disconnected activity for which words can offer a clarifying corrective.

In *chapter 5* ("What the *fahrenden Gesellen* Told Him") I consider the much different case of the First Symphony, in which Mahler borrows substantially from two of the songs in his early cycle *Lieder eines fahrenden Gesellen,* in order to fashion a much different narrative, one considerably more optimistic than that of the cycle. In his First Symphony, Mahler stands in a quite different relationship to his (self-)borrowed materials; in these adaptations, to a much larger extent than in his next three symphonies, context alters the significance of the borrowed material. A central concern in this chapter is Mahler's preoccupation, especially in these early symphonies, with the task of representing his own subjectivity in a public genre, a task that entailed both projecting that self in some objective detail and creating a prevailing sense of "I." As detailed further in *chapter 6*, these two components of the task were not always equally possible—they were, in fact, somewhat at odds with each other. This circumstance was reflected in Mahler's choice of source material, which ranged from the objectifying perspectives of the *Wunderhorn* songs that he developed into the scherzos of his Second and Third Symphonies to the overtly subjective perspective of his *Lieder eines fahrenden Gesellen*, evoked twice in the First Symphony. To some extent, Mahler's reliance on his own folklike songs, whether originally in an objective or a subjective mode, entails projecting the self simply by invoking the traditions and ethos of the German *Lied* as it was developed in the nineteenth century. Thus, the mere act of his reusing these songs carries with it a more immediate sense of the personal than could his relying solely on newly composed "symphonic" material, which tends inevitably toward objectivity. In this respect, "Das himmlische Leben" provides a particularly suitable conclusion to Mahler's symphonic tetralogy, with its intriguing mix of subjective and objective perspectives. Also important to the process of re-cycling his songs as central components of these symphonies is Mahler's intricate, ongoing response to the material he reuses (hence, "What Music Told Him"), which imparts to that material a sense, oddly, of a specifically *musical* subjectivity. It is as if it were the music's self, now conceived separately from his own, that Mahler is responding to and that therefore may be seen to drive the process.

Chapter 7 ("What the World Told Him") serves as an epilogue for the study. In it I reconsider Mahler's evocation of childhood in his Fourth Symphony in a variety of contexts ranging from the musical and the programmatic to the personal and cultural. Musical details in this work, which completes Mahler's tetralogy of symphonies by cycling back, implicitly, to the "Days of Youth" that launched his First Symphony, point to a deeply nostalgic yet also deeply troubling view of childhood as a time of extreme vulnerability. The idealized innocence that forms the core of Mahler's treatment reflects a number of cultural archetypes of childhood ranging from unsexualized purity to the erotically charged. For Mahler, the depiction of a specifically Christian childhood is colored profoundly as well by his own experiences, both within a family of assimilating German Jews in Bohemia riddled with child-death (although he was not yet a father himself, he had for some years acted as the effective head of his birth family), and within a culture that proved itself capable of resurrecting and taking seriously the ancient "blood libel," which accused Jews of the ritual murder of Christian children.

My experience of writing this book has been colored by another, much more disturbing parallel to Mahler. In the spring of 1999, the article version of the final chapter appeared in *Nineteenth-Century Music*. Titled "Suffering Children," it discussed along the way Mahler's troubling dance with the specter of child-death, which culminated in the death of his beloved daughter Marie some years after writing his Fourth Symphony and the *Kindertotenlieder*. Earlier in 1999, while the article was still in press, my sixteen-year-old son Dashiell was diagnosed with acute lymphocytic leukemia. I briefly considered, for superstitious reasons, the possibility of changing the title of my article, but chose not to. I began writing this book shortly after he was diagnosed, and indeed wrote most of it away from home, during the many months of 1999 I spent on the East Coast in order to be near Dashiell while he struggled against this insidious disease and gamely endured a course of treatments that seemed at times even more devastating than the disease itself. I have no doubt that some of my observations about Mahler's music, particularly concerning his projection of a subjective self in the midst of a chaotic and often threatening environment, were colored by this experience. In early January 2000, I completed my draft of the book in Virginia while Dashiell was preparing to undergo what would be a last-ditch effort to save him: a bone-marrow transplant, with his sister Rachel as donor. Although the transplant initially seemed successful, the leukemia returned at the end of March, and Dashiell died in early April.

Because of these circumstances, I must offer my thanks for this book first and foremost to those many who made such a tremendous positive difference during the year of Dashiell's struggle: To everyone at the Grafton School, but especially Kim and Tony Sanders, John and Natasha Roberts, Agnes Horwich, Morgan Reed, Rick Sjostrom, Stephanie Hostler, Stephanie Digman, Barbara Varney, and Michelle Grubb, who gave Dashiell the chance to reach true maturity during his last year of life. To Johanna Elliott and Jack Hencke of Blacksburg High School, who continued their valuable support throughout. To the medical staff at the University of Virginia Medical Center in Charlottesville, particularly Kimberly Dunsmore, Rajesh Malik, Pedro de Alarcon, Peter Waldron, Taylor Troischt, Margy Sennett, Barb Blow, and Karin Eshleman, whose directness and respect for Dashiell mattered almost as much as their expertise. To his teachers in Charlottesville, particularly Marta Gilliam, Ginger Ellingwood, and Susan Weir, who from the first made such an effort to enrich Dashiell's experiences in the hospital. To Jennifer LoCasale and Mellicent Blythe, who so often and with so little fuss simply made things happen. To Andrew Chancey, Elizabeth Smiley, and Mary Kirwan at the Ronald McDonald House of Charlottesville for their kindness and support. To everyone at the Primary Care Clinic, who was always so welcoming and encouraging, but especially Pat Cobb, Gwen Porterfield, Janet Lombardi, Jackie Shifflett, Betty Criser, and Beth Jackson. To the nurses and support staff at Seven West, the Bone Marrow Transplant Unit, the PICU, and above all Seven Central, whose tremendous contributions can neither be measured nor adequately described, and whose teamwork I slight by singling out individuals to thank particularly: Bobby Casteen and Kristin Adams, whose gentle firmness first helped Dashiell to accept the rigors of his treatment; Jennifer Thomas, who took a leadership role in Dashiell's management without suppressing his need to express himself; Mary Ann Kelly, Melissa White, and Stacey Meyer, who hooked up so well with Dashiell's unusual sense of humor; Kathy Sullivan, Amy Knox, Cathy Sides, Kim Leake, Susan Payne, Susan Boston, Tina Robinson, Sandy Dean, Anne Stadelmaier, Julie Walraven, Barb Sauer, Marilyn Poling, Cheryl Ostrowski, Jennie Sowers, Marilu Dixon, Lisa Hunter, Colleen Williams, Lauren Calder, Patricia Casper, Marc Gilgannon, and Jody Smith, whose deep sense of caring always came through; and the many who took the time to foster a special relationship with Dashiell—Flo Taylor, Nita Giroux, Mel Horton, Anne-Bee van Meter, Barb Hettinger, Teresa Williams, Charlie Stratos, Eliza Haskins, Sydney Reed, and most especially Sheila Williams, who was Dashiell's link to the world and major supplier of eggs. To my teaching colleagues who supported me and made my frequent absences from the University of California, Los Angeles, possible, especially Susan McClary, Mitchell Morris, Elisabeth LeGuin, Rob Walser, Francesca Draughon, Nadya Zimmerman, Stephen Baur, Jacqueline Warwick, Maria Cizmic, Cecilia Sun, Mel Surdin, and Hui-ling Lui. And to those closest to me and to Dashiell, who helped tighten his circle of support, Rachel and Genevieve, Daniel and Rebecca, Ahuva, Robert and Judy, Dashiell's grandparents, and above all his mother, Shoshana.

Thanks also go, of course, to those who had a more direct role in the book: To Susan McClary, Mitchell Morris, Francesca Draughon, Larry Kramer, Richard Leppert, Tamara Levitz, and Mark Martin, who not only inspired my work on the book and contributed materially to it, but also provided sympathetic readings and useful comments. To the editors, designers, and readers associated with Wesleyan University Press, especially Darwin Campa (for designing a cover Dashiell would have loved), Chris Crochetière, Leonora Gibson, Barbara Norton, Leslie Starr, and Suzanna Tamminen. To Kate Bartel, Durrell Bowman, Jonathan Greenberg, Gordon Haramaki, Jon Hofferman, René Jagnow, James Kennaway, Rachel Knapp, Andrea Loselle, Dan Sallitt, Erica Scheinberg, Eva Sobolevski, Griffin Woodworth, and Judy Yantis, for their helpful contributions along the way. To the brave undergraduates in Music History 127E at UCLA—neophyte Mahlerians all—whose discussions helped launch this study. And to Ahuva Braverman for much more than I can say or ever repay.

But my main thanks—and the dedication of this book—go to my son Dashiell, whom I miss terribly, but who taught me, especially during his last year, so much about what it means to be a good human being: about raw courage, about the special grace of acceptance, about hope, about candor, about maintaining perspective and a sense of humor, and above all about connecting with people and truly making a difference in their lives. In all these ways, he was tenaciously himself to the end, and he lives on within those whose lives and souls he touched. And because he has mattered so much in the writing of it, I believe he will also live on in the pages of this book, and be reawakened in the hearts and minds of those who read it.

Note Regarding
Musical References

References to Mahler's scores in this book will specify measure numbers for his songs and for the Fourth Symphony. For his first three symphonies, where measure numbers are not readily available, I will adopt the following notational shorthand unless the passage in question lies near the beginning of its movement:

r4.1–4   (rehearsal number 4, mm. 1–4)

r5.6–r6   (the sixth measure of rehearsal number 5 to rehearsal number 6)

References in the examples to symphonic movements will be of the following form:

Symphony No. 3, third movement

In most cases, I have provided timings as well as references to Mahler's scores. Depending on the recording you are using, and especially for longer movements, actual timings may differ substantially from those I have provided here. For the symphonies, where this consideration is most important, I have based my timings on a fairly inexpensive and reliably good set of recordings. All timings given in this book have been derived from the following recordings, listed here by the referenced work(s):

Ablösung im Sommer:

Thomas Hampson and Geoffrey Parsons. *Lieder aus Des Knaben Wunderhorn: Mahler, Brahms, Mendelssohn, Strauss, Schumann, Loewe, Schönberg, Weber, Zemlinsky.* Teldec Classics 244 923-2 ZK, 1989.

Des Antonius von Padua Fischpredigt and Das irdische Leben:
Christa Ludwig, Walter Berry, Leonard Bernstein, and the New York Philharmonic. *Mahler: Des Knaben Wunderhorn.* Sony Classical SMK 47590, 1993 (reissue from 1969).

Lieder eines fahrenden Gesellen:
Janet Baker, John Barbirolli, and the Hallé Orchestra. *Mahler: Kindertotenlieder, 5 Rückertlieder, and Lieder eines fahrenden Gesellen.* EMI Classics 7243 5 66981 2 3, 1999 (reissues from 1968 and 1970).

Symphonies 1–4:
Georg Solti with the Chicago Symphony Orchestra. *Mahler: The Symphonies.* Second Symphony with Isobel Buchanan, Mira Zakai and the Chicago Symphony Chorus. Third Symphony with Helga Dernesch, Women of the Chicago Symphony Chorus, and the Glen Ellyn Children's Chorus. Fourth Symphony with Kiri Te Kanawa. Decca 430 804-2, 1991 (reissues from 1981, 1983, and 1984).

Chapter 1

Songs into Symphonies: Problems and Rationales

Mahler's conspicuous tendency to depend on preexisting songs for much of the material in his first four symphonies has generated more puzzlement and disapproval than approbation. The very designation that has frequently been attached to these works, "song-symphony," defines his early symphonies as something other than true symphonies. It also implies that it was an ill-considered presumption on his part to depend as heavily as he did on the relative inconsequence of a folklike song idiom to carry the weight of a large-scale symphony.[1] Even if Mahler's cultural status has risen during the last decades to the point that his peculiar self-dependency is no longer questioned as regularly as it once was, we have yet to hear either a cogent defense or a convincing rationale for what seems to have been a decidedly odd compositional crutch; we are left instead with only a long, rather awkward critical silence, punctuated occasionally by dim echoes of early, mostly ineffectual apologists.[2] Meanwhile, Mahler's re-cyclings continue to disconcert in two ways: not only does his early reliance on song, whether as an external source or, more directly, as an expressive medium, point to what many still regard as an inadequate symphonic sensibility, but his substantial reuse of preexisting material suggests as well a certain laziness, or perhaps a failure of creative imagination. Taken separately, each of these criticisms seems to undermine Mahler's pretensions as a major symphonist; together, they can seem irretrievably damning.

Mahler's procedures have been well documented and seem to speak for themselves. With apparent disregard for symphonic propriety, he shuffled orchestral versions of his songs into and back out of his first four symphonies, sometimes reusing whole songs as symphonic movements, at other times recasting song material into purely instrumental form as part of a larger movement or, more locally, simply alluding to known songs (usually but not always his own). Of the nineteen individual movements in these symphonies, thirteen either involve vocal forces or derive in part from song:

four are outright songs, four others quote significantly and substantially from either his *Lieder eines fahrenden Gesellen* or his *Des Knaben Wunderhorn* settings,[3] and the remaining five either incorporate newly composed vocal music or refer to specific vocal music through allusion.

Although not all of these instances will be of equal interest here—for reasons that will become clear shortly—it is useful to document the range and extent of his practice, both to establish a larger context for those examples we will consider more closely, and to document the extent of a practice that virtually disappears from Mahler's symphonies after the turn of the century.[4] Figure 1-1 lists, hierarchically, Mahler's most obvious derivations from song in his first four symphonies, ranging from those movements that are orchestral songs outright (far left), those that quote extensively from his songs within an instrumental setting (middle left), those that either pursue a more conventional approach to allusion or present a vocal setting too elaborate to be described as song (middle right), and those song-inspired movements that were once included but were eventually dropped from the plan of a particular symphony (far right).

Figure 1-1. Song derivations in Mahler's first four symphonies

Key:	orchestral songs
	instrumental treatment of songs
	song allusions / more elaborate vocal settings
	dropped songs or other recyclings
	[brackets indicate newly composed vocal settings]

Symphony No. 1:	i	instrumental treatment of "Ging heut' Morgen übers Feld" from *Lieder eines fahrenden Gesellen*
		allusion to "Waldmärchen," discarded first movement of his *Das klagende Lied* (recalled in iv)[5]
	(ii)	dropped: "Blumine," a movement derived from the now-lost *Der Trompeter von Säkkingen*[6]
	ii	allusion to his "Hans und Grethe"
	iii	extended minor-mode instrumental treatment of "Bruder Martin" (folk song)
		instrumental treatment of "Die zwei blauen Augen" (final section) from *Lieder eines fahrenden Gesellen*
	iv	triumphant chorale derived in part from the "Hallelujah" Chorus in Handel's *Messiah*

Symphony No. 2: i	allusion to *Dies irae* (recalled in v)
iii	instrumental treatment of "Des Antonius von Padua Fischpredigt" from *Des knaben Wunderhorn*
iv	"Urlicht" (from *Des knaben Wunderhorn*)
v	[setting of Klopstock's "Aufersteh'n," with additional verses by Mahler]
Symphony No. 3: i	allusion to "Burschenschaftslied" (folk song)
iii	instrumental treatment of "Ablösung im Sommer" from *Des knaben Wunderhorn*
iv	["O Mensch! Gib acht!" (from Nietzsche's *Also sprach Zarathustra*)]
v	["Es sungen drei Engel" (from *Des knaben Wunderhorn*)]
(vii)	dropped: "Das himmlische Leben" from *Des knaben Wunderhorn* (see 4.iv)
Symphony No. 4: i	allusion to "Ablösung im Sommer" from *Des knaben Wunderhorn*
(ii)	dropped: "Das irdische Leben" from *Des knaben Wunderhorn*; "Es sungen drei Engel" (see 3.v) was apparently also considered for this symphony
iv	"Das himmlische Leben" (from *Des knaben Wunderhorn*)

Explanations for Mahler's practice might reasonably begin from a number of starting points. The introduction of vocal music into nineteenth-century symphonies inevitably recalls the finale of Beethoven's Ninth Symphony, a connection reinforced in Mahler, on the one hand, by the fact that all of the vocal movements listed above involve either a folklike style or serve as dramatic culmination (both true of Beethoven's finale) and, on the other, by Wagner's arguments regarding Beethoven's Ninth Symphony and, more generally, the relationship between symphonic and folk music.[7] Moreover, the practice of basing symphonic music directly on folk styles, independent of Wagner's arguments, has a long history going back at least to Haydn. By Mahler's time, this practice had been enlisted as support for two interrelated ideological functions that had become associated with the symphony, enhancing its ability to serve as a high-art vehicle for either democratic expression or nationalist sentiment (if, indeed, these two are really distinguishable from each other in the late nineteenth century; for example, one easily finds a nationalist agenda in what is most often taken as an expression of democratic feeling in the finale of Beethoven's Ninth).[8] And we may find, with Carl Dahlhaus, that Mahler's practice helps him to achieve a kind of musical realism: by grounding his symphonic discourse in the "found objects" of (mainly imitation) folksong, Mahler is able to suggest a direct connection to the natural, and thus to nature itself.[9] And, more concretely, Mahler's use of particular song sources in his symphonies may provide substantial clues to his intended meanings.

Yet none of these explanatory approaches has led to a real feeling of comfort about Mahler's practice. To begin with—and surely this is the core of our discomfort—Mahler does not really conform to any of the Beethovenian, Wagnerian, democratic, and/or nationalistic models he seems to evoke. Beethoven's use of folklike song in the Ninth Symphony is integrated much more fully than Mahler's, serving initially as culmination to more extended thematic processes and eventually extending itself to vocal idioms that overtly displace the manufactured folk idiom of his *Freudenthema*.[10] Wagner's arguments against absolute music and appropriated folk idioms are often directly at odds with what Mahler seems to be trying to achieve. And both democratic and nationalistic aims appear either alien to Mahler's highly individualized, even autobiographical approach to the symphony at this point in his career, or difficult to parse, given his own profound sense of alienation, as (eventually) a converted Jew from the provinces—specifically, from a region whose national status would long remain in question—working within an increasingly anti-Semitic Viennese culture whose claims of German nationalist preeminence were themselves rapidly being usurped by a pan-Germanism (for which Mahler had strong sympathies) centered considerably to the north.[11]

Moreover, despite the intrinsic appeal and partial success of Dahlhaus's correlation of folk and nature, and of the notion of cross-referencing Mahler's symphonies with their song sources, these approaches, too, fail to account for a great deal in Mahler's practice. Although Mahler does, on occasion, represent nature through re-cycled folklike song, there are many counterinstances, either of folk idioms being used for quite different purposes—in the finale of the Fourth Symphony, for example, or in the penultimate movement of the Third—or of nature being evoked through other means, as in much of the opening movement of the Third Symphony, which, even if we take its march idioms as folklike in Dahlhaus's sense, derives its expressive power more from how those idioms are deployed than from the idioms themselves.

Nor does cross-referencing help as much as we might like it to, for it raises at least as many questions about musical meaning as it seems to answer. Thus, are we to hear the exuberant nature images in the opening movement of the First Symphony "straight" (as most commentators do) or ironically, as they are obviously meant in "Ging heut' Morgen übers Feld"? What does a futile sermon to fishes have to do with the situation Mahler has described as part of his explanation for the middle movement of the Second Symphony, the familiar romantic trope of a ballroom dance being observed in despair from outside? And how do the allegorical obscurities of "Ablösung im Sommer"—a reactive account of the death of a cuckoo from the perspective of an unspecified first-person plural—extend into the more elaborate, and apparently quite different, scenario of the "Forest" movement in the Third Symphony?

These added questions have, for the most part, ready answers. In "Ging heut' Morgen übers Feld," it is the words, along with the established perspective of disappointed love, that cast an ironic cloud over the exuberant musical depiction of nature; without the words, and in a different setting, the cloud evaporates.[12] In "Des Antonius von Padua Fischpredigt," it is not the fish so much as their pointless, endlessly circling motion, and a sense of estrangement between that circling motion and the perspective of the un-heeded preacher, that are depicted by the music in Mahler's setting (respectively, the accompaniment and the pedantic contrast offered by the vocal setting); these may easily be mapped to the circling motions of dancers at a ball, especially as seen from the estranged, unsympathetic perspective of their solitary observer. And we may surmise from the music of "Ablösung im Sommer"—even without the clarifying title Mahler provides for the symphonic movement based on this song, "What the Creatures of the Forest Tell Me"—that the "we" in the song is the animating spirit of the forest, perhaps even merging the wind in the trees with the bustling activity and sounds of its creatures; it is this animating force that Mahler borrows for the third movement of his Third Symphony.

But new questions quickly arise to replace any we might find (temporary) answers for; indeed, we may expect such questions to swirl forever around these settings, which share so much music yet do not seem to mean quite the same thing by that music. And the questions are quite distracting, imposing themselves (even when left unasked) in the unceasing intrusions of one setting and its associations on another, making it impossible for us to hear any of this music "on its own terms." It is scarcely surprising that early audiences, deprived of the illusion that they were being presented with newly minted "absolute" music, demanded explanations from Mahler; nor is it surprising that such explanations as he provided proved to be woefully inadequate for many. Surely, it would have been better and more honest for Mahler to have composed new music for his symphonies. Why could he not have assumed the responsibility of fashioning new musical representations—of exuberant nature, of mindlessly circling motion, of a collectively animated forest—and saved us all a lot of trouble?

The question is not one of avoided responsibility, of course. How could Mahler ever be seen this way, with his ceaseless worrying over the details of his scores and the meticulous control he exercised as a conductor? Rather, the question concerns what, precisely, is being represented within the networks of meaning that are created and/or modified when music is transplanted from one setting to another. Part of such a network is a pattern of mutual reinforcement and negation, which bears some resemblance to the complex patterns that emerge when similar sound waves, but with slightly different wavelengths, interact with each other. Thus, whatever meanings might be projected within one setting will generate patterns of intensification and attenuation when brought to bear on another, depending on how and to what extent the settings reinforce some meanings and negate others.

The sense of distraction we feel in Mahler's early symphonies regarding the mutual interference of multiple settings of the same music has much in common with the frequently distracting effect of Mahler's instrumentation, which so often seems designed to defamiliarize the familiar.[13] Both his unusual approach to instrumentation and his song-based re-cyclings pull our awareness level to a point somewhat outside our inclination to accept his music at face value—that is, as what its more conventional features project it to be—while at the same time intensifying some aspects of the more normalized experience that is being denied. This effect of pulling us in two directions at once, the one more abstract, the other more particularized, in both cases leads us to question the straightforward communicative power of music, its capacity to present in immediately felt, absolute terms. Moreover, we have this experience whether we are more heavily invested in absolute or programmatic explanations of what music actually communicates, for the literalness of programmatic explanations becomes, through Mahler's procedures, as problematic as the premise that the meaning of music is basically abstract and self-referential.

Mahler's ambivalence about providing programs for his symphonies echoes the twofold reception of music for many, if not most listeners. On the one hand, music suggests (or, at least, easily aligns itself with) specific, seemingly extramusical meanings, and this suggestive capacity can be enhanced and given focus by the addition of words, whether directly, as in the text of a song, or indirectly, through titles or other separate explanations. On the other hand, music does seem to possess its own logic, and a significant part of its effect on us stems from our ability to sense and follow its musical logic; indeed, without this dimension, its status as music, or at least its comprehensibility, would seem to be in jeopardy. Mahler's music heightens the paradox that these two frames of reference often seem in direct conflict with each other, but with neither having the capacity to effectively eclipse the other. If it is this central paradox that motivates Mahler's own ambivalence, it also lends extraordinary and surprising power to those moments—whether created through denaturalized instrumentation, re-cyclings, or some other means—when he challenges, simultaneously, our ability to engage cleanly with either side of the dichotomous structure of musical meaning.

Despite the similar results of such procedures, the disorienting effect of Mahler's instrumentation has considerably more admirers than his re-cyclings of musical material.[14] Part of the reason for this undoubtedly stems from a confused sense of Mahler's own attitudes toward composing, at least as expressed to Natalie Bauer-Lechner: "Composing is like playing with bricks, continually making new buildings from the same old stones. But the stones have lain there since one's youth, which is the only time for gathering and hoarding them."[15] Mahler's description may easily (if not necessarily) be taken to imply that his "bricks" have substantial meaningful content, so that composition, for him, involves manipulating not only musical units, but units of associative meaning as well. It is tempting, and initially plausible, to extend this interpretation with the presumption that Mahler is referring expressly to his re-cyclings; this is, for example, how Constantin Floros understands Mahler's comment.[16] Yet the analogy works poorly when extended to the larger units of Mahler's more prominent re-cyclings. Rather, Mahler's analogy to "bricks" seems more likely to refer to meaningful musical gestures and/or procedures—in Mahler, one thinks of topics such as funeral-march rhythms, cuckoos, and the like, or of his unusual manipulations of standard forms—which might be construed as building blocks in a way similar to how words and plot devices might be understood as the building blocks of a novel.[17] Moreover, Mahler's allusion to youth does not fit the often fairly contemporary multiple settings that he elaborates or envisions for his re-cyclings, although we may take this reference metaphorically, as to an earlier stage of musical development, when these "bricks" originally took shape, rather than specifically to Mahler's own childhood.

The paths by which Mahler arrived at some of his more unusual orchestrations reveal an interplay of tensions involving, on the one hand, an apparent desire to mask somewhat the clarity of a basic, often generic gesture and, on the other, a desire to underscore (through exaggeration) a specific attribute of that gesture. While these conflict on one level—the one seeks to obfuscate associative meaning, the other to heighten it—their coordination is often quite close, since the latter provides an eminently practical means to accomplish the former. But substantial risk remains; because exaggeration calls into question the ready comprehension of the basic gesture, the strategy must be employed so as not to wholly mask that gesture. In a typical application, Mahler starts with a fairly straightforward setting and layers a disorienting effect on his original conception; thus, in the introduction to the first movement of the First Symphony (to cite a particularly well-documented case), the opening string harmonics were a later inspiration, and the substitution of clarinets for muted horns in the first fanfare a still later one.

The latter example illustrates Mahler's management of the conflict particularly well. In his revisions to the opening sequence of emergent fanfares, originally given only to horns and trumpets, Mahler dramatizes a dialogic component that is otherwise somewhat concealed within a strong sense that there is, in this extended passage, essentially only one thing taking shape. Thus, in reworking the opening, Mahler gave the first of the three main fanfares to *pianissimo* low-lying clarinets climbing into their weaker midrange (0:44), which are answered by offstage trumpets ("in the far distance"; 1:28), the horns being withheld until they can assume their distinctive lyrical identity (1:59). In the individual fanfares, as well, the dialogic aspect is heightened, with the distinctive sound of the bass clarinet responding to the clarinets in the first fanfare and, in the second, an onstage, deeper-voiced trumpet (in B♭ rather than F) responding to the offstage trumpets. From being a fairly insignificant supporting element within a more homogenous development, instrumental exchanges are thus brought into the foreground, where they largely eclipse the clarifying harmonic profile (♭VI–V–I). Moreover, allowing the first fanfare to emerge from the instruments that have already been introduced heightens the effect of the trumpets' later intrusive addition to those instruments (with the second fanfare), and gives their entrance the added function of clarifying that we are, indeed, to understand the clarinet figure as a precursor of the brass fanfare, a more primitive or elemental—

perhaps even fetal—version of the familiar topic. Indeed, fanfare itself acquires an added significance in Mahler's revised instrumentation, developing from a fairly generic vehicle for formal articulation and the introduction of new instruments—that is, from a well-worn topic—into a gesture that more vividly recalls its roots as a practical device for communicating over distance. Thus, from the first bars of his First Symphony, Mahler uses his instruments regressively, to suggest the ancestral meanings of more conventional topics, a temporal regression that serves him as well here as later, suggesting temporal distance, even timelessness, in addition to the physical distance that he specifies in his performing instructions.

The conventional view that Mahler's orchestration is primarily one of refinement,[18] so that he arrives gradually at an instrumental realization of a conception that has been present in his mind from the beginning, seems inadequate to describe this process. Rather, the process must be understood in two phases. In one, Mahler creates a coherent musical environment. In the other, he responds creatively to that environment, making explicit some of its implications and masking its derivation from the conventional. It may well be this two-part process that Mahler is indirectly referring to in an oft-quoted remark to Bauer-Lechner: "The inception and creation of a work are mystical from beginning to end; unconsciously, as if in the grip of command from outside oneself one is compelled to create something whose origin one can scarcely comprehend afterwards."[19] Part of what he is describing is an odd sense of estrangement from a completed musical structure, such that his later orchestral manipulations of these structures would inevitably seem a matter more of composing anew with found objects than of extending the original process.

Mahler's re-cyclings follow a similar two-phase process, in which he responds to his original musical setting as he transplants it to a different context. Indeed, the decision to transplant is itself his first critical response to his original creation, and it often seems as if that response is no longer simply that of its creator, but of a third party responding to someone else's creation or, at least, to something that has acquired an independent life of its own and is no longer fully answerable to its creator. Mahler's frequent expressions of awe at his own creations are particularly revealing in this light, for they show precisely the kind of estrangement one often senses between him and his re-cycled materials. It is useful, therefore, to view his re-cyclings from two quite different perspectives, asking not only how and what they represent, but also what it is that Mahler is responding to in the original when he decides to reuse its material and proceeds to elaborate a new con-texture—a new context and/or form, often involving a newly conceived in-frastructure of meaningful relationships—for that material.

In view of this duality, we must also consider where Mahler's own subjec-tivity lies within these works and, more specifically, within these re-cyclings. If, as he describes, he composes "as if in the grip of command from outside oneself," what then becomes of our familiar notion, encouraged over and over by Mahler himself, that his music is deeply autobiographical? Spe-cifically, he claims during this period that each new symphony completes his musical presentation of his own life's story, that the Second takes up and continues the story of the hero introduced in the First and that, together, they presented "everything that I have experienced and endured,"[20] that the Third completed his "Passion trilogy,"[21] and that the Fourth combines with its three predecessors "to create a definite unified tetralogy."[22] Yet, the more we see him in an estranged relationship to his materials (whether through instrumentation or re-cyclings), the more suspect his almost automatic merg-ing, of self and artistic creation, becomes.[23]

In order to delineate the ways in which these perspectives—contexture, selfhood, and what I term the autonomy of musical presence—operate in Mahler's re-cyclings, I will in the following chapters examine some of the more elaborate of them as case studies. This is necessary in part because al-though each case is unique, when considered together, they reveal important aspects of the complicated interpenetration of these perspectives as they pro-duce musical meaning, with application not only to misunderstood aspects of Mahler's music, but also to the creation and reception of musical mean-ing more generally. To begin, in chapter 2 I will consider the movement that boasts the most volatility of projected uses, "Das himmlische Leben," which ultimately takes its place as the finale to the Fourth Symphony and, by an extension encouraged by Mahler, to this entire group of works. The issue will be one of musical montage, of how different meanings might be sug-gested or emphasized for a musical construct through its contextual place-ment. Next, I will take up Mahler's most elaborate recomposings of songs into purely instrumental contexts, beginning with the scherzo movements from the Second and Third Symphonies (chapters 3 and 4, respectively) and continuing with the first and third movements of the First Symphony (chapter 5). It is with regard to these three cases that critical issues will be raised regarding what musical meanings are transferred within Mahler's re-cyclings; what meanings are uncovered, lost, or created "in transit"; and what actually bears these meanings from one context to another. Overall, then, I progress in fairly straightforward manner from the least to most complex revisions of actual borrowed material. The fact that this order virtually reverses chronology is an apparent paradox that I will consider at the end of this part of the study, in chapter 6, when I will return once again to the vexing question of Mahler's troubled relationship to his musical material, as it plays out in his symphonic re-cyclings.

I have sought to ground the following discussions of Mahler's music as fully as possible in both musical analysis and careful consideration of previous important discussions of the music and its context. I hope thus to enter into an ongoing conversation with other studies of these works, not to displace those studies with something pretending to more authority. But I do claim a particular kind of authority too often lacking in discussions of music (and deliberately so): an *authority* deriving specifically from the conspicuous presence of an *author* whose observations are grounded both in a personalized perspective and in careful assessment of the observations and readings already on offer. No readings can (or should try to) represent the whole truth of the full range of possible musical experiences a particular work or body of work might provide. While my readings constitute no more and no less than a part of the truth, that part is particularly valuable because it brings us into intimate involvement with musical gesture in a way that illuminates both the experience at hand and wider issues of musical meaning.

I begin the next two chapters with discussions referent to another medium: film. In chapter 2 I draw upon theoretical discussions dating back to the "silent" era, and in chapter 3 I describe and interpret particularly vivid representations of music within a single film. Film offers a richly fertile starting point for discussing Mahler because of significant parallels between his music and the filmic world, parallels that mark each apart from similar experiences that had come before. Thus, unlike most earlier forms of enacted narratives, film allows, and eventually even seems to demand, the kind of discontinuities that mark Mahler's symphonic music to an extent that was then unprecedented; fragmentation, eclecticism, dramatic juxtaposition, and the difficulty of maintaining a sense of continuity across surface disjunctures, are only some of the features the two media share.[24] Yet, while early filmmakers working in the generation just after Mahler's death were brought to these things through practical necessity, since they were learning to work within a developing medium that required this kind of manipulative engagement with their materials, Mahler's medium was scarcely new and seemed, in fact, to proscribe such manipulations. Nor could he be thought here to be learning directly from developments in filmmaking. Although film in Mahler's later years was developing into a medium that might have held some fascination for him, I am working here with only his early works; the specific filmic techniques I discuss were developed only after he died. If Mahler's music is necessarily like film, that necessity has deeper roots than technology and may be traced most convincingly to issues of cultural estrangement. It is the latter that plays out vividly in the example I use at the beginning of chapter 3, and it should not be surprising that film, in coordination with music, provides an ideal vehicle for its representation. More abstractly, as Mahler attempted within symphonic discourse to introduce disruptive elements and techniques analogous to those then being developed in other arts, the nature of his medium brought him close to the concerns, and to some of the solutions, of filmmakers a generation later.

Chapter 2

Montage and Contexture

"Das himmlische Leben" and the
Third and Fourth Symphonies

The Kuleshov Effect

In a famous experiment during the silent-film era, inspired in part by the cutting techniques of D. W. Griffith's landmark films from the 1910s, Lev Kuleshov (1899–1970) demonstrated that cinematic images were perceived differently according to context. In the first surviving account of the experiment, V. I. Pudovkin (1893–1953) reports that when the same image of a "neutral" face of a well-known actor (Ivan Mozhukhin) was placed separately before images of soup, a dead woman in a coffin, and a little girl playing, so that it would appear that he was looking at each in turn, audiences "raved about the acting of the artist," noting "the heavy pensiveness of his mood over the forgotten soup," "the deep sorrow with which he looked on the dead woman," and "the happy smile with which he surveyed the girl at play."[1] This experiment, which vividly demonstrated what is now usually referred to as "associational montage" or the "Kuleshov effect," helped launch the Soviet "montage" movement, in which the technique of juxtaposing images is used to manipulate an audience into relating the images to each other either in an imagined "real time" or through abstract association; in its extreme form, a filmmaker could juxtapose completely unrelated images in order to enforce an abstract analogy or provide unspoken commentary (e.g., cutting from a police officer to a butcher in Sergei Eisenstein's *Strike* [1924]).

The experiment Pudovkin recounts has often been taken, somewhat naively, as a demonstration of the unlimited power of montage to falsify reality, to make an audience believe something that has no basis in fact.[2] What matters most in this interpretation is the neutrality of the facial image, so that whatever meanings a viewer ascribes to the face will stem more or less entirely from its juxtaposition with other images. Yet, the idea that the face of a famous actor could be considered "neutral" is patently untenable. Not only would the targeted audience already be empathetically invested in the actor Mozhukhin through familiarity, but the very qualities that helped make him famous—having an "expressive" face that audiences would tend to care about—would also most likely guide even an unfamiliar audience to the kind of responses Pudovkin describes. The nature of the problem becomes clear if we imagine a much different "neutral" face, instead of Mozhukhin's, being used in the experiment and project how easily quite different interpretations might thus have been elicited. An uninflected but less warmly expressive face might have seemed, for example, less pensive than simply hungry before the soup, less grief-stricken than coldly indifferent to the dead woman, and, perhaps, less happy than sinister regarding the child, who would be seen to play in blissful unawareness of a potentially menacing presence. Kuleshov's experiment works because it balances neutrality and definite character within its starting condition, presenting an image that can seem neutral in one context (among other images of the same actor's face) yet tremendously charged in another (e.g., among assorted images of various actors' faces or, more globally, among random filmed images). While it may seem that, for each component of the experiment, the subsequent image "writes" itself onto the blank slate of Mozhukhin's relatively neutral expression, the interaction of the two images within each combination is much more complex than that.

But the seeming lack of subtlety in most descriptions of the experiment is mostly a construct of reception. Thus, early on, Sergei Eisenstein (1898–1948), without attacking the experiment directly, derided Kuleshov's theorizing about montage for its naiveté, so that he could erect a more elaborate theoretical structure of his own devising (one that was in fact not so very different from Kuleshov's).[3] More generally, many who refer to the experiment have been especially eager to emphasize the overriding power of montage to manipulate audiences and thus to determine the true content of film. Historical circumstance has played a large part in this, especially with regard to the latter emphasis. Postrevolutionary Russians (and many others, if more for cultural than political reasons) felt impelled to establish that making films was, indeed, an art, rather than a means of recording the art of others, and so were led to emphasize above all else the most obvious signature control exercised by the filmmaker.[4] Moreover, with the advent of synchronized sound, many were afraid that the enforced artificiality of silent film—for them the key to film's claim to the status of high art—would be swamped by the more persuasive illusion of realism provided by sound film.

If, as André Bazin later claimed, "montage . . . did not give us the event; it alluded to it,"[5] then sound film risked losing this dimension altogether by seeming more directly to "give us the event." For some, silent film was art precisely because montage, with its deliberate artificialities, was its central technique. In order to serve as the central emblem of this position, the Kuleshov effect was reduced, monolithically, to its simplest meanings.

If, however, we understand Kuleshov's experiment—which was but one among many similar experiments—not as an attempt to be scientific, but rather as a pragmatic attempt to create a convincing "artificial landscape" (Kuleshov's own term) by combining images that were created independently,[6] then we may see an interesting parallel to some of Mahler's re-cyclings. The parallel becomes more vivid when we consider the admonition Pudovkin delivers at the end of his account:

> But the combination of various pieces [of film] in one or another order is not sufficient. It is necessary to be able to control and manipulate the length of these pieces, because the combination of pieces of varying length is effective in the same way as the combination of sounds of various length in music, by creating the rhythm of the film and by means of their varying effect on the audience. Quick, short pieces rouse excitement, while long pieces have a soothing effect.[7]

What is striking about this passage—aside from its intriguing (if simplistic) analogy to music—is the emphasis Pudovkin places on manipulating the "neutral" image whose meanings are most central to a particular application of the technique (i.e., Mozhukhin's face), remembering that, however much control the other images exert, it is the perceived emotions of the actor that will seem to matter most, which we will perceive as if they were inherent in his image alone. If we construe a transplanted song or movement in Mahler as analogous to the manipulated piece of film in Kuleshov's experiment—to Mozhukhin's face, as it were—then we may also construe Mahler's project, in each case, as creating an "artificial landscape" for his recycled music, one that will seem to impart new meanings to the transplant. Typically, Mahler will substantially rework the music he re-cycles, in line with Pudovkin's admonition that it is not the juxtaposition of images alone that creates meaning. In one particular case, however, Mahler envisioned and carried out, by stages, a musical transplantation in such a way that the stringent conditions of Kuleshov's experiment came very close to being met (aside from the chimerical "neutrality" of the image, that is).

"Das himmlische Leben" is heard today primarily in only one context: as the finale of Mahler's Fourth Symphony. Inevitably, our understanding of the song *qua* song is colored by our only available experience of it. Yet, there are at least three other contexts for which Mahler at one time or another intended it: simply as a song, as the second of a pair of songs (preceded by "Das irdische Leben"), and as the finale of his Third Symphony.[8] All too easily, even when we mentally consider these other settings, we transplant our experience of the song from the Fourth Symphony relatively intact, forgetting that the Kuleshov effect—no less a factor for music than for film—would have produced a quite different experience for us in each of the abandoned alternative settings. Even in the setting Mahler eventually chose for the song, its meanings are richly ambiguous: does it project the sensibility of a child directly, or of an adult singing a lullaby? Are its strange yet comforting images to be taken at face value, or are they meant as a projection against present realities? And are these (projected) comforts to be actualized through sleep or through death?[9] Given such ambiguities even within a single setting, we might well speculate concerning the even more divergent ways the song would have presented within Mahler's three earlier plans. To this end, we must reimagine the song independent of its eventual setting in the Fourth Symphony.

As a stand-alone song, "Das himmlische Leben" projects in the simplest of terms an untroubled scenario involving a healthy child and an adult fully capable of transporting the child into a comforting sleep. Given the foregrounded presence of a solo female voice, the song by itself is basically a lullaby, a sung narrative with a comforting tone and trajectory, whose success as a lullaby is signaled unmistakably with the change of key from G to E major near the end. Coupled with "Das irdische Leben" (in which a child dies of starvation), on the other hand, the "lullaby" is radically transformed, projecting no less vividly than its companion *Lied* a parallel chronicle of a child's mortal hunger (hence its images of abundant food) and the inadequacies of its adult caretakers to provide for its wants. We know with this pairing that the child dies, and that it is the adult audience, not the child, who finds comfort in the song's revelation that its needs will be met in heaven. However, when the song is restored to its position of finale to the Third Symphony, its childly perspective becomes its most vivid characteristic. Newly titled "What the Child Tells Me," the song here projects its relative textural simplicity against the contrapuntal complexities of the immediately preceding sixth movement ("What Love Tells Me"); moreover, this juxtaposition replays the displacement of an adult perspective with a more naive sensibility, as enacted just before in the fifth movement ("What the Angels Tell Me").[10] Serving as the concluding movement of the Third Symphony, then, the song cloaks the mysteries of the afterlife—the final link in the chain of Mahler's "happy science"—behind a veil of relative innocence, reminding us that from the perspective of an achieved heaven, our adult projections of paradise will seem as naive as do the child's from ours; implicitly, the combination of song and setting recalls the familiar words of St. Paul: "When I was a child, I spake as a child, I understood as a child, I thought as a child: but when I became a man, I put away childish things. For now we see through a glass, darkly; but then face to face: now I know in part; but then shall I know even as also I am known" (I Corinthians 13:11–12; King James version).

Lullaby

Of these earlier settings, the straightforward, stand-alone lullaby is probably the hardest for us to reimagine, partly because its later associations have taught us to hear considerably more than that in it, and also because its favored position as finale, particularly in the two symphonic settings, has encouraged us to probe deeper, to hear something we can take as more significant and weighty than mere lullaby. But if we had not been thus pushed to discover its disturbing ambiguities, we might have found in it little more than a delightful, narrative-based interaction between mother and child at bedtime. Adeptly, and with a sureness evidently borne of long experience, the singer playfully intermixes the seeds of pleasant dreams with recurring strains of soothing lullaby (see Figure 2-1).

As shown, the song has the structure of a bedside story, filled with amusing fancy and shaped in a diminishing spiral so as to lead naturally to quietude and sleep. The first cycle takes us the farthest afield, with the slaughtering of lamb and oxen made graphically amusing by the exaggerated orchestral mimicking of their protests. This is also the most elaborate cycle in formal terms, with internal closure provided for the second, more adventuresome vocal span ("E" in Figure 2-1) through a return to the chorale/sleigh-bells structural unit ("C–D"), thus articulating a balanced twofold

Figure 2-1. Translation and formal layout of "Das himmlische Leben" (as lullaby)

(A1)   Wir genießen die himmlischen Freuden,   We delight in heavenly joys,
        D'rum tun wir das Irdische meiden.   And therefore avoid the earthly.
        Kein weltlich' Getümmel   No worldly turmoil
        Hört man nicht im Himmel!   One does (not) hear in Heaven!
        Lebt Alles in sanftester Ruh'!   Everything lives in the gentlest quiet!

(B1)   Wir führen ein englisches Leben!   We lead an angelic life!
        Sind dennoch ganz lustig daneben!   Are at the same time still quite merry!
        Wir tanzen und springen,   We dance and spring,
        Wir hüpfen und singen,   We jump and sing,
(C1)   Sankt Peter im Himmel sieht zu!   Saint Peter in Heaven looks on!

(D1—sleigh bells, extended interlude)

(E)   Johannes das Lämmlein auslasset!   John lets the little lamb out!
        Der Metzger Herodes drauf passet!   Butcher Herod watches for it!
        Wir führen ein geduldig's,   We lead a patient,
        Unschuldig's, geduldig's,   Innocent, patient,
        Ein liebliches Lämmlein zu Tod!   A dear little lamb to death!

        Sanct Lucas den Ochsen tät schlachten,   Saint Luke would slaughter the ox,
        Ohn' einig's Bedenken und Achten,   Without any doubts and qualms,
        Der Wein kost' kein Heller   Wine costs not a farthing
        Im himmlischen Keller,   In the heavenly cellar,
(C2)   Die Englein, die bakken das Brot.   Angels bake the bread.

(D2—sleigh bells)

(A2)   Gut' Kräuter von allerhand Arten,   Good vegetables of all kinds,
        Die wachsen im himmlischen Garten!   Grow in the heavenly garden!
        Gut' Spargel, Fisolen   Good asparagus, beans
        Und was wir nur wollen!   And whatever we might wish!
        Ganze Schüsseln voll sind uns bereit!   Completely full platters are ready for us!

        Gut' Äpfel, gut' Birn' und gut' Trauben!   Good apples, good pears and good grapes!
        Die Gärtner, die Alles erlauben!   The gardeners allow them all!
(B2)   Willst Rehbock, willst Hasen,   If (you) want a deer, or want a hare,
        Auf offener Straßen   In the open street
        Sie laufen herbei!   They run here!

        Sollt ein Festtag etwa kommen,   Should a holiday arrive,
        Alle Fische gleich mit Freuden   All fish will joyfully come swimming!
            angeschwommen!
        Dort läuft schon Sankt Peter   Already Saint Peter runs there
        Mit Netz und mit Köder   With net and with bait
        Zum himmlischen Weiher hinein.   Into the heavenly fishpond.

(C3)	Sankt Martha die Köchin muß sein!	Saint Martha must be the cook!
(D3—sleigh bells)		
(A3)	Kein Musik ist ja nicht auf Erden,	No music exists on earth,
	Die unsrer verglichen kann werden.	That could be compared to ours.
	Elftausend Jungfrauen	Eleven thousand maidens
	Zu tanzen sich trauen!	Venture to dance!
	Sankt Ursula selbst dazu lacht!	Even Saint Ursula herself laughs!
	Cäcilia mit ihren Verwandten	Cecilia with her relatives
	Sind treffliche Hofmusikanten!	Are splendid court musicians!
	Die englischen Stimmen	The angelic voices
	Ermuntern die Sinnen!	Enliven the senses!
(C4)	Daß Alles für Freuden erwacht.	So that everything awakens to joy.

0:33	A1: Initial soothing music in G, including orchestral introduction (text: heavenly peace)
1:07	B1 (m. 25): Quickening pace, G moving towards e (text: play of the angels)
1:28	C1 (m. 36): Chorale phrase 1 (modally inflected e): St. Peter looks on —
1:43	D1 (m. 40): Wild sleigh-bells interlude in e (17 bars): sense of adventure
2:17	E (m. 57): Continued adventure, in e (text: slaughtering of lamb and ox, accompanied by orchestral bleats and bellows)
2:47	C2 (m. 72): Chorale phrase 2 (cadence to e): Angels bake bread —
3:03	D2 (m. 76): Less extreme sleigh-bells interlude (only 4 bars)
3:12	A2 (m. 80): In G, no introduction, modulating and accelerating (text: heavenly garden)
3:44	B2 (m. 95): In e, modulating further (text: deer, rabbits, and fish)
4:03	C3 (m. 106): Chorale phrases 1 and 2 (in d): Saint Martha as cook —
4:38	D3 (m. 115): Return to wilder sleigh-bells interlude, but fading (7 bars)
4:59	A3 (m. 122): E major, with more elaborate introduction (text: heavenly music)
7:23	C4 (m. 169): Simpler, cadential chorale phrase: Joyful awakening

structure with chorale phrases concluding each half. The second cycle (beginning in m. 80) abbreviates this structure to about half the length. Although somewhat less stable harmonically, it leaves out the more adventuresome second span ("E"), substitutes friendly images of deer, rabbits, and fish—all of which run free yet are readily available, eagerly offering themselves as a meal for the hungry—for the heavily symbolic animals of the previous span. It also retreats in its projected activities from slaughter to what amounts to mere gathering. Moreover, the closure provided by the chorale is this time more complete, extended from four to nine measures and combining the two earlier phrases into an extended culminating statement. The third and final span (beginning in m. 122) moves with a firm finality to E major, replays more overtly the full structure of the soothing opening section ("A," complete with orchestral introduction), and leaves out entirely the more disruptive sections of the previous cycles ("B," "D," and "E"). Moreover, the shift to E major carries with it two qualities that enhance its projection of a successful lullaby. First, the added indication of *geheimnisvoll* (*misterioso*), along with new textures that are more "dreamlike" than the opening, an extremely soft dynamic that rises to *forte* only to set the laughter of St. Ursula (m. 151), and an abrupt textual shift from bodily concerns (food) to spiritual concerns (music), delineates an affective shift from "comforting" to "comforted"; our perspective seems to transfer here from mother to child. And second, the harmonic shift and reconfigured textures suggest the peculiar, fuzzy heaviness of child sleep; we sense that by the end, the child is fully asleep, and that the mother is singing the final chorale phrase in benediction, as much for herself as for the child.

As sung by a woman to a child, the exaggerated images of "Das himmlische Leben" represent precisely the kind of play that typifies the familiar activity of an adult amusing a child. The profundities of the chorale phrases are made arch by their progressively less profound texts, descending from "Sankt Peter im Himmel sieht zu!" and "Die Englein, die backen das Brot" to "Sankt Martha die Köchin muß sein!" However appropriate a chorale setting may be for St. Peter and bread—the latter a traditional object of sanctification—treating the cook to the more exaggerated gravity of the extended chorale, replete with textual repetition, retrospectively returns bread to its more prosaic function as food, with the mockery of exaggerated gravity serving to revoke the previous blessing. The joke of casting Herod as butcher ("Der Metzger Herodes drauf passet!") is surely not above the heads of most children, nor is St. Peter's eager reversion to his former profession of fisherman ("Dort läuft schon Sankt Peter / Mit Netz und mit Köder / Zum himmlischen Weiher hinein"). Even if the irony of St. Luke slaughtering his ox for food, or of St. Ursula being provoked to laughter, is above the heads of most children (and, today, many adults), the spirit of fun that infects the whole, with its absurdist modeling of dreamlike irrationality, makes the ethos of these references, if not their specific referential content, accessible to all (cf. Lewis Carroll's sometimes sophisticated political satire).[11] Moreover, what matters throughout the song is not so much the specific content of each saintly image, but rather the activity of domesticating these rather scary religious figures, so that the child might laugh at what must normally be either taken seriously or even feared; *this* is why Herod fits so easily, even essentially, into the picture, and why the irony of St. Ursula's laughter is only obliquely marked as anomalous, through a briefly swelling melisma.

"Das irdische Leben"

"Mutter, ach Mutter, es hungert mich!	"Mother, oh mother, I am hungry!
Gib mir Brot, sonst sterbe ich."	Give me bread, or I will die!"
"Warte nur! Warte nur, mein liebes Kind!	"Only wait! Only wait, my dear child!
Morgen wollen wir ernten geschwind!"	Promptly tomorrow we will harvest!"
Und als das Korn geerntet war,	And as the grain was harvested,
Rief das Kind noch immerdar:	The child cried without ceasing:
"Mutter, ach Mutter, es hungert mich!	"Mother, oh mother, I am hungry!
Gib mir Brot, sonst sterbe ich!"	Give me bread, or I will die!"
"Warte nur! Warte nur, mein liebes Kind!	"Only wait! Only wait, my dear child!
Morgen wollen wir dreschen geschwind!"	Promptly tomorrow we will thresh!"
Und als das Korn gedroschen war,	And as the grain was threshed,
Rief das Kind noch immerdar:	The child cried without ceasing:
"Mutter, ach Mutter, es hungert mich!	"Mother, oh mother, I am hungry!
Gib mir Brot, sonst sterbe ich!"	Give me bread, or I will die!"
"Warte nur! Warte nur, mein liebes Kind!	"Only wait! Only wait, my dear child!
Morgen wollen wir bakken geschwind!"	Promptly tomorrow we will bake!"
Und als das Brot gebakken war,	And as the bread was baking,
Lag das Kind auf der Totenbahr!	The child lay dead upon the bier!

In Mahler's projected coupling of "Das irdische Leben" with "Das himmlische Leben," which persisted as a possibility in his planning even after he had completed the Third Symphony,[12] the latter song's emphasis shifts somewhat from its soothing frame to the urgencies of the "adventuresome" music launched by the sleigh bells. Enforcing this shift in emphasis is, above all, the close relationship between the sleigh-bells motive and the background churning of "Das irdische Leben," representing at once the fatalistic inevitability of the child's death and the methodically oblivious machinery of food production (thus the tempo indication in the original version, for piano and voice: *doch in stetig gleicher Bewegung*), which is ultimately too slow to save the child. When the songs are placed together, the sleigh bells offer an amplified echo of the opening and prevailing accompaniment of the previous song, intensified and made to seem more urgent, converting what is a departure within the song itself into a forceful return within the larger span. The musical parallel, as shown in Example 1, is pointed and specific: in each case,

eighth-note reiterations of the open fifth on the dominant are inflected by chromatic neighbor-notes, above in "Das himmlische Leben," and below in "Das irdische Leben." Because of this musical assonance, the textual assonance between the songs is drawn out as well, so that "Das himmlische Leben" seems to be less about heaven than about food preparation, presenting a feverish parody of the mechanical obsessions of "Das irdische Leben,"[13] inspired, presumably, by the delirium of prolonged hunger.

The endings to the two songs will also register as parallel. We are prepared for the death of the child in "Das irdische Leben" by a purely orchestral passage nearly three times the length of any previous interlude (mm. 95–110; 1:48), by a decrease in tempo for the first time in the movement (*Etwas zögernd*, m. 111; 2:06), and by an additional four-bar interlude that in-

terrupts the thematic return itself (m. 115–118; 2:12). In "Das himmlische Leben," too, by far the longest orchestral interlude occurs before the E major
vocal entry (mm. 112–141; 4:59); again, there is a substantial decrease in
tempo, marking an arrival in this case in E major. What these arrivals mean
is explicit in "Das irdische Leben" and implicit here: the child has clearly
moved beyond its need for food at this point. The text in "Das himmlische
Leben" confirms this, turning from the appointment of St. Martha as cook
to a description of heavenly music. In this pairing of the two *Lieder*, then,
the change of key at the end of "Das himmlische Leben" may be seen more
clearly to "change the subject" (not to mention the venue), presenting an escape from the foregoing preoccupation with food that can be interpreted
only as death. As if to forestall doubt in this matter, a thematic link between
the two songs emerges briefly at this point: with the first hint of the minor
mode since the shift to E major in m. 122, Mahler introduces a melodic motive (m. 148) directly evocative of the opening cry of the child in "Das ir-

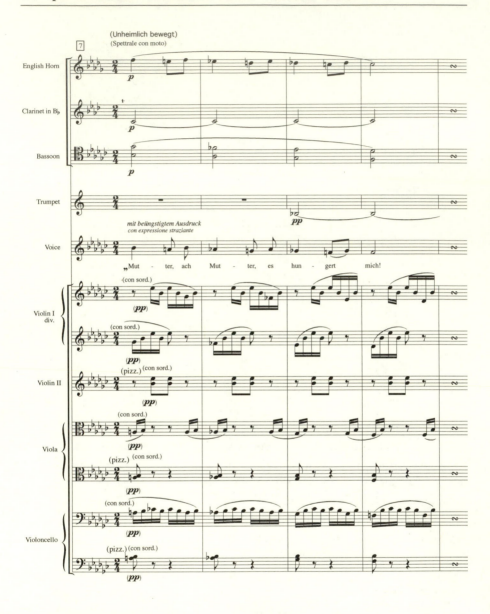

dische Leben"; as shown in Example 2a and 2b, each phrase descends chromatically from $\hat{5}$ in a distinctive dactylic rhythm. (Since he wrote "Das irdische Leben" after "Das himmlische Leben," Mahler must have composed
the child's cry out of the chorale, so as to set up this moment late in "Das
himmlische Leben" as a revelatory recollection.) While the text here offers

no further connection, the dactylic rhythm and the portentous descent also recall the chorale phrases heard earlier in the song, reinforcing the implicit connection between the child's pleas in "Das irdische Leben" and the prayerful chorale phrases of "Das himmlische Leben." The latter two of these phrases resonate particularly well with the focal point of the drama in "Das irdische Leben": the preparation of bread (see Example 2c). Thus, the recurring chorale phrases of "Das himmlische Leben," which projected an elaborate mockery of religiosity in the lullaby version of the song, are recast as an ominous echo of want; conversely, the child's pleas in "Das irdische Leben" may be heard, in retrospect, as chromatic, anguished versions of these chorales. Significantly, no food is actually consumed in "Das himmlische Leben"; we are instead tantalized by a continuous series of descriptions of how food *might* be produced.

The overturning of significance detailed here is by no means total; "Das himmlische Leben" retains, even in this coupling, the basic quality of a lullaby. Thus, in this musical version of associational montage, we can recog-

nize Mozhukhin's facial expression as fundamentally unchanged even if at the same time another dimension, a hidden care behind its basic geniality, is forcefully revealed to us. But "Das himmlische Leben" offers its companion considerably more than the simple contrast described in the parallel titles Mahler gives the two songs.[14] Thus, "Das himmlische Leben," obliquely replaying much of the earthly trauma of "Das irdische Leben," provides an integrated narrative completion to its predecessor in order to suggest, through its heavenly alternative, a more gratifying conclusion. Conversely, "Das irdische Leben" gives its successor a depth of associative meaning it could scarcely have managed as a stand-alone lullaby, allowing a disturbing subtext to emerge within "Das himmlische Leben" itself that unfolds a stark counterpoint to the song's otherwise comforting sanguinities.

The Third Symphony

If the distinctive chorale phrases of "Das himmlische Leben" serve as a fairly subtle link between the two songs in the pairing with "Das irdische Leben," they provide the focus for a nearly pervasive motivic presence in the Third Symphony, where dactylic rhythms abound in a variety of guises and settings, often implying either a folk-based vocality or actual chorale.[16] The most overt anticipation of these chorale phrases—indeed, of "Das himmlische Leben" in general—occurs with the penitent's pleas in the fifth movement ("Es sungen drei Engel"), where the entire two-part chorale phrase is used to set the core of the entreaty: "Ich hab' übertreten die zehn Gebot.

Figure 2-2. Formal layout of Mahler's Third Symphony, with program, text, and translations[15]

Part 1

   I. Kräftig. Entschieden (Pan Awakes—Summer Marches In)

Part 2

  II. Tempo di Menuetto. Sehr mässig (What the Flowers in the Meadow Tell Me)

 III. Comodo. Scherzando. Ohne Hast (What the Creatures in the Forest Tell Me)

 IV. Sehr langsam. Misterioso. Durchaus **ppp** (What Night [or Man] Tells Me)

O Mensch! O Mensch!	O man! O man!
Gib Acht! Gib Acht!	Take heed! Take heed!
Was spricht die tiefe Mitternacht?	What says the deep midnight?
Ich schlief! Ich schlief!	"I slept! I slept!
Aus tiefem Traum bin ich erwacht!	I am awoken from a deep dream!
Die Welt ist tief!	The world is deep!
Und tiefer, als der Tag gedacht!	And deeper than the day imagined!
O Mensch! O Mensch!	O man! O man!
Tief! Tief!	Deep! Deep!
Tief ist ihr Weh! Tief ist ihr Weh!	Deep is your woe! Deep is your woe!
Lust, Lust tiefer noch als Herzeleid!	Joy, joy deeper still than heartache!
Weh spricht: Vergeh! Weh spricht: Vergeh!	Woe says: Begone! Woe says: Begone!
Doch alle Lust will Ewigkeit!	But all joy desires eternity!
Will tiefe, tiefe Ewigkeit.	Desires deep, deep eternity."

                 (Nietzsche, adapted by Mahler)

  V. Lustig im Tempo und keck im Ausdruck (What the angels tell me)

—Bimm bamm—	—Ding dong—
Es sungen drei Engel einen süssen Gesang;	Three angels were singing a sweet song;
Mit Freuden es selig in dem Himmel klang,	It rang blissfully with joy in heaven,
Sie jauchzten fröhlich auch dabei,	They also happily shouted for joy,
Dass Petrus sei von Sünden frei.	That Peter was free from sin.
Und als der Herr Jesus zu Tische sass,	And as Lord Jesus sat at table,
Mit seinen zwölf Jüngern das Abendmahl ass:	Eating supper with his twelve disciples:
Da sprach der Herr Jesus:	Thus spoke Lord Jesus:
—Was stehst du denn hier?—	—Why do you stand here?—
"Wenn ich dich anseh', so weinest du mir!"	"When I look on you, you weep at me."
"Und sollt' ich nicht weinen, du gütiger Gott?	And should I not weep, thou gracious God?
—Du sollst ja nicht weinen!—	—You surely should not weep!—
Ich hab' übertreten die zehn Gebot.	I have broken the Ten Commandments.
—Bimm bamm—	—Ding dong—

Ich gehe und weine ja bitterlich.	I go and weep quite bitterly.
—Du sollst ja nicht weinen!—	—You surely should not weep!—
Ach komm und erbarme dich über mich!"	Oh come and have mercy on me!"
—Bimm bamm—	—Ding dong—
"Hast du denn übertreten die zehen Gebot,	If you have broken the Ten Commandments,
So fall auf die Knie und bete zu Gott!	Then fall on your knees and pray to God!
Liebe nur Gott in alle Zeit!	Love only God for all time!
So wirst du erlangen die himmlische Freud'."	Thus will you attain heavenly joy!"
Die himmlische Freud' ist eine selige Stadt,	Heavenly joy is a blessed city,
Die himmlische Freud',	Heavenly joy,
die kein Ende mehr hat!	which no more has end.
Die himmlische Freude war Petro bereit't,	Heavenly joy was granted to Peter,
Durch Jesum und allen zur Seligkeit.	Through Jesus, and to all salvation.
—Bimm bamm—	—Ding dong—

(*Des Knaben Wunderhorn*, adapted by Mahler)

VI. Langsam. Ruhevoll. Empfunden (What Love Tells Me)

[VII. "Das himmlische Leben" (What the Child Tells Me)]

. . . Ach komm und erbarme dich! Ach komm und erbarme dich über mich!" (r4.1–4 and r5.6–r6; 1:29 and 1:55). When "Das himmlische Leben" serves as the finale to the Third Symphony, it seems to recall these penitential cries with some specificity before each onslaught of sleigh bells, recreating—in the ensuing turbulence and eventual return to the soothing opening strains of the song—the cycle of penitence and forgiveness enacted in "Es sungen drei Engel."[17] Yet, pointed as this striking anticipation is, and however central to Mahler's recontextualizing of "Das himmlische Leben," it remains a relatively small part of an intricate network of anticipations of the song in the previous six movements; moreover, "Es sungen drei Engel" itself provides a much richer referential nexus than this single thematic anticipation, regarding both general issues of referential content and other specific musical anticipations of "Das himmlische Leben."

"Es sungen drei Engel"

Although ostentatiously naive in style and well under half the length of any other movement in the Third Symphony, "Es sungen drei Engel" is nevertheless one of Mahler's more intricately woven creations. The original poem is straightforward enough: three angels sing of Peter being free of sin, and of Jesus forgiving a penitent who has broken the Ten Commandments. The poem strongly implies that the penitent is Peter himself, and that the Peter in question is St. Peter—one of the first and easily the most famous of sinners redeemed through Jesus' intervention—but it is not fully explicit about these identities. Mahler, characteristically, takes full advantage of this circumstance, first by framing the narrative of the penitent as a separate episode, with Peter's redemption serving as inspiration and model, and second by casting the lines of the penitent for solo alto, suggesting even more strongly that the penitent may not be St. Peter himself.[18] Yet this by itself does not settle the matter, for the part is sung by the same alto who, in the previous movement, had intoned Nietzsche's "O Mensch! Gib Acht!," a movement Mahler had once called, "What Man Tells Me"; Mahler's choice of singer here indicates some willingness on his part to allow "man," and by extension a man, to speak through an alto voice. But if the penitent in "Es sungen drei Engel" is not St. Peter, the suggestion of a continuity of persona between songs becomes all the stronger, so that the identity of the penitent merges with that of the solitary in the previous song. Moreover, if what the alto voice meant for Mahler, at least in this symphony, was not specifically feminine, we may perhaps understand the choice of singer as qualitative and emblematic since, in both songs, the alto voice is associated with the troubled soul; thus, the soul, as such, is given a feminine identity, while the deepness of the voice signifies its troubled condition. And, by further obscuring the specific identity of the penitent, Mahler allows him or her to serve more generally for humankind; it is thus humankind who has broken the Ten Commandments but who may nonetheless be redeemed.

The literal continuity of voice also serves to underscore the fact that both songs follow the same basic path—rejecting pain in favor of eternal joy —however differently they project that path, and however contrasting their poetic sources may be (Nietzsche's *Also sprach Zarathustra* and *Des knaben Wunderhorn*, respectively). Moreover, once this connection is made, the role of "Es sungen drei Engel" in the symphony is clarified, and in such a way that "Das himmlische Leben" might later serve a similar act of clarification in its position of finale. Thus, "O Mensch! Gib Acht!", while rejecting pain in favor of joy, does not really project a consummated quest for joy. We are left instead with an aching sense of need in the presence of deep midnight: within a "deep dream," in a "deep world," "deeper than the Day imagined," in the midst of "its deep woe," a "deeper joy" (*Lust*) "desires deep, deep eternity!" We aspire to joy but sink ever lower into Mahler's stark, low-lying textures, pulled down with each of Nietzsche's seductive reiterations of *tief* into a realm so overwhelmingly dark that there seems little chance of actually achieving the eternal joy ostensibly being sought. At one stroke of its opening bell, however, "Es sungen drei Engel" seems to solve Nietzsche's quandary; in *Mahler's* "happy science," if not in Nietzsche's, Christian redemption is not only possible, but freely given to all who seek it appropriately.[19]

This juncture between song movements, then, represents the crossroads of the Third Symphony, where an achieved Christian joy abruptly displaces the traditionally unrequited romantic longing that lies at the bottom of Nietzsche's quest for eternity, a quest that achieves its aching power from the very impossibility of its consummation. In making the solitary *cum* penitent an intruding voice within the song and restoring equanimity so readily thereafter by allowing an easily won salvation, "Es sungen drei Engel" laughingly mocks Nietzsche's dark alternative.[20] Not that this solitary and brief repudiation of darkness is sufficient in itself to displace Nietzsche— for, surely, we are not disposed simply to leave aside the compelling beauties of the previous song however much we may welcome a shift from its dark eternities. But the fundamental gesture of "Es sungen drei Engel" will be re-enacted in various ways throughout the later movements: most dramatically in the sixth movement, with its overcoming of multiple crises; emblematically at the juncture between the sixth and seventh movements, which affectively replays the juncture between the fourth and fifth movements; and with childish exaggeration in "Das himmlische Leben," which moves with mostly unmotivated exuberance from one replayed dramatic mode to the next, careening with wild abandon through its cycle of penitence, crisis, and absolution. In retrospect, we may see the *Wunderhorn* song as more a posed alternative than an enforced decision to change course, for it will take all of these later reenactments to fully displace Nietzsche. And so we may find, in the final version of the Third Symphony (without "Das himmlische Leben"), a much more ambivalent balance between the alternatives posed by this song pair.

Critical to the success of "Es sungen drei Engel" in projecting an alternative to the potentially endless cycle of unrequited longing introduced in "O Mensch! Gib Acht!" is the dialogic component Mahler draws out of the *Wunderhorn* poem. The contrast between the worlds of these two songs recalls the contrast between poem and novel as delineated by Bakhtin: thus, from the monologic sensibilities of Nietzsche's midnight poem, we emerge into the heteroglossia of "Es sungen drei Engel."[21] To be sure, this heteroglossia results from Mahler's manipulation of the source poem, rather than from the poem itself. But Mahler's manipulation of the poem seems to stem naturally from its simple and direct style, whose folkish naiveté is further enhanced through being juxtaposed with Nietzsche, so that it emerges, as it were, from the shadow of the previous art poem. In contrast, the high seriousness of Mahler's setting of "O Mensch! Gib Acht!" does not permit a real departure from the single-minded sensibilities established at the outset, even though that poem, too, is potentially dialogic, with its nested internal quotations. Significantly, the possibility of joy, for Mahler, is opened only with the introduction of a novelistic heteroglossia involving a dramatic negotiation among separate personae. Thus, in Mahler's setting of Nietzsche, we are trapped, without this sense of multiple voices, by the general tendency of poetry to project inwardly focused, obsessional mental states as natural and even inevitable—states that would tend to be identified, in more mundane contexts, with mental illness and more generally sickly modes of existence.[22]

The predilection of "serious" music, with its allied concepts of organic unity and absoluteness, to align with this obsessional tendency of poetry is part of what becomes for Mahler a much larger problem, stemming in part from his many and fundamental cultural ambivalences, as I will argue later. Without completely forgoing the advantages of working within these "absolute" traditions, and of having their established capacity to project sustained, powerfully felt emotional states at his disposal, Mahler nevertheless works against the monologic tendencies of absolute music, endlessly subverting its presumptive position at the center of musical expression. Yet, if "Es sungen drei Engel" represents just such a subversion, Mahler's ambivalence in the matter is made clear in the following movement, and in his ultimate decision to end there, without progressing thence to the naiveté of "Das himmlische Leben" and its aggressive denial of such adult constructs. If Mahler's decision to drop "Das himmlische Leben" was thus in part a decision to remain grounded in the absolute-music alternative, however, it was not because of a simplistic desire to distance himself from programmaticism, as his motivation for this choice has too often been construed. Rather, Mahler seems to have been content that the cycle of crises overcome in "What Love Tells Me" satisfactorily grounds the victory asserted in "Es sungen drei Engel"—indeed, more satisfactorily than a return to its naive sensibilities might have accomplished, since the aesthetic of "O Mensch, Gib Acht!" is largely restored in the process. Thus, Mahler structures his sixth movement around one of the characteristic tropes of absolute music, in which threats to an opening condition are ultimately put aside by an irresistibly enhanced return whose manner and culminating position assert its claim to the status of eternal truth. "What Love Tells Me," then, like its immediate predecessor, renounces the Nietzschean alternative, but this time on its own turf. Thus, it clings no less obsessively to a single monolithic vision, even if the quality of that vision offers a radical alternative made possible only through the intervention of the multiple voices of "Es sungen drei Engel."

The heteroglossia of "Es sungen drei Engel" embraces three distinct "voices," including an invested narrative voice, the angels themselves, and the penitent.[23] The basic narrative is sung by a three-part women's choir. While they might initially be taken to be the "three angels" of the title, they primarily narrate in the third person, so that it would be more appropriate, perhaps, to hear them as a figurative earthly reflection of the three angels. What we hear most distinctively from the beginning of the song, and what must surely be understood as the three angels that the women sing about, is a two-part boys' choir, placed unconventionally at the top of the score and *in der Höhe postiert* within the concert hall, along with the tuned bells that accompany them intermittently. As angels, these are, perhaps, oddly configured, as one part bell and two parts boys who are directed to imitate the sound of bells,[24] but they align easily with the tradition of representing angels through bells and also reflect the text, which describes their "sweet song . . . ringing" in Heaven ("süssen Gesang . . . in dem Himmel klang"). As is often the case in Mahler, staging is critical, as are also role-playing and even score placement. At the beginning of the song, the bells/boys and the women frame the score, since Mahler does without violins entirely and brings in the lower strings only with the plaints of the penitent (at which point the strings are placed, as is traditional, beneath the women's choir in the score).[25] Clearly delineated in function for the opening of the song, the women and boys gradually intermix their role-playing. During the middle section, the women accompany the penitent with (often dissonant) imitation bell sounds. Later, with the redemption of the penitent by yet a fourth voice representing the redemptive force of Jesus, which overwhelms the doubt of the penitent in r6.5–r7.5 (2:19) and offers a foretaste of the next movement, the boys suddenly become articulate as well, echoing the rejoicing words of the women (2:59). This gradual transference as both groups respond mutually to Jesus' redemptive presence carries with it the strong sense that it is specifically the innocent joy of the angels as much as Jesus' redeeming power that makes redemption possible; in terms of vocal forces, it is the child, ultimately, that is heard to redeem the adult. Although the boys do not return in "Das himmlische Leben," their innocent perspective is vividly projected throughout, and the outlandish, absurdist images engendered by this perspective provide an acceptable image of heaven specifically and solely through their unsullied innocence.

Besides the anticipation of the chorale phrase itself, there is a network of anticipations of "Das himmlische Leben" in "Es sungen drei Engel" that sets the stage for the chorale, all stemming from the section in "Das himmlische Leben" that concerns the slaughtering of the lamb, and associated in "Es sungen drei Engel" with the initial words of the penitent. Specifically, the penitent's first phrase, "Und sollt' ich nicht weinen, du gütiger Gott?" (And should I not weep, thou gracious God?) is greeted by a series of anticipations of "Das himmlische Leben," including wailing cries in the oboe directly evocative of the lamb's bleats (r3.6–10 and mm. 58–62 in Example 3), a dissonant echo of the angels' "Bimm bamm" by the women's choir modeled on parallel accompanimental voices in the later song (e.g., the flute's and bassoon's F against the English horn's concert E in m. 59), and a response to the penitent absent from the original *Wunderhorn* poem, "Du sollst ja nicht weinen! Sollst ja nicht weinen!" (You surely should not weep! Surely should not weep!), which is sung by the women to the same nervous melody that will later carry the words, "Wir führen ein geduldig's, unschuldig's, geduldig's ein liebliches Lämmlein zu Tod!" (We lead a patient, innocent, patient, a dear little lamb to death!). As may be seen in Example 3, these fairly obvious references to "Das himmlische Leben" are supported by others: the rising sixteenth-note figure in the clarinet, the anticipation of the sleigh-bells motive in the muted horn, and the melody of the penitent's first phrase, which departs only slightly from the introductory vocal phrase in "Das himmlische Leben," "Johannes das Lämmlein auslasset! / Der Metzger Herodes drauf passet!" (John lets the little lamb out! / Butcher Herod watches for it!).

Working backward from "Das himmlische Leben" to "Es sungen drei Engel," we might well find a serious referential nexus involving the multiple associations of the lamb with Jesus, who serves as figurative shepherd to humanity, as Lamb of God, and, more obliquely but relevant here, as special advocate for the privileged status of youthful innocence[26] (and whose own nativity was, moreover, watched over by lambs and shepherds). Of these, the second is relevant in a particularly pointed fashion, since, as the Lamb of God, Jesus trod a sacrificial path that is heralded by the prophecies of John the Baptist, who first described him as the "Lamb of God," and who thus, indeed, "das Lämmlein auslasset." Moreover, John the Baptist is in turn to be slaughtered at the hands of "der Metzger Herodes"; ultimately, of course,

Example 3a. Mahler, "Es sungen drei Engel," r3.5–r4.4 (1:18)

Jesus himself is sacrificed to secure the salvation of all repentant sinners, so that, in a sense, it is indeed "we" who lead the "liebliches Lämmlein" to its death. Potentially, this connection darkens almost unbearably the comic exaggeration of "Das himmlische Leben," which may be seen thus to treat the central narrative of Christian belief as a burlesque. And the pain of the penitent in "Es sungen drei Engel" is similarly intensified to the breaking point, echoed musically in ways that point specifically to the sufferings of Jesus, who has just expressed mild bewilderment at the penitent's weeping and whose "voice" carries Mahler's added text, "Du sollst ja nicht weinen!" (cf. r2.7–8: "Was stehst du denn hier?" [0:54]; and r3.9–10: "Du sollst ja nicht weinen!" [1:25]); within this frame of reference, the penitent's suffering is made to seem like an exaggeration born of self-importance, approaching blasphemy in its being paraded thus before Jesus' serene acceptance of his own suffering.

Yet, this dark reminder of what underwrites Christian salvation, implicit in Mahler's settings of both *Wunderhorn* texts, and of which Mahler clearly took note with his web of musical connections, is not really given a voice in the symphony. It is accessible only on reflection and, perhaps, with repeated

hearings (and Mahler could scarcely have envisioned, especially with this mastodon of a symphony, the current easy accessibility of such rehearings). The reason for this is straightforwardly pragmatic: we are not, in the seven-movement plan for the Third Symphony, meant to hear "Es sungen drei Engel" in light of "Das himmlische Leben," but rather the reverse, since the one precedes the other in performance. There is thus no hint in "Es sungen drei Engel" that the penitent's sufferings should not be taken as very real and heartfelt, especially in the wake of "O Mensch! Gib Acht!" Rather, the penitent's pain is taken quite seriously indeed, grounded in the morose chorales of the lower strings (r3.1–4, r4.1–7, and r5.7–11; 1:09, 1:28, and 1:55) and echoed in the dissonant "Bimm-bamm" of the women and the wailing cries of the oboes, which are in turn echoed shortly thereafter in the lower register as part of the lower-string support for the penitent (thus anticipating "Das himmlische Leben," but without the comedic, animalistic rationale of the lamb's bleats followed by the ox's bellows). Moreover, the penitent is quickly and urgently reassured by Mahler's textual inerpolation, "Du sollst ja nicht weinen!," which occurs long before the more measured response provided by the original poem. It is impossible to hear the oboes' cries as a lamb's bleats, the penitent's first phrase as evoking either John the Baptist or Herod, or the penitent's confession as implying a connection to Jesus' suffering and death unless we have first heard "Das himmlische Leben." And, from the reverse direction, all the specific musical references connect the latter to the episode of the penitent and may not be construed as a burlesque of Jesus' suffering unless we have first heard the penitent's suffering in that way. Indeed, without these associations in place, we automatically assume the "John" in "Das himmlische Leben" to be St. John the Evangelist rather than John the Baptist, and the Herod in question to be the enraged king who ordered the deaths of all young boys under the age of two in order to be sure of Jesus' death, rather than the reluctant ruler who, betrayed by his own lust, ordered the death of John the Baptist. Moreover, we would also connect the lamb more readily to the child, whose perspective is being presented, than to Jesus, who is not even mentioned.[27] Just as "Es sungen drei Engel" ultimately puts aside the pain of the penitent through absolution and joy, the burlesque of "Das himmlische Leben" does so by recalling the penitent in a gently mocking parody of the earlier song, in which the penitent's first line now presents the absurdist pairing of St. John and Herod; the penitent is then recast as an exaggeratedly innocent lamb ("ein geduldig's, unschuldig's, geduldig's ein liebliches Lämmlein"), whose culminating confession is mapped to the mock-serious projection of the lamb's death.[28] Perhaps most telling in the temporal interplay of the two passages is the punning recollection of the word "weinen," the focus of Mahler's urgently interpolated phrase: in the final recurrence of the melodic phrase that carries this interpolation in "Das himmlische Leben," the penitent's tears are teasingly converted into wine, dispensed freely from heaven's wine cellars: "der Wein kost kein Heller im himmlischen Keller" (see Example 4).[29]

While the darker side of these associations is thus held firmly in check by temporal order and tone, it is still there to be read by an astute listener and could potentially cast a rather ominous, perhaps even impious cloud over the otherwise innocent celebrations offered by "Das himmlische Leben" as finale to the Third Symphony. Perhaps herein, too, may be found a partial explanation for Mahler's decision to transplant the song one more time, this time to a setting—the finale of his Fourth Symphony—that steers clear of this kind of possible reading by introducing death first within the realm of

dreams (in "Der kleine Appell" in the development of the first movement)[30] and then of fantasy ("Freund Hein" of the second movement), making no reference whatever to the sufferings of Jesus. Nevertheless, the decision to transplant remains a curious one in light of the enormous energy Mahler expended to ensure that "Das himmlische Leben," rather than "What Love Tells Me," might serve as culmination for the symphony as a whole.[31]

The Motivic Design of the Extended Narrative

Two of the most prominent musiconarrative threads that Mahler weaves into the Third Symphony, so as to reach a point of culmination in "Das himmlische Leben," are the dactylic rhythms referred to above and a distinctive, constantly evolving oscillating motive. The latter, in turn, subdivides into two distinct strands that become intertwined, once again, in the finale. Thus, the oscillating motive both merges with a similarly evolving use of bell sounds and emerges, separately, as a childlike rocking motive that will serve on either end of the affective range of "Das himmlische Leben," bestowing on the quieter sections a sense of soothing lullaby and inflecting the disruptive sleigh-bells music with a raucous grace-note figure. Although there are many models for this kind of evolutionary motivic procedure in the nineteenth-century symphonic tradition, the central figure is clearly Beethoven, and the central model the "quest" narrative in the Ninth Symphony.[32] The shape of Mahler's quest scenario is, however, highly individual; while it seeks, like Beethoven's staged quest for the *Freudenthema* of his finale, something that might be understood as both aspiring to the highest level of artistic expression and stemming from the simplest musical material, Mahler has constructed his quest narrative so as to highlight a series of well-defined stages of arrival—the "chain of being" he delineates as a blueprint for his "happy science"—with each arrival along the way celebrated individually. Although something like this strategy may be seen to operate as well in Beethoven's Ninth, the series of supplanted arrivals there occurs only in the finale,[33] whereas in Mahler the arrivals are spread across the entire symphony, articulated as separate movements.

The sleigh bells of "Das himmlische Leben" provide a culmination that will serve to illustrate these processes. Regressive in their childish exuberance and in their general association with childhood, they claim a higher place even than the angel's bells of "Es sungen drei Engel," which in turn supplant the dark midnight bells of "O Mensch! Gib Acht!" Each stage in the process both elevates and regresses, moving back from an angst-ridden adult seriousness, through an angelic joy that cannot countenance pain, to unabashed childishness, but moving upward as well, from earthly concerns to heavenly serenity, ending with a view of heaven refracted through the purifying lens of childlike innocence.

Mahler grounds these stages within symphonic processes of motivic evolution so as to reinforce the sense of an evolving teleology; he lays the foundation for this in the sprawling first movement (see Example 5). Thus, the rocklike solemnity of the trombone chords early on introduces the oscillating motive (Example 5a), which evolves into more bell-like flute tones (Example 5b; labeled "Pan sleeps" in Mahler's notes); the sequence of events here anticipates the beginning of "Es sungen drei Engel," in that the bells offer a refreshing escape from the preceding gloom, and quickly become background for an ingenuous, folklike melody. Immediately thereafter, a grace-note

figure provides the first clear harbinger of the childlike tone that will emerge full-blown in the two *Wunderhorn* song movements (Example 5c; labeled "the Herald" in Mahler's notes); here, it serves to launch the first of many marches that will usher in Mahler's "Summer." This first attempt, however, is not sustained; only after a varied repeat of this entire sequence of events does the first sustained march get under way. Although bell sounds contribute to this first extended march (which is coextensive with the sonata-form exposition), these involve mainly the triangle and piccolo, which arise generically from the militaristic march-metaphor Mahler has adopted for the onset of summer. But along the way he also introduces the glockenspiel, which will emerge more distinctly, as bells, in the quieter first part of the developmental march (Example 5d), and which is allowed, near the end of the movement, a more privileged moment of its own within the celebratory recapitulation

Example 5b. Mahler, Symphony No. 3, first movement, r11.1–4 (4:52)

Example 5c. Mahler, Symphony No. 3, first movement, r12.1–3 (5:24)

(Example 5e). The latter provides another significant anticipation of later events, especially as it offers both audible and symbolic contrast to the use of the tam-tam earlier in the movement, in association with the "frozen" sounds that the march of summer displaces; in "Es sungen drei Engel," a similar deployment will associate the tam-tam with the central episode of the penitent, and the glockenspiel with the celebratory framing music— distinguished, however, from the angels' bells sounding above.

The second movement ("What the Flowers Tell Me") directly anticipates many elements of "Das himmlische Leben," thus underscoring the obvious associative bonds that connect flowers to children and heaven, involving not only purity, innocence, and mysterious beauty, but also—and not least in Mahler's view—an extreme vulnerability.[34] Thus, a sleepy innocence is betokened in both movements through a pervasive intermixing of triplet and rocking dotted-note figures within a relaxed tempo and major mode, and, in

both movements, a threatening presence is introduced through abrupt shifts to faster sections in the minor, marked by repeated eighth-note chords inflected by grace notes. While bells, as such, are absent from the second movement, its minor-mode episodes provide a model, in both their dramatic positioning and motivic framework, for the sleigh-bells episodes of the finale. Nevertheless, the parallels between these movements serve most importantly to highlight the *differences* between flowers and children, or at least as these are made to function in this symphony. In the second movement, the threatening minor-mode presence is clearly that of an intruder, overwhelming the established gentle flow of the flowers music (which is, however, miraculously restored when the intruder vanishes, at least initially). Yet, by the time of the finale, children have been established as the most reassuring element in the symphony, after their appearance in the guise of angels in the fifth movement virtually compels the redemption of the troubled adult sinner. In "Das himmlische Leben," at least when it functions as finale to the Third Symphony, the sleigh-bells episodes are not so much intruders as the more exuberant dimension of its childly vision, offering what amounts to a playful re-creation of past trauma. In this setting for the song, then, the sleigh bells are more a token of childhood than a threat to it. Consequently, the finale inverts the central dramatic element of "What the Flowers Tell Me," recalling and merging their trauma with that of the alto solo in movements four and five, and dispelling both in the same burst of high spirits.

The central role of bells in the denouement of the symphony, foretold in the emergence of the glockenspiel in the first movement, emerges fully only with the fourth movement. Here, the midnight tolling of bells is rendered with a kind of sonic slow motion, in the deep oscillations of the low strings (see Example 6a). While not literally using bells in this movement, Mahler with this opening suggests the reverberating slow "beats" characteristic of deeper bells, and as well recalls the rocky landscape of the first movement, where this oscillating motive was first introduced as an emblem of lifeless nature. So, too, does this transmutation from lifeless nature to deep midnight bells continue to evolve, as the initial warning, "O Mensch! O Mensch! Gib Acht! Gib Acht!" seems to emerge from the stylized bell sounds.[35] Mahler's original name for this movement, "What Night Tells Me,"[36] reflects this orientation; this is not yet a fully human voice. As the song continues, the oscillating-bell motive will reinforce certain words or phrases in Nietzsche's original poem, as specifically representing the voice of midnight: "I slept, I slept. . . . The world is deep. . . . O Man! O Man! Deep! Deep!"; in this, Mahler follows both Nietzsche's literal indications ("What says the deep mid-

night?") and responds to a recurring four-syllable rhythmic assonance in the original poem. But this is a selective response, for Mahler avoids this oscillating motive with the key phrase, "Weh spricht: Vergeh!" ("Woe says: Begone!"). Thus, where Nietzsche probably meant for the voice of woe to resonate with that of midnight, Mahler slides past this easy identification, not only by avoiding the distinctive motivic connection, but in two other ways as well. First, Mahler repeats the phrase intact, as narration, which mitigates the sense of an actual voice sounding within the song; thus, we hear, "Woe says: Begone! / Woe says: Begone!," not "Woe says: 'Begone! Begone!'" Second, Mahler sequences the phrase instead of simply repeating it as with the tolling of a bell; moreover, the sequence points toward a sense of warm arrival for the next word, "Doch," so as to emphasize the putting aside of death as an alternative (see Example 6b). Significantly, just before this line, Mahler introduces a faster, higher oscillation—a higher bell sound that will echo through the remainder of the vocal part (see Example 6b)—to project the hopeful alternative of *Lust* "deeper still than heartache." Clearly, for Mahler, midnight does not map directly to either *Weh* or *Lust*, but seems instead to represent something eternal yet inaccessible, to be neither evaded nor fully achieved. And, because a human voice seeking joy gradually emerges from out of the voice of midnight, we sense this eternity both as a dark exterior and as a measureless depth within the soul; yet, specifically, the internal dimension of eternal midnight does not embrace the voice of woe, so that the impulse toward joy is presented as internal, and the impulse toward death as external.

The tolling of the midnight bell is instantly transmuted, at the beginning of "Es sungen drei Engel," into a pealing of heavenly bells. If the former marks the birth of the human soul, both emerging out of eternity and seeking eternity, it is the specificity with which the "angels" echo the oscillating beats of the previous movement that stakes a human claim to their heavenly joy. Similarly, the return of the oscillations in "Das himmlische Leben," in the form of a rocking lullaby motive, maps a sense of Nietzsche's eternity onto the heavenly sleep that the music and words project in themselves. And, notably, while the sleigh bells emerge in "Das himmlische Leben" as the most extreme representation of bells in the symphony, they are used sparingly in the early stages of the movement; more pervasive is the sound of the triangle, which serves as a direct link between the early oscillations and the minor-mode episodes, and also recalls the angels of the fifth movement (thus appearing, even within the chorale phrase, on the word "Englein" in "die Englein, die backen das Brot" [angels bake the bread], m. 72).

If the bells thus reach their defining moment in the fifth movement and their culmination in the seventh, yet take part in thematic networks that span the symphony, nearly the same may be said of the distinctive dactylic chorale phrases. "Es sungen drei Engel" marks the first emergence of true chorale in the symphony and presents two contrasting chorale phrases, each to be taken up again in the finale.[37] The penitent's minor-mode phrases are most overtly reclaimed, but their major-mode predecessors are also important; these sing piously of Peter being redeemed: "Petrus sei von Sünden frei" (Peter was free from sin; see Example 7a), and of Jesus querying the penitent: "da sprach der Herr Jesus: Wenn ich dich anseh', so weinest du mir!" (Thus spoke Lord Jesus: When I look on you, you weep at me!); later, a final reference to Peter's redemption through Jesus recalls the major-mode version and brings it to an emphatic and joyous conclusion: "Die himmlische Freude war Petro bereit't, durch Jesum und allen zur Seligkeit" (Heavenly joy was granted to Peter, / Through Jesus, and to all salvation; see Example 7b). The pious tone of all of these passages is surely to be understood as genuine and is consistently applied whenever Peter and Jesus are mentioned in the song.

Yet, "Das himmlische Leben," which most often (though not always) also matches its chorale phrases with mentions of saints, seems to parody this pious mode—even if, incidentally, the first of these seems to confirm that the Peter of "Es sungen drei Engel" is indeed St. Peter. As culmination, then, "Das himmlische Leben" offers an odd profile, unless we assume—as well we might—that true piousness is simply too adult a pose to claim the last word here.

As with the bells, the chorale narrative begins, somewhat obliquely, in the first movement, where it derives idiomatically from folksong. In merging folksong with chorale, Mahler follows prominent nineteenth-century symphonic traditions, although the Third Symphony is somewhat unusual both in using an actual, easily recognized song as its starting point and in unfolding a narrative of emergence, in which chorale emerges only gradually from folksong; in Mahler's most important models, the fusion presents itself as axiomatic at a point of dramatic culmination. Here, at the very outset of the first movement, the horns intone the opening phrase of "Wir hatten gebauet ein stattliches Haus," which begins with a forceful dactylic gesture and later treats the dactylic rhythm in diminution.[38] In both these features, the tune resembles the *Freudenthema* of Beethoven's Ninth and the main theme in the finale of Brahms's First Symphony (see Example 8a). Significantly, the folk tune in question figured prominently not only in Mahler's life,[39] but also in Brahms's; the latter used it conspicuously in his *Academic Festival Overture* and as a probable secondary model for the finale theme of his First Symphony. In Mahler's Third Symphony, the tune serves not only to launch the first movement, but also to suggest, early on, the march idiom that will dominate the movement. Later on, after more energetic dotted rhythms have been established as the central march idiom, the tune returns in the style of a hymn, imparting a religious tone to the prevailing militaristic march topics (see Example 8b). In thus grounding religious sentiment in folksong, Mahler builds on a paradigm of authenticity that, in this application, links Christianity to pastorale, nature, youth, and—especially given the political connotations this particular folksong had by then acquired—both populism and nationalism. Thus, in Mahler's Third Symphony, "Summer Marches In" beneath the banner of a folksong long since appropriated by pan-Germanist student movements; as victory seems assured, the marchers sanctify their triumph by briefly folding their hands in prayer, so that the banner acquires as well the emblem of a Christian cross. Whether a political movement has assumed the mantle of preordained nature or nature has adopted the style and manner of a political movement is not entirely clear, but it is in either case religion, construed as the common ground between nature and humanity, that binds them together.

The emergence of the folk tune in a chorale guise late in the first movement is an important event for the symphony as a whole, particularly in its gesture of softening an established hardness. This gesture will be much repeated; more specifically, after the dactylic chorale motive has assumed a pious profile in "Es sungen drei Engel," it will be taken over in the sixth movement as the embodiment of love, dominating the rhythmic profile of the opening

melody and its many variants (see Example 9). "What Love Tells Me," then, provides a much different kind of culmination for the chorale narrative than "Das himmlische Leben," embedding it as the touchstone of the movement's structure and principal affect, whereas its successor recalls it from a more detached perspective, seemingly oblivious to the depth of feeling it so recently conveyed. Perhaps "Das himmlische Leben" does not quite negate "What Love Tells Me," having no real capacity for either affirmation or ne-

gation of an adult emotional perspective that is essentially beyond its purview. But it does, in an important sense, push this movement off to the side; with "Das himmlische Leben" as finale, love seemingly does not have the capacity to embrace the child—or, better, the child does not have the sensibility to acknowledge and value the embrace of love. This may be a great truth about childhood innocence—that it needs yet does not comprehend such adult emotions. Ultimately, however, this narrative/affective dimension may well

Brahms, Symphony No. 1, fourth movement, mm. 62–65 (melody only)

"Burschenschaftslied" ("Wir hatten gebauet ein stattliches Haus"), mm. 1–8

have been decisive in Mahler's removal of "Das himmlische Leben" from the Third Symphony, making his later chagrin over the fact that "nothing came of the profound interrelationships [among] the various movements" as he had originally planned[40] seem hierarchically less important than avoiding the subtly ruinous tempering with which "Das himmlische Leben" inflects the powerful message of the sixth movement.

Had "Das himmlische Leben" remained in place as the symphony's finale, it would have seemed to be, as Mahler's design for the symphony had carefully prepared and enabled, the inevitable culmination of the various musiconarrative strands traced here. Even without the specific meanings that the movement takes on through these referential networks, it carries the weight of assimilated recollection by virtue of its being, on the one hand, an independently compelling statement and, on the other, a patchwork of recalled gestures drawn from all the previous movements. In terms that conventionally pass for purely musical, these recollections within a secure environment (and what could seem more secure, at least in tone, than a lullaby?) are reassuring tokens of unity, of a musical voice that has remained in control of the diverse facets of its story, of a narrative safely concluded; this impression is largely a matter of motivic work and other musical processes and need not be connected directly to specific notions of what that story has been or of what a conclusion of such a story ought to look like. In short, "Das himmlische Leben" conventionally assumes the guise of a symphonic finale, refer-

ring to and grounding the diversity of music that has preceded it. These, too, are meanings the song does not have as a stand-alone lullaby or when paired with "Das irdische Leben"; moreover, they add a depth to the song's other meanings that a mere song setting could impart in no other way in the late nineteenth century.

While these musical resonances and deepenings function with seeming autonomy, they are themselves deepened and reinforced by the sense that the symphony's "extramusical" preoccupations with the place of humanity in the cosmos—that is, in nature, among other forms of life, and within a projected afterlife—are also addressed by the manner in which these issues

Example 9. Mahler, Symphony No. 3, sixth movement, mm. 1–8

are taken up and assimilated in "Das himmlische Leben," especially and spe-cifically as they have been delineated, one by one, within part two of Mah-ler's symphonic structure (movements 2–7). As discussed, the flowers from the second movement are recalled in both the structure and detail of "Das himmlische Leben"; significantly, as well, they are recalled in the latter's ref-erence to a "himmlischen Garten." In the third movement (which will be discussed in more detail later), specific musical figures connect the forest an-imals to the roebuck and rabbits of "Das himmlische Leben" (note the simi-lar chromatic bariolage-like figures in the flute, shown in Example 10). As discussed, the finale replays the dynamic between "O Mensch! Gib Acht!" and "Es sungen drei Engel." The sixth movement, though affectively de-tached from "Das himmlische Leben," offers both musical and figurative preparation in its D major chorale basis. It is unclear whether Mahler's last-minute changes to the ending of the sixth movement, so as to allow it to serve more effectively as the finale, introduced the existing breakthrough effect or merely retained and simplified it;[41] as it stands, this concluding breakthrough is similar to the one he would fashion near the end of the third movement in the Fourth Symphony, although thematically less spe-cific. Absent Mahler's revision, a quiet close on D major would have made the succeeding G major opening of "Das himmlische Leben" seem inevit-

able, in local terms much like the transition Mahler would fashion for the Fourth Symphony, particularly if, as suggested by Mahler's comments about the revision, the harmonies had occluded the tonal orientation (as they do in the Fourth). The chorale phrases that come later in "Das himmlische Leben" and their association with saints serving as caretakers and providers remind us musically of the love music of the sixth movement, and associatively of how indispensable love is to the security of the child, however much the child may seem to take that love for granted.

Perhaps the oddest cross-reference Mahler works into the Third Symphony occurs in the third movement, which briefly combines the pervasive dactylic chorale rhythm with a chromatic figuration in order to produce a near-quotation of "Das irdische Leben" (see Example 11a; cf. also Example 2 above). As shown in Example 11, the fully chromatic version of the chorale rhythm emerges through a step-by-step process of derivation from the original flute phrase until it is nearly identical to the child's initial cry, "Mutter, ach Mutter, es hungert mich!" (Mother, oh Mother, I am hungry!). We may find in this obviously contrived reference—for the derivation is too clearly mapped out, and the resemblance too close, for us to take it as coincidence —a variety of possible explanations. Perhaps, in line with our immediate concerns here, Mahler is attempting to set up a resonance between this movement and the later, more chromatic chorale phrase in "Das himmlische Leben," in parallel to the resonance discussed above between the paired *Wunderhorn* songs (see Example 2). Perhaps he is simply alluding to a song he might reasonably expect his audience to know. Or perhaps he is responding to something in the melodic gesture itself, and to a more abstract parallel between this moment in the Third Symphony and the source passage, a parallel strong enough to compel the use of the same melodic figure. While the first two of these explanations seem most plausible—most relevant to our discussion, and most easily shown to be at least partially true—the last is nevertheless the most intriguing and may arguably be more relevant than the others, and even more basic to our larger concerns.

This is not to say that the passage does not allude to "Das irdische Leben," or that it does not point ahead, within the symphony, to "Das himmlische Leben." As allusion, the passage is, first of all, well grounded within the movement. The dactylic rhythm relates easily to one of the principal melodic figures, which, moreover, characteristically traces the descending tetrachord from $\hat{5}$ to $\hat{2}$ (see Example 11c); thus, when the manipulations of the dactylic rhythm crystallize into a recollection of "Das irdische Leben," we are at the same time also returned to a characteristic melodic shape within the movement. As allusion, the passage resonates with the child's cries in "Das irdische Leben," for the phrase concludes a series of parallel phrases by tracing a melodic shape typical of lament: a descending chromatic tetrachord. It also serves an appropriate function within the movement, forewarning of the intrusion to come (the posthorn), and articulating, in a slightly altered version, the first rather queasy reaction after the first episode with the posthorn is complete (see Example 11b). Moreover, there is ample reason for the finale to recall this phrase in particular, as it represents one of a series of anxious moments in the symphony, analogous to the minor-mode episodes in the "Flowers" movement and the episode of the penitent in "Es sungen drei Engel." Given the function of the finale within the overall plan of the symphony, it is thus more than reasonable for Mahler, at least gesturally, to recall this earlier anxiety. But these relatively easy explanations do not go as far as we might like them to in accounting for what is, after all, a very telling moment within the third movement itself.

One of the fascinating aspects of the third movement is its evocation early on of a multitude of roughly equivalent voices, creating a conversational con-

fusion as a metaphor for the animate forest. Within this fairly balanced het-eroglossia, the often overlapping individual phrases are given to distinctive in-struments or groupings so that no particular instrument or grouping occupies the foreground more than briefly. This is a very different kind of heteroglossia than what Mahler will introduce two movements later—more diffuse and less sharply defined, evoking a multivoiced foreground as the starting condition for the forest that the highly individuated posthorn will later intrude upon.[42] But this heteroglossia is not presented as a stable, "natural" environment simply waiting for the advent of an "unnatural" intruding voice; rather, its multitude of voices registers significant agitation and mounting anxiety even before the posthorn makes its appearance. We hear descending minor-mode tetrachords and falling chromatic lines well before the allusion to "Das irdische Leben," so that the allusion itself appears as part of a continuing presence; what mark the allusion as special within the movement are its appearance just after a crisis has already marred the equanimity of the forest (see r8.23–24; 3:48), and its posi-tion at the end of a series of more measured phrases. While not yet chorales,

these phrases seem more articulate than have previous "voices" in the movement; one senses a more measured discussion taking place, culminating, as if
inevitably, in the lamenting voice that recalls the child in "Das irdische Leben."

There is thus a dynamic at work within the movement that offers a dialogic parallel to "Das irdische Leben," involving a plaintive voice foretelling
catastrophe ("Gib mir Brot, sonst sterbe Ich!") and a denial of crisis based
on self-deluding bravado. The basically celebratory attitude that marks each
arrival in Mahler's "happy science"—flowers, forest creatures, angels, love

(only midnight is not basically cheerful)—disguises somewhat the fact that each arrival is also undermined by a foretaste of what will come next and supplant it. Thus, Mahler's "great god Pan" presents an unanswered threat to the flowers of the second movement in preparation for the forest creatures of the third movement, while the love of the sixth movement is prophesied by Jesus in the preceding movement, providing the energizing force for the return to angelic celebration. Here in the third movement, the sense of something amiss, even before we are given a real taste of what is to come, is subtly conveyed by the emergence of a quasi-rationalist dialogue, anticipating the declamation of the chorales to come and aspiring, as it were, to a semblance of humanity in its measured discourse and responsive structure. Thus, the strong parallels from phrase to phrase serve as a marker of rationality; these "voices" not only speak, but they also listen attentively and pa-

tiently, and respond in kind, so that the same thematic processes through which the allusion is derived, step by step, are also an advance token of human discourse.[43] But, recalling "Das irdische Leben," this discourse foretells an uneasy existence, moving between unquenchable need and inadequate bravado without the resolution that Mahler's "science" will eventually project through Christian faith and the innocence of childhood.

On this deeper level, then, each setting for the allusive phrase establishes a close relationship to "Das himmlische Leben." Remarkably enough, even given the more literal connections forged between "Das irdische Leben" and "Das himmlische Leben," the third movement of Mahler's Third Symphony forms the nexus of a more enriching context than the straightforward solace offered in the earlier pairing, that the earthly suffering of the innocent will be supplanted by heavenly plenty. The somewhat odd allusion to "Das irdische Leben" serves in this way as a critical pointer to what seems to have been a fundamental motivation for Mahler in devising a succession of ever more elaborate settings for "Das himmlische Leben": to enrich its meaningfulness without actually discarding meanings that were established within previously conceived contexts. Significantly, then, "Das himmlische Leben" remains a lullaby when paired with "Das irdische Leben," and its heavenly/childly preoccupation with unrequited earthly needs continues to inform the song as it concludes the Third Symphony, even as it remains essentially a lullaby.

But Mahler's motivation can be stated differently, and more truly, if we imagine that the complexities of "Das himmlische Leben" that Mahler reveals with each new setting were, for him, an integral part of the song all along, so that his continued obsession with finding the most effective context for the song is at bottom a desire to bring out as richly as possible its latent meanings. It is as if, having perceived the richness of Mozhukhin's face and wishing to convey that experience more completely to an audience, Kuleshov had devised a setting that would reveal Mozhukhin to be responding to the soup, the corpse, and the child not separately and differently, but all at once, with a rich interplay of potentially conflicting meanings. For, as discussed above, Mozhukhin's face is never a blank slate, but rather a cornucopia of potential meanings, so that the Kuleshov effect may be best understood as a process not of creating meaning, but of revealing meaning implicit in the image itself. Musical images are, however, considerably more flexible than visual ones. While it is hard to see how Kuleshov might have managed the kind of polymorphic simultaneity imagined above, even with so richly evocative material as a human face, music is capable, as Mahler demonstrates, of precisely this kind of super-Kuleshov effect.

The Fourth Symphony

When "Das himmlische Leben" assumes its ultimate position as the finale of the Fourth Symphony, it retains most, if not all, of the meanings discussed here in relation to its previously designed settings, but with considerable enhancement. Its function as lullaby, for example, is reinforced markedly by the appearance of a lullaby-like sequence in the first movement, which leads to the less than comforting "sleep" of the development section and its nightmarish elaborations of previously unthreatening material;[44] the enhancement is twofold, as its lullaby function is confirmed and its heavenly alternative all the more welcome for following a failed earthbound lullaby (this time, we will "awaken to joy" rather than to the funereal music that closes the dream sequence in the first movement). The subtext of child hunger is also reclaimed more fully than in the Third Symphony, since the Fourth Symphony twice forecasts the death of a child: at the end of the development section in the first movement and within the Freund Hein narrative of the second. And, as a symphonic finale, it finds a more satisfactory (if less grandiose) placement in the Fourth Symphony than in the Third, since in the later work its significant features register as implicit from the beginning, and since it does not have to compete for dramatic position with a parallel culmination in the preceding movement.

Key to Mahler's success in holding on to meanings from earlier imagined settings is his ability to fashion substitutes for their central activating triggers, those earlier musical moments that "Das himmlische Leben" will seem to recall with renewed significance. Thus, the intruding sleigh bells in the first movement are an even more explicit substitute for the urgent refrains of "Das irdische Leben" and the threatening minor-mode sections of "What the Flowers Taught Me." The stark contrast of the *Wunderhorn* pairing is reformulated as the contrast between earthly nightmare in the first movement and heavenly dream in the finale. Mahler also establishes an earlier ending to parallel that of "Das himmlische Leben," one no less pertinent than that of "Das irdische Leben": the arrival in heaven (the completion of the "death process," as it were) is first accomplished near the end of the Scherzo, and through a parallel harmonic shift (from F to D in the Scherzo, from G to E in "Das himmlische Leben").[45] The penitent of "Es sungen drei Engel" seems to reappear in the third movement of the Fourth Symphony (see especially the E minor section beginning in m. 62; 4:40), redeemed, as in the Third Symphony, by what is sufficiently evocative of "What Love Tells Me" for us to identify it securely as heavenly love. Indeed, this latter substitution is among the most obvious; once again, "Das himmlische Leben" is introduced through a "love" Adagio, warmed by intense string counterpoint and sanctified by the predominance of dactylic chorale phrases. On a somewhat deeper level, Mahler also manages in his Fourth Symphony to fashion a close parallel to Beethoven's Ninth, even if Mahler does without the evolving folk-tune scenario of the Third Symphony—not to mention the latter's D minor opening movement, which seems, like Beethoven's D minor opening movement, to depict creation itself in the starkest terms possible, and whose pervasive D minor march topics inevitably recall as well Beethoven's second movement. In Mahler's Fourth Symphony, we are presented (as in Beethoven's Ninth) with a familiar four-movement structure, but with the Scherzo placed second, followed first by a warm Adagio in a freely evolving variation form, and then by a Utopian finale joining voice to instruments.[46]

There are, to be sure, inevitable losses. The subtext of Jesus' sacrifice, muted in any case in the Third Symphony, is virtually unsupported in the Fourth, except, perhaps, by our uneasiness as "we" are so cheerfully made to lead the lamb to slaughter, to inaugurate the finale's projected carnivory with the blood of the lamb. Indeed, although the Fourth Symphony ends in a distinctly Christian heaven, however perversely rendered, religion itself is downplayed: death is secularized through the folkish figure of Freund Hein, and religious figures are treated with irreverent familiarity. The tradeoff for Mahler is not having to reconcile adult religion and childly innocence, as he tried to do in the Third Symphony. Nor does the Fourth Symphony engage with Nietzsche in any direct sense;[47] by extension, romanticism and unrequited adult yearnings play no significant part, either (hence the frequent, if somewhat misguided, descriptions of this symphony as Haydnesque). Like religion, these are adult preoccupations, difficult to reconcile with childly innocence; Mahler may thus be seen here in retreat from the ambitions of the Third Symphony, where he sought to reclaim innocence after thoroughly ingesting it. Politics, too, are quietly put aside, although the basic maneuver of folk-based pastorale as the path to utopia surfaces often enough, particularly in the trios of the second movement. Remarkably, though, his desire to have "Das himmlische Leben" serve as evolutionary pinnacle is more fully realized here than before, at least in the sense that Mahler claimed for the Fourth Symphony as a whole the role of completing his symphonic tetralogy. Within the symphony itself, however, the basic evolutionary narrative is sharply curtailed. The narrative centering around evolving bell sounds disappears entirely, since Mahler begins with his culminating sleigh bells; similarly, the extended chorale narrative is considerably condensed, although here, at least, there is a commensurate payoff. Since dactylic chorale phrases do not appear until the penultimate movement and so cannot be heard as the completion of processes begun earlier, Mahler avoids the conflict of parallel culminations he faced in the Third Symphony.

Whether it may be counted as a loss or gain, Mahler also manages to sidestep the conflict between absoluteness and heteroglossia this time around by staging, within the third movement and serving as its culmination, an anticipatory breakthrough that implicitly embraces the informalities of an earned relaxation. Two things distinguish his procedures here from his strategies in the Third Symphony: by enfolding the one within the other, he not only avoids the stark opposition he created in the Third Symphony between "O Mensch! Gib Acht!" and "Es sungen drei Engel," but also avoids having to choose between two culminating movements of subtly opposed sensibilities. Indeed, Mahler's enfolding of the finale within the "love" of his preceding Adagio provides another sort of payoff, not only effecting an audible bridge between the two movements, but also evolving—or, rather, recapturing—the topic of childishness through the "absolute" musical processes of thematic variation. Thus, long before the final breakthrough, Mahler presents a dizzying spiral of accelerations from one variation to the next (after m. 238; 14:01), in which prominent tokens of childish disregard for absolute decorum appear with gleeful abandon (after m. 263; 14:37), including a triangle, a rowdy clarinet, and the raucous laughter of a muted trumpet, before order is restored through the strong fatherly presence of the horns after m. 282 (14:58).[48]

And, of course, there are new riches. Most obviously, the overall structure of the Fourth Symphony, with its framing use of sleigh bells, creates a much more satisfying place for "Das himmlische Leben," at least in conventional "organic" terms as they are generally construed for symphonic music after Beethoven. (This kind of organic unity was a feature Mahler placed great store in; he lamented its loss in the Third after he removed the finale and extolled its presence in the Fourth.) Unlike the spiraling structure of the Third Symphony, which could plausibly conclude at more than one point of culmination, the structure of the Fourth traces a narrative circle in which the finale reclaims and stabilizes the innocent naiveté with which the symphony began. The lullaby spiral of "Das himmlische Leben" itself, retreating into a quiet center as discussed above, is balanced by the opposite shaping principle in the Scherzo, in which Freund Hein "fiddles us up to heaven" in ever widening spirals.[49] Besides the obviously pleasing symmetry these complementary shapes create (which bear some analogy to the parallels involving the "Flowers" movement in the Third Symphony), Mahler gently underscores an understated parallel to the Nietzsche-inspired, Janus-faced eternities of the Third Symphony, in which heavenly peace is suggested through dual projections of eternity, one extending without, the other lying deep within the human soul.

"Der Himmel hängt voll Geigen"

The ambiguities mentioned near the beginning of this chapter regarding the orientation of "Das himmlische Leben" as the finale of the Fourth Symphony are a product of Mahler's individual application of an enhanced Kuleshov effect. Perhaps most emblematic of these ambiguities is the role played by the sleigh bells, which may arguably be construed, with equal justification, as an emblem of childish exuberance, a nostalgic evocation of an idealized childhood (following some aspects of their use in the first movement), an intrusion signaling mortal danger, or even a mocking projection of such an intrusion. With the aural equivalent of a double image, the sleigh bells seem to mock childhood by projecting childish excitement with a tone of amused condescension, at the same time mocking adult seriousness with childish laughter while fiendishly despoiling the religious icons of adulthood. And there is really no way to parse these ambiguities, to choose one set of meanings over another, without substantial loss to the rich network of referential meanings Mahler has created.

Perhaps the most intriguing new twist Mahler introduces in his final setting for "Das himmlische Leben" involves, once again, the chromatic chorale phrase near the end, which in the Fourth Symphony refers not to a hungry child or to the anxious creatures of the forest, but to the chromatic slippages of Freund Hein. As in the earlier settings, a previous moment of distress is recalled and grounded within a comforting chorale phrase; this time, however, there are two surprising consequences. First, Freund Hein, who is traditionally depicted as more devil than angel, and so is represented in Mahler's Scherzo by a *scordatura* solo violin, is retroactively sanctified; amazingly, a personage who cannot always be distinguished from Satan himself is, no less than the butcher Herod, to be given a place in heaven, perhaps even a presiding place. And second, because we hear this phrase so soon after the words have begun to tell us of heavenly music, we are oddly reminded that we have been led to this place through the still more unusual music—in Mahler's word, the "uncanny" music—of Freund Hein.[50] The conflation is telling, for it suggests that once again we have been seduced by unearthly music, however more congenial the strain.

Freund Hein's appearance this late in the proceedings is thus oddly disconcerting. It obliquely recalls to mind the similarly disconcerting original title of this *Wunderhorn* poem, "Der Himmel hängt voll Geigen" ("Heaven Hangs Full of Violins"). The phrase is a cliché of sorts, long used to describe unwavering and, perhaps, unfounded optimism. In serious applications, it resonates with images of angelic choirs; more playfully, it implies delusional optimism or, more simply, delusion, occasionally suggesting as well mere simplemindedness or even drunkenness.[51] Although Mahler has shifted the context for the poem by mapping these conditions and attitudes, serious and playful alike, onto childly innocence in each of his settings, primarily through giving the song itself the cast of a lullaby, he does not completely put aside the original title. In particular, "Es sungen drei Engel" in the Third Symphony resonates rather obviously with the original title—even if silently, since Mahler nowhere uses that title for "Das himmlische Leben," and since there are no literal resonators for the original title within the poem itself, which refers to heavenly music without once mentioning violins. Similarly, and even more subtly, the presence of Freund Hein in the Fourth Symphony also connects to the original title, but with a startling twist. The violin, which has a long history of symbolizing both the sacred and the profane, may be appropriately played by either angels or demons. The late echo of Freund Hein's fiddle, taking its place however faintly within the heavenly music-making near the end of the Fourth Symphony, underscores this ambiguity, reminding us as well that this is perhaps a fool's heaven:[52] if Herod is to be allowed to butcher the lamb with impunity, so, too, will Freund Hein provide the dance music.[53] According to English usage (if not German), we might note that this version of heaven does indeed hang full of "fiddles" (if not violins), which appear throughout the poem in the devilish havoc it plays with Christian doctrine.[54] In Mahler's final application of the Kuleshov effect, he introduces, without changing a single note of the song[55]— or a single wrinkle in Mozhukhin's face—yet one more fiddle that is present in none of the previous contexts he had created for the song: that of Freund Hein, whose part, in the second movement, is to be played "wie eine Fiedel."

Chapter 3

Representing Alienation: "Absolute Music" as a Topic

"Des Antonius von Padua Fischpredigt"
and the Second Symphony

> Empty activity devoid of autonomy is the never-changing. . . .
> It is a hell of absolute space. . . . Yet simply through the internal
> logic of the composition, Hegelian justice so far guides the com-
> poser's pen that the world's course takes on something of the
> self-propagating, enduring, death-resisting force of life itself, as
> a corrective to the endlessly protesting subject. . . . Counterpoint
> for Mahler was the self-alienated form of music that imposed
> itself on the subject.
>
> —THEODOR ADORNO, *Mahler: A Musical Physiognomy*

Sybil: Classical Music and Alienation

Near the beginning of the film *Sybil* (1976, directed by Daniel Petrie),[1] the title character returns to her apartment building dismayed to find that a pi-ano has been moved in downstairs from her. Throughout this and the ensu-ing sequence, we hear the instrument thundering Chopin's "Winter Wind" Etude (Op. 25 No. 11, in A minor) as Sybil vainly attempts to escape the op-pressive, unrelenting drive of the music. Intermittently, various sounds in the foreground compete with the continuing background sound of the pi-ano: ambient street noise, Sybil's conversation outside the building, a baby crying from another apartment, Sybil's feet as she walks and then runs up the stairs, her key in the lock, her door closing, the ticking of a clock. And twice, when the presence of the piano seems strongest—as she passes the piano on the way to her room and again, at the end of the sequence, when she lies in a fetal position on the bed, hands over ears—we hear electronic manipulations of the piano's sound that seem to project both its extreme disorienting effect on Sybil and her unsuccessful attempt to block out the sound. But always, relentlessly, we hear Chopin's etude continuing in the background, doggedly indifferent to her struggle to escape it.

In a parallel scene near the end of the film, during an enactment of Sybil's memory of a repeated childhood trauma, we see her as a small child, leashed to a piano leg after receiving an enema, admonished by her monstrosity of a mother who is playing a grandiose transcription of the finale of Antonín Dvořák's Symphony No. 9 (*From the New World*) on the piano, "Don't you let go, young lady . . . hold your water till the very last note." The music is majestic, overpowering, relentless, as inexorable in its forward momentum as the Chopin etude earlier in the film; as it builds, we see water trail across the floor and are left to imagine, with the child, the terrible punishment that must follow the music, knowing she must dread its conclusion as desperately as she needs to escape its awful oppression.[2]

In between these two scenes, we learn that Vanessa—one of the seventeen personae of the adult Sybil, who has recently been told that she has Multiple Personality Disorder (MPD)—has retained her ability to play piano, a skill Sybil thinks she has lost, and we watch Sybil listen to a recording of her alter ego playing the elegant beginning of Mozart's Sonata in F Major, K. 332 (breaking off before the minor-mode episode in m. 23f). At various points, we also hear her express particular dread for the music of Bach, Beethoven, Brahms, and Dvořák; in one sequence, we see her respond badly even to a fairly benign transcription for two guitars of the Prélude to Bach's Third English Suite in G Minor (BWV 808), just after she has delighted in a comic rendition of "Follow the Band" by the same performers. With the recollection of the *New World* Symphony near the end of the film, we finally learn why she has this pronounced aversion to what most would regard as "serious" music; we understand, implicitly, that these composers, who rank among the "heaviest" representatives of the classical tradition, were the particular favorites of her mother, who used their obsessive minor-mode bombast as part of a regular regimen of terror and torture.

On one level, then, Mozart and the bits of show tunes we hear Sybil play or respond positively to are lighthearted, carefree, and whimsical, and so offer an obvious contrast to her mother's much heavier repertory. But the severity of her mother's music is at best only part of its ability to terrorize Sybil; long before we know the sadistic acts for which it has provided accompaniment, we experience this music from Sybil's perspective and readily accept—perhaps as an extension of a standard Hollywood trope[3]—its ability to frighten her as utterly consistent with its nature, even if our normalized response to it is quite different from hers. What is at issue—what is conveyed unmistakably to us in the Chopin sequence—is a quality that this kind of music can present to an outsider over whom it exerts its will; typically minor mode, given to close motivic work or ostinato, spinning itself out with a self-generating, unstoppable, self-propelled logic, this music assumes the role of a terrifying monstrous *presence*, oblivious, self-absorbed, and beyond reach. It is, in fact, the opposite of the music Sybil/Vanessa likes, music that seems both to provoke and to thrive on its listener's delight. During Sybil's barely coherent babbling while she confronts the horrors of her childhood, along with the names of Brahms, Beethoven, Bach, and Dvořák, which she recites in panic, we hear also, in panting gasps, how she experiences their music: "and the music, it goes around, and around, and around, and around and over and down, like that, and then like that, and you can see it, you can see it, you can see it, . . . and it's like that, and like that, and it goes over, and around, like that, and like that, and you can hear it, and you can hear it." Clearly, it is much more than the association of this music with her mother—rather, it is the music itself that terrifies Sybil, and what allows it to retain this potency long after her mother's death is its threefold *absoluteness*: its inaccessible removal from outside control, its seeming ability to generate indefinitely its own continuation, and its unassailable power to impose itself on its listeners.[4]

It is precisely these qualities of musical absoluteness that Mahler exploits in the scherzo of his Second Symphony in order to evoke a sense of extreme alienation. Mahler here re-cycles material from his *Wunderhorn* song, "Des Antonius von Padua Fischpredigt," which he was completing while working simultaneously on the related symphonic movement.[5] Indeed, the somewhat puzzling link between song and scherzo, which ostensibly enact markedly different scenarios, involves a particular attitude toward musical absoluteness basic to Mahler's aesthetic, an attitude deeply ambivalent and, to some extent, divided against itself. In this respect, Mahler's sensibilities seem at times remarkably similar to Sybil's. Even if his many ambivalences—as Nietzschean Christian, as Austro-Bohemian pan-Germanist, as provincial Jew aspiring to Viennese high culture, among others—do not compare to Sybil's multiple personalities, he, too, took refuge in a kind of cultural MPD, alternating antithetical attitudes that were, individually, indelibly inscribed upon his psyche, yet never truly integrated. On his musical psyche, in particular, were etched two diametrically opposed attitudes toward music at its most absolute.

There have been many attempts to explore the link between "Des Antonius von Padua Fischpredigt" and the scherzo of Mahler's Second Symphony; these tend, predominantly, to proceed from the implicit premise that the closer to the programmatic surface we might locate this link, the more satisfying the result will be. Thus, even the relatively deeper probings of Constantin Floros concern themselves more with the situations suggested by Mahler's various programs than with particular features or attributes of the music itself.[6] The tendency to focus on the program in this way is natural, given the relative ease with which specific textual referents may be mapped to musical motives and gestures within the song version. Thus, in general, the incessantly circling sixteenth notes seem to represent swimming fish; the more pompous and angular eighth notes (i.e., when the voice first enters), the didactic voice and manner of St. Anthony. Moreover, the often close coordination of these two motivic elements may be taken for the close attention the fish pay to the preacher's sermon; the exaggeratedly pleasant melodic exchanges (e.g., mm. 41–48; see Example 12a) for the shallowness of the fish's pleasure in the sermon; the grotesque parody of the preacher's more ordered sequencing (cf. mm. 37–40 and mm. 49–53, e.g.; see Example 12a) for the failure of the fish to grasp the sermon in any meaningful way;[7] and so on. Some of this maps easily enough to the explanations Mahler provided for the symphonic movement, which are typically (if wrongly) reduced to the familiar scenario of an excluded outsider observing a dance from afar. In particular, the empty circling of the fish becomes the whirling of dancers to unheard music, the solitary observer assumes the perspective of the unheeded preacher, and the parodic sequencing continues to express the estrangement between the two.[8]

But there are several problems with this approach. Most immediately, the removal of a singing voice in the transmutation of song into symphonic movement has a number of consequences. Because the vocal line and accompaniment thus merge into one basic entity, we are left without an authoritative locus in the opening texture of the scherzo and, moreover, cannot easily place the perspective of the lonely observer within the movement except obliquely, in the satirical tone that provides the arch "filter" through which we watch the dancers. More disturbingly, the responsive dynamic between individual and group is overturned, with results that are hard to accommodate to a surface-oriented link between song and scherzo. Thus, in the song, the fish respond to the preacher (if inadequately), whereas in the

Example 12a. Mahler, "Des Antonius von Padua Fischpredigt," mm. 37–53 (0:40)

scherzo, the dancers are completely oblivious to the observer, so that the originating perspective for the satirical clarinet lines (mm. 49–53 in the song; see Example 12a) is diametrically inverted, offering its comic distortion in the song to underscore the lack of comprehension of something heard, and in the scherzo of something unheard yet understood all too well. Allusive detail, too, provides a puzzling overlay: references to Bruckner's Fourth Symphony (cf. Examples 12a and 12b) are seemingly more appropriate to the song, with the unappreciated Anton Bruckner mapping to the preacher Antonius, whereas a reference to Schumann's "Das ist ein Flöten

und Geigen" seems more appropriate to the scherzo, with its scenario of a wedding dance observed in despair from afar by the bride's rejected suitor. Yet, both allusions maintain reasonably high profiles in each setting. The more fundamental problem with this kind of detailed mapping, though, has to do with how easily it eclipses our sense of what song and scherzo are individually "about," and of how Mahler's musical treatment projects and responds to not just the respective sensibilities of fish, dancers, preachers, and outsiders, but also, and more important, a much deeper stratum of meaning, which, as it happens, is where song and scherzo may be most satisfyingly linked.

"Des Antonius von Padua Fischpredigt"

Antonius zur Predigt	Anthony, ready for his sermon,
Die Kirche find't ledig!	Finds the church empty!
Er geht zu den Flüssen	He goes to the river
Und predigt den Fischen!	And preaches to the fish!
Sie schlag'n mit den Schwänzen!	Their tails flicker!
Im Sonnenschein glänzen!	Glittering in the sunshine!
Die Karpfen mit Rogen	The carp with their spawn
Sind all' hierher zogen,	Have pulled all to this place,

Hab'n d'Mäuler aufrissen,
Sich Zuhörn's beflissen!
Kein Predigt niemalen
Den Fischen so g'fallen!

Have raised up their snouts,
Intent on their listening!
No sermon (n)ever
Pleased the fish so!

Spitzgoschete Hechte,
Die immerzu fechten,
Sind eilends herschwommen,
Zu hören den Frommen!
Auch jene Phantasten,
Die immerzu fasten:
Die Stockfisch ich meine,
Zur Predigt erscheinen.
Kein Predigt niemalen
Den Stockfisch so g'fallen!

Sharp-nosed pike,
Which are always fencing,
Are swimming here in haste
To hear the pious one!
Also that visionary,
Which is always fasting:
I mean the cod,
Appears at the sermon.
No sermon ever
Pleased the cod so!

Gut Aale und Hausen,
Die Vornehme schmausen,
Die selbst sich bequemen,
Die Predigt vernehmen!
Auch Krebse, Schildkroten,
Sonst langsame Boten,
Steigen eilig vom Grund,
Zu hören diesen Mund!
Kein Predigt niemalen
Den Krebsen so g'fallen!

Good eels and sturgeon,
Which high society feast on,
These condescend
To hear the sermon!
Also crabs, turtles,
Otherwise slow apostles,
Rise quickly from bed
To hear this speaker!
No sermon ever
Pleased the crabs so!

Fisch' grosße, Fisch' kleine,
Vornehm und gemeine,
Erheben die Köpfe,
Wie verständ'ge Geschöpfe!
Auf Gottes Begehren,
Die Predigt anhören!

Large fish, small fish,
High-born and common,
Raise their heads,
Like understanding creatures!
On God's wish,
Listening to the sermon!

Die Predigt geendet,
Ein jeder sich wendet.
Die Hechte bleiben Diebe,
Die Aale viel lieben;
Die Predigt hat g'fallen,
Sie bleiben wie Allen!
Die Krebs geh'n zurükke;

The sermon ended,
Each one wends his way.
The pike remain thieves,
The eels letch;
The sermon has pleased,
They remain like everyone!
The crabs go backward;

Die Stockfisch' bleib'n dikke,	The cod remain thick,
Die Karpfen viel fressen,	The carp devour too much,
Die Predigt vergessen!	Forgetting the sermon!
Die Predigt hat g'fallen,	The sermon has pleased,
Sie bleiben wie Allen!	They remain like everyone!

Curiously, in his only surviving "explanation" for the song, conveyed to us through Natalie Bauer-Lechner, Mahler seems especially pleased with the precision of his pictorial imagery, and only hints at deeper meanings:

> In the "Fischpredigt" . . . the prevailing mood is one of rather bitter-sweet humor. St. Anthony preaches to the fishes; his words are immediately translated into their thoroughly tipsy-sounding language (in the clarinet), and they all come swimming up to him—a glittering shoal of them: eels and carp, and the pike with their pointed heads. I swear, while I was composing, I really kept imagining that I saw them sticking their stiff immovable necks out from the water, and gazing up at St. Anthony with their stupid faces—I had to laugh out loud! And look at the congregation swimming away as soon as the sermon's over: "Die Predigt hat g'fallen / Sie bleiben wie alle" ("They liked the sermon / But remained unchanged"). Not one of them is one iota wiser for it, even though the Saint has performed it for them! But only a few people will understand my satire on mankind.[9]

The pictorial dimension of this song as Mahler describes it was undoubtedly reinforced for him by a reproduction of this scene as painted just one year earlier by Arnold Böcklin (1827–1901) (see Figure 3-1), which he placed on the wall of his Hamburg studio.[10] Thus, Mahler mentions precisely those fish that are both described in the poem and reasonably identifiable in Böcklin's painting (eel, carp, pike) and describes their listening attitude in terms that more closely match the painting than the poem.[11] Moreover, since Böcklin's painting presents itself as an altarpiece, with a lower predella that depicts the fish returning to their old ways, even this aspect of Mahler's pictorial description might have been based at least as much on Böcklin's painting as on the poem and his setting of it.

On one level, Mahler's "satire on mankind" is virtually transparent, as the fish are apportioned the easily recognized features and foibles of an all-too-human congregation. Few could miss that humanity is being indicted as behaving on the whole like fish, smugly self-satisfied that they have appreciated a sermon they have not begun to understand. On the other hand, the quasi-pictorial musical detail in the song operates on a more subtle level than Mahler's brief description suggests. The allusion to Bruckner (Example 12b), for example, is part of the most grotesque episode in the song (Example 12a), during which smugly complacent instrumental interchanges convey the self-satisfaction of the fish, who believe that they have easily grasped the (seemingly pleasant) message of St. Anthony's preaching ("Kein Predigt

Figure 3-1. Arnold Böcklin, *Der Heilige Antonius Predigt den Fischen* (1892)

niemalen den Fischen so g'fallen!"). These are followed, however, by the screeching clarinet line of mm. 49f (labeled "mit Humor"; in the symphony, this line is given even more bite through being set in the E♭ clarinet rather than the less strident B♭ clarinet of the song); the parodic tone reveals just how inadequately they have absorbed the sermon. The allusion to Bruckner, which informs the melodic profile of the interchanges, is one of the most insipid phrases in all of Mahler, a quality that is clearly meant to serve as an emblem of the simple-minded naïveté of the fish. This would thus seem to be an odd moment to be referring to the revered Bruckner, who was nearing the end of his life when Mahler was composing the song. Yet, for those who might recognize the reference and who might recall as well its placement in Bruckner's symphony, the passage thereby acquires an additional sting—one that Mahler might well have expected at least some listeners to appreciate, since Bruckner's Fourth Symphony had been one of his few genuine successes. (Indeed, Mahler himself conducted the work between the completion of the song and the first performances of the symphony, which would have established an even more secure basis for his allusion.[12]) Bruckner's pastoral trio, a *Ländler* he devised to offer a respite from the dynamic heroism of the scherzo, represented an aspect of Bruckner's background that many saw (and many still do see) as basic to Bruckner, both as a person and as a musician: the sensibility of an Austrian peasant, good-hearted but irretrievably naive. The exaggerated naïveté of Mahler's allusion, purged even of Bruckner's exotic modulation,[13] takes the most reassuringly accessible element of Bruckner's art and lets it stand for the whole, as if to say that this is the Bruckner we prefer, and that we, like the fish, will be content to accept it as the essence of the master, simply because it fits more easily into our limited field of vision than his actual message.

But allusion is not the only way Mahler finds to forge intimate connections between interpretive nuance and musical detail, or between the pictorial dimension and deeper meanings. The highly profiled ascending third across the opening two eighth notes in the first full bar of the vocal line (C–E♭; see Example 13) provides a particularly subtle example. As may be seen, this melodic gesture is distinctive to the vocal line, although derived by combining separate motives from the opening texture (e.g., between the first and second bassoons). Except for returns of the opening phrase, however, this motive is taken up on only two other occasions in the song, to suggest the reflection of the sun from the swimming fish in the first stanza ("Sonnenschein glänzen"; mm. 21–26 [0:24]), and again in the final stanza,

Example 13. Mahler, "Des Antonius von Padua Fischpredigt,"
mm. 1–27, 180–185 (3:15)

where it is first extended to an upper sixth before returning to its earlier form; here, the motive is used to set the text "die Karpfen viel fressen, die Predigt vergessen!" (mm. 180–185). Mahler thus draws an oblique parallel between the reflection of the sun, whose rays bounce off the fish while enhancing their appearance, and the forgotten words of the preacher, whose sermon has similarly been "reflected." The motive has a strong pictorial component, in that it seems to "ricochet" off a reflective surface (an effect due both to its ascending thirds and its echolike sequential repetitions), reminding us that the repeated word "glänzen" (shine) connotes reflected light, and that what we are actually "seeing" is reflected sunlight.

But the link between the two applications is itself neither pictorial nor even verbal, but rather metaphorical and conceptual. Mahler's musical setting, which links the key words "glänzen" and "vergessen" through parallel

sequenced repetition of the characteristic motive, draws attention to this hidden dimension of the original poem and hints as well at a sense, in each case, of dissipating strength, as of an echo fading away within the parallel descending sequences. Moreover, into this already subtle connection between the outer stanzas of the song, Mahler incorporates a significant difference in detail. In the first stanza, the vocal motive presents an angular counterpoint

schlag'n mit den Schwän-zen! Im Son-nen-schein glän-zen! Im Son-nen-schein, Son-nen-schein glän-zen, sie

to the ubiquitous sixteenth-note swimming motive by straddling the pedantic two-part bassoon accompaniment (surely, at least at this point, meant to represent St. Anthony), which mechanically traces an ascending cycle of rising melodic thirds within a downward sequence; in the final stanza, however, the vocal motive seems to derive directly from the swimming motive, which at this point incorporates the motive of the cuckoo as it appears in the earlier *Wunderhorn* song, "Ablösung im Sommer" (an emblem, perhaps, of the pretentiousness of the fish's aspirations).[14] Reflected in this shifting affiliation is a quasi-pictorial shift in emphasis, from the shining of the sun's reflected light in the first stanza—a visual analog for the unheeded sermon to come—to the oblivious fish in the last, who have basked in the sermon as fatuously as they had in the sun.

Both the nature of this assonance and its change of focus are at the heart of the "satire on mankind" that Mahler conceived this song to be. The content of St. Anthony's sermon is itself never the issue (and absolute music is thus its ideal vehicle, since his actual words are irrelevant); rather, what matters is that the sermon has no effect and makes no vital connection, even if both sides are apparently satisfied that something useful has taken place. But, while St. Anthony's sermon does not matter as such, his enthusiastic delivery of it does (for both Böcklin and Mahler); moreover, we are wrong

to think that only the fish are involved in the satire, while St. Anthony is exempt. His sermon alternates between pedantic sequencing and the grotesque clarinet passages Mahler labeled "mit Humor" and described to Natalie as "completely drunken, slurred, . . . and confused"; clearly, this is not a sermon likely to benefit any congregation, least of all one made up of fish (no wonder his own church stands empty!). The fish's aimless circlings and the preacher's pontifications mesh so well because they both involve a pointless, self-absorbed posturing that congratulates itself as participating in a lofty act of enriching communication—in which, however, nothing is actually being communicated.

We may hear in this song, then, alongside an apparently respectful salute to Anton Bruckner as the unappreciated preacher (an image that will be resurrected and extended by Luciano Berio, with reference to Martin Luther King, Jr., in the scherzo movement of his *Sinfonia*),[15] a veiled criticism of the aging composer, whose own "church" stood empty not only because of the inadequate sensibilities of his congregation, but also because his own "sermons" pretended to a loftiness that was not consistently achieved. While Mahler's implied criticism of Bruckner is, at best, vaguely stated, it is nonetheless surely deliberate and goes a long way toward explaining both why there are so many sequences in the song and why the most outwardly grotesque moments (the "mit Humor" clarinet passages) always follow the overt allusions to Bruckner. But Bruckner is largely a side issue. More generally, Mahler satirizes all who are content to preach to fish and their like (which is to say, to preach at all), when the activity is on the one hand pointless, since congregations, however constituted, will inevitably remain unchanged, and on the other a mere vehicle through which the preacher may be accorded praise and estimation as a wise and holy man. Notably, the praise of the fish is the one palpable result of St. Antonius's sermon; moreover, there is no suggestion whatever that he is dissatisfied with the results of his sermon.

Mahler's setting thus faults both sides of the attempted communication, and ultimately finds cause for its failure in the nature of humanity. Even had the preacher's sermon been of genuine value, it would have been, by that very token, inaccessible to his congregation, just as—to extend the song's metaphor—one cannot look directly at the sun, but must be satisfied to see it only at reduced intensity, as when it is being reflected. As for the fish (which is to say, the rest of humanity), they understand too little about even themselves to appreciate something that extends beyond their own experience. What the song is "about," then—what it is chiefly and fundamentally concerned with in the story it relates—is the projection of a (necessarily) sham act of communication, in which the participants are oblivious to its falseness.

"In ruhig fliessender Bewegung"

Carolyn Abbate, in her essay on Mahler's Symphony No. 2,[16] connects the scherzo movement ("In ruhig fliessender Bewegung") to the idea of deafness, tracing the roots of one of the explanations Mahler provides for the movement to familiar nineteenth-century preoccupations, including both the horrified fascination that deafness holds for musicians, with Beethoven at the center and Wagner serving as the principal articulator, and the romantic trope of the excluded outsider observing a celebration involving his beloved unfitly paired with another (of these, Adam Mickiewicz's Gustav has seemed the most immediately relevant to Mahler,[17] but earlier obviously relevant examples are Goethe's Werther and the *Wunderhorn* poem from which Mahler derived the first of his *Lieder eines fahrenden Gesellen*). While her emphasis is based on a misreading of Mahler's explanation (as will be argued below), the notion of at least partial deafness—something unheard that would allow sense to be made of what otherwise seems grotesque—is indeed part of the link that connects song to scherzo. Indeed, the grotesqueness of Böcklin's painting stems in part from its silence: since we cannot hear the preacher's words, his posture and gestures seem all the more outlandish. Similarly, in the explanations Mahler provided for this movement, his recurring example is the music that guides dancers at a ball but is inaudible to an observer; since the music that would make their movements sensible is not heard, they seem incomprehensible and grotesque. But it is worth noting that Mahler's scenario is offered only as an *example* for a more general feeling or response to the human condition, not as an actual scenario for the movement. And we should recall that there was a specific context for this kind of feeling in some of the debates taking place in the later nineteenth century concerning absolute music—too esoteric, perhaps, to serve as a generally accessible example for a programmatic explanation, but entirely relevant to this movement. As the debate was mounted by Wagner around mid-century, the very possibility of rationality in music, even music's legitimacy, hinges on the guiding presence of words; Wagner's argument against absolute music centers on the necessity of the feminine Music yielding to the legitimizing will of the masculine Poet.[18] And in both Mahler's song and scherzo, as in Böcklin's painting, there is indeed something verbal that is missing, something vital to its logical foundation that is not heard. In "Fischpredigt," it is the *Fischpredigt* itself we do not hear; instead, we hear musical gestures simulating the sermon and the reactions of the fish that hear it. In the symphonic scherzo, we hear, literally, a song without words, whose characteristic melody, moreover, has been mostly effaced.

The grotesque clarinet passages in "Fischpredigt," which Mahler singles out specifically as representing Antonius's sermon (sounding, as he describes it, "completely drunken, slurred, . . . and confused"), are central to Mahler's casting of the entire song as a "satire." Without these passages and their overtly parodic tone, the absurdities conveyed by the text would not be grounded musically, so that the music might appear to be a mere foil of sorts for the words. Significantly, it is in these passages that we most clearly "hear" the sermon—or, rather, we hear its sound and basic gesture without its words. The grotesquerie of the clarinet passage is implicitly a manifestation of this absence (our deafness, following Abbate's usage); thus, even if the words are not at issue, since the fish are incapable of understanding them, the absence of the words is precisely to the point, since our failure to hear them places us for that moment in full alignment with the perspective of the uncomprehending fish and so underscores for us the absurdity of the situation.

In giving his music two independent settings, Mahler evidently sought to take a specific setting of irredeemable alienation, presented as a "satire on mankind," and recast it in more general terms, as a more general statement about the human condition. While the song has an amusing surface to respond to, so that it is possible to be simply diverted by the song and fairly oblivious to its deeper meanings, Mahler's music, as he presents it anew in the symphony, seems to embody more directly these deeper meanings. The absence of a specific scenario allows these meanings to emerge from behind the scrim of a specific narrative. It is ironic, then, that Mahler's explanations have been read primarily for the clues they offer to those who would reduce the movement to its "program." Seemingly, Abbate's reading is deeper than most, as she tries to find resonance with issues of some import both historically and within her larger project in *Unsung Voices*, which is to probe our perception of "voice" in nineteenth-century music. Unfortunately, she begins her discussion of this movement with a distortion, by placing a key phrase in one of Mahler's three main surviving explanations for the movement in italics (thus, "you *can't hear the music they dance to!*"; she only briefly refers to Mahler's other two explanations, in separate footnotes). To be sure, she acknowledges these italics as hers, but it is impossible to read the result as anything but a seeming cry from the heart by a musician tormented with the horrific prospect of deafness.[19] Without her italics, the terror conveyed by the passage, if there is terror, has less to do with deafness—which is, in any case, a selective deafness, the result of physical distance—than with the apparent futility of making sense of life's seemingly pointless animation, for which dancers' movements to unheard music serve merely as illustration.

The extensive history of reading Mahler's explanation as a specific scenario for his scherzo, involving an excluded outsider observing a dance from afar, is supported in a number of powerful ways. Mahler alludes at the end of both song and scherzo to Schumann's "Das ist ein Flöten und Geigen" from *Dichterliebe*, which traces a similar scenario—in which, however (as Abbate points out), the dance is heard but not seen, an inversion of Mahler's sensory deprivation. And the triple meter and general flow of the music make it seem sufficiently waltzlike for us to accept it as such, albeit not a representative example; however, this, too, is problematic since (again, as Abbate has argued) it seems strange for Mahler to set an unheard waltz as one we can actually hear. But, even putting aside Abbate's clearly relevant objections, none of these supports is as strong as it seems. Unlike the Bruckner allusion, which takes part in a repeated sequence of events vital to the overall musical statement, the Schumann allusion appears only at the end, as a brief parting assonance with the end of Schumann's song; significantly, too, the passage he alludes to seems to represent not the dance, but rather the weeping of the angels that Schumann's protagonist imagines at this point, which is heard, like Schumann's (and Mahler's) descending chromatic line, "in between" ("dazwischen") the din and clamor of the dance (see Example 14). Moreover, the apparent parallel in situation conceals a difference that should be seen as fundamental, since Schumann's protagonist makes all too much sense of what he hears, grotesque though it may seem. And, finally, although passages in the scherzo are indeed dancelike, its overall character and most telling moments are not.

"As If Deformed by a Concave Mirror"

Even so, we need not simply put aside Mahler's three extant explanations for this movement as being, each considered individually, a poor fit for what seems to be happening in the music. Quite the opposite—his explanations can be extremely helpful if we read them more carefully, with an eye for both differences and similarities among the three. Here, then, are his three

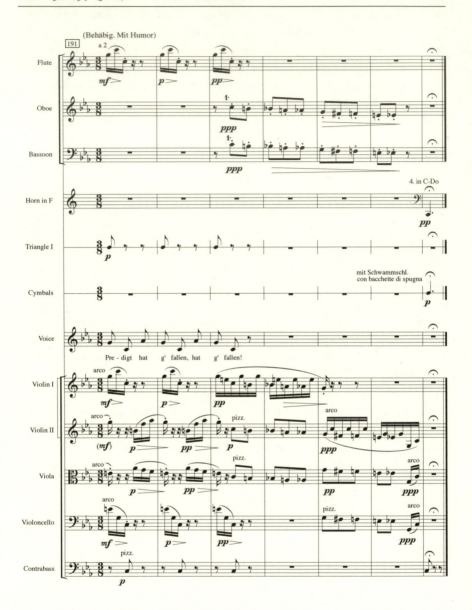

explanations in chronological order, the first two taken from fairly contemporary private letters (the quotation Abbate cites is the first of these, given here in her translation, but without her italics and with Mahler's original emphases restored), the third from a nearly suppressed program note dated some years later:

> When you wake out of this sad dream, and must re-enter life, confused as it is, it happens easily that this always-stirring, never-resting, never-comprehensible pushing that is life becomes *horrible* to you, like the motion of dancing figures in a brightly-lit ballroom, into which you are peering from outside, in the dark night—from such a *distance* that you can *not* hear the *music* they dance to! Then life seems *meaningless* to you, like a horrible chimera, that you wrench yourself out of with a horrible cry of disgust.[20]

> The second and third movements are episodes from the life of the fallen hero. The Andante tells of his love. What I have expressed in the scherzo can only be described visually. When one watches a dance from a distance, without hearing the music, the revolving motions of the partners seem absurd and pointless. Likewise, to someone who has lost himself and his happiness, the world seems crazy and confused, as if deformed by a concave mirror. The scherzo ends with the fearful scream of a soul that has experienced this torture.[21]

> A spirit of disbelief and negation has seized him. He is bewildered by the bustle of appearances and he loses his perception of childhood and the profound strength that love alone can give. He despairs both of himself and of God. The world and life begin to seem unreal. Utter disgust for every form of existence and evolution seizes him in an iron grasp, torments him until he utters a cry of despair.[22]

The immediate context for the scherzo is set by the previous movement, a "sad dream" about the protagonist's lost love, from which the scherzo represents a discomfiting awakening.[23] The cause of the disorienting effect of the scherzo, which each explanation describes in different ways is to be understood as that of an unbearable reality, made so by an intensified awareness of the absence of the love recalled in the previous movement.[24] In each explanation, Mahler also suggests other, less specific absences that make "life" and/or "the world" seem "meaningless, like a horrible chimera," or "crazy and confused, as if deformed by a concave mirror," or, more simply "unreal," to the extent that a crescendo of disgust results in a "horrible cry," "fearful scream," or "cry of despair." These absences range from repose and comprehensibility in the first explanation, to self and happiness in the second, to the perception of childhood and the strength of love in the third, the latter to the point that self and God are also renounced. With each successive explanation, Mahler elaborates these absences more fully while simultaneously curtailing and eventually dropping the analogy that most interpretations have seized upon as the programmatic scenario for the movement, that is, dancing figures without the music that rationalizes their movements.

"Absolute Music" as a Topic

As differences in Mahler's descriptive accounts make clear, the expressive thrust of the movement is not concerned with the specific *content* of what is missing so much as with the effect of incomprehensibility engendered by its absence. The absences noted in especially the latter two of these explanations—love, happiness, self, God, and the perception of childhood—include what many would regard as the central things that can make life worth living, that have the capacity to give order and meaning to an otherwise chaotic existence. Put differently, these are the principal experiences through which "life" and "the world" return a sense of worth to the individual soul, the central avenues of communication through which the world provides positive reinforcement. The main point of Mahler's movement, then, is to project the grotesqueness of what remains when these things are gone, when communication between the world and us breaks down, when we lose our sense of connection to reality.[25] The outer explanations use the most compelling phrases for the qualities that the world exhibits from this perspective—"this always-stirring, never-resting, never-comprehensible pushing" and "the bustle of appearances"—which together convey a sense of ongoing, self-propelled motion that is alien to us and takes no notice of us, and whose logic is inaccessible. If this is, indeed, what the main sections of Mahler's scherzo are meant to project, it is also well in line with the "threefold absoluteness" I referred to earlier in connection with Sybil's panicked response to certain types of classical music, an absoluteness that consists in "its inaccessible removal from outside control, its seeming ability to generate indefinitely its own continuation, and its unassailable power to impose itself on its listeners."

Mahler's expressive strategies and musical procedures in this movement may be likened to his evoking "absolute music" as if it were itself an established topic in instrumental music, carrying with it a set of specific associations and musical properties. While a referential musical background for such a topic is difficult to trace for either Mahler or his audience, the split between "classical" and "popular" music in the twentieth century has since made the topic a familiar one, albeit within a fairly wide range of expressive functions that do not always align with Mahler's usage.[26] Thus, within modern popular culture in general, but especially in films, serious classical music is routinely evoked as an emblem of high culture; here, we might reasonably speak of a "classical music" topic. Within this broader topic, which embraces any number of associations this kind of music might have for us and the characters in the film, however, there is a prominent strand that corresponds closely to Mahler's practice in his "Fischpredigt" scherzo, in which "classical music" appears as something foreign and unnatural, even alien to whatever has been established in the film as "human." In these applications, the music we hear is typically either instrumental music or vocal music in a foreign language, and we, as audience, are assumed not to have any special knowledge of that music.[27] In less extreme cases, this use of absolute music might register as an affectation on the order of a character's introducing foreign phrases into casual conversation, not so much to communicate content as to communicate his or her own learnedness. The piano music in the earliest of the scenes from *Sybil* described above, however, represents a much more extreme case, in which absolute music is experienced not as a mere affectation that might be easily disregarded but as a genuine threat. Even so, there is a disparity in proportion; when Sybil tries vainly to escape the sound of Chopin's etude, we identify (or at least seem meant to identify) with her sense of oppression, but know as well that the extremity of her reaction is something that will require eventual explanation. Her exaggerated response heightens the sense of a shared topic with Mahler's scherzo, for the music seems to be more than simply oppressive; it seems as well to represent and intensify Sybil's confused alienation from the world, which could well be described, from her perspective, as an "always-stirring, never-resting, never-comprehensible pushing."

As a topic, absolute music can impart a sense of alienation by projecting both self-contained activity and a vantage point from which that activity seems disengaged; it does not, however, in itself determine precisely how that sense of alienation registers. Thus, in Mahler's scherzo, as in *Sybil,* the topic suggests a world that takes no notice of a subjective center and whose bustling activities seem disjointed and confusing as a result; we, as audience, are placed in the position of the alienated individual. In "Fischpredigt," however, the alienating effect is rendered more objectively than subjectively, so that we witness the alienation from somewhere above or outside, as something to deplore rather than something to feel as an extension of our own experience; thus, we do not identify with the fish (even if we are, implicitly, of their number), nor do we cry out in protest against them—although, to be sure, the angels do weep at the end, with the allusion to Schumann.

A better correlative for "Fischpredigt" than *Sybil* in later twentieth-century popular culture is the 1966 Beatles song "Eleanor Rigby." Unusual in its instrumentation and accompanimental style, "Eleanor Rigby" is dominated by the sound of closely miked lower strings playing in an agitated minor mode and contrapuntal texture evocative of baroque music, so that style, instrumentation, and texture are all obviously referential to classical music at its most severe.[28] This assonance is especially prominent during the recurring phrase that launches the song, with each rendering of its single repeated lyric, "Ah, look at all the lonely people," descending from the initial cry into the register of the lower strings. Thus, the vocal line "points" to this music at the same time that the words direct us to "look." Clearly, the baroque-like music is meant to represent the larger collection of "lonely people" of whom Eleanor Rigby and Father McKenzie are representative, as well as, perhaps, the baroque details that betoken their lonely, (metaphorically?) celibate lives ("darning his socks in the night"). Here, the lyric indicates a perspective outside the empty, baroque gyrations of the "lonely people," although, as in "Fischpredigt," identification is also possible.

If perspective is not itself built into the topic, there must nevertheless be an established vantage point through which the topic may be perceived as alienated (or alienating) activity. In the two songs, this is established largely through lyrics and structure; thus, in "Fischpredigt," a clear verbal narrative is enacted musically, while in "Eleanor Rigby," a fairly dispassionate narrative in the verses mutates during the refrain—"All the lonely people, where *do* they all come from?"—into an exhortation to pay attention to their plight and that of others like them. Indeed, the similarity in perspectives is given peculiar focus through a striking textual assonance, when in the central verse of "Eleanor Rigby" we encounter a parallel to Antonius in "Father McKenzie, writing the words of a sermon that no one will hear"; while it seems quite unlikely that Paul McCartney was thinking of Mahler's song while composing his own song of alienation, he nevertheless found analogous expressive means.[29] (What he *was* thinking about may be inferred, with some help from Mahler's contemporary Sigmund Freud, from the fact that until quite late, the unheeded preacher was to be named "Father McCartney.") But "Eleanor Rigby" is, if anything, more objectifying than "Fischpredigt," for it more explicitly establishes its vantage point above its alienated subjects, musically as well as verbally. Thus, the baroque topic of a descending minor-mode tetrachord provides a melancholy overlay to the refrain,[30] which is gradually intensified over the course of the song, leading in its second appearance back to the opening demand to "look" and combining contrapuntally with that demand in its third and final appearance, which closes the song. The mutation is progressive, from dispassionate narration, to the posing of the questions, to the forthright demand for us to look at them—all the while enacting and intensifying a shift in perspective toward what might be construed as yet another vestige of the baroque: the smugly grandiose pathos inherent in the act of sympathetic observation.

In *Sybil*, too, an embracing narrative will eventually flesh out an explanation for her perspective on the music that disturbs her, but more subjective immediacy is achieved by merging the experience of the music with nonverbal tokens of its oppressive effect: her unsuccessful flight from its sound and the intermittent electronic distortion applied to it. For absolute music to function as a topic of alienation, then, there must be both highly profiled musical elements that serve as identifiers and a perspective located outside the topic from which it will seem alien. Before detailing how these are established in Mahler's scherzo, however, it is worth considering why such a topic might show up in the late nineteenth century symphony and, more particularly, in Mahler.

Many earlier models for the split between classical and popular music in the twentieth century may indeed be seen as its precursors. These typically involve a distinction between serious and comic (especially in opera), or between religious and secular. During the late eighteenth century, particularly with Mozart, it became increasingly possible to explore various manifestations of these splits within a single work. This practice is most fully developed in opera and the symphony, each of which routinely uses or evokes a number of contrasting styles in fairly close juxtaposition. Mozart's use of *opera seria* elements in his comic operas, for example, has been widely discussed, and his use of seemingly incompatible topics in some of his symphonies has been usefully explored as well.[31]

If, with Mozart, the symphony becomes an arena for presenting a dramatic interaction among musical elements that had become identified as mutually incompatible and antagonistic, it became in the nineteenth century a place where larger issues were even more trenchantly addressed. Especially by the later nineteenth century, the symphony had become the focal point for discussions of music's place among the arts, and one of the principal genres for expressing a sense of national difference—capable, like opera, of the most elevated and public expression and drama, yet more universally accessible than opera, which had to contend with an unavoidable language barrier. Wagner's mid-century claims for the inherent failure of absolute music—which had, he claimed, resulted in the death of the symphony—are central here, in part because he identified ways in which music could seem absolute even when it was associated with a text, thus separating absoluteness from the issue of explicitly intended meanings.[32] Even more important was Wagner's identification of "absoluteness" as a quality that music could or could not have, which represented a decisive move away from asserting it (or something like it) to be an inherent aspect of music, however incompletely realized, or identifying it as what set music apart from other arts. While, for the most part, composers and commentators would continue to operate as though music intrinsically either was or was not essentially absolute in some sense, the idea of a binary-like choice in the matter would later be critical to Mahler's evocation of absolute music as a musical topic.

Yet, absolute music had for Wagner a decidedly different profile than for Mahler, since, for the former, the feminine "music" appropriated a folk element in its attempt to forge an independently viable art form (an attempt that was doomed to fail because the vitality of the appropriated element could not survive this kind of expropriation). For Mahler, on the other hand, elements stemming from the core of high art music—motivic work, counterpoint, sequence, and so on—would make up the core features of absolute music treated as an alienating musical topic. An explanation for this disparity (and an explanation is surely needed, given Mahler's reverence for Wagner) may be grounded in the developing debate over music's absoluteness, late-nineteenth-century symphonic practice, and Mahler's own cultural position.

Eduard Hanslick's claims for music's inherent absoluteness, which followed close on the heels of Wagner's denunciations of music's absolutist presumptions,[33] were based on music's capacity to make sense on its own—to behave autonomously, as if it were a closed system. As a result, abstract processes stripped of extramusical meanings, rather than a folk basis, came to be widely seen as the foundation for an absolute musical practice. On the other hand, folk material became in the later decades of the nineteenth century the core ingredient of a nationalist symphonic practice, the principal means by which "emerging" nations could assert a vital and viable difference between their music and the Germanic traditions that had by then laid claim to the (most often absolutist) mainstream.[34] Mahler's own attitudes, not always acknowledged, were formed within this theoretical and practical milieu, and, moreover, could scarcely escape one of the most palpable results of his ethnic background: musically, the absolute mainstream of German music, which he aspired to dominate as both conductor and composer, was nevertheless something very much outside his own cultural heritage. In a real sense, absolute music was for Mahler a second language, the inevitable result of his provincial background and also of his tendency throughout his life to assume the role of cultural outsider. This in turn led to a fundamental ambivalence in Mahler that would make it possible for him to establish, almost by default, an outsider's perspective as well on absolute music, even though he remained committed to its central traditions and would on many memorable occasions tap directly and without apparent qualms into its expressive power (as, for example, in the finale of the Third Symphony). Indeed, Mahler's ambivalent attitudes extended as well to his deployment of absolute music as a topic, which, as we will see in subsequent discussions, quite often took on a considerably more sympathetic cast than in the "Fischpredigt" scherzo.

Some of the descriptive phrases given earlier for the music to which Sybil responds poorly may also serve as a descriptive account of absolute music as Mahler evokes it as a topic, especially when it is given negative connotations: "relentless, inexorable in its forward momentum"; "typically minor mode, given to close motivic work or ostinato, spinning itself out with a self-generating, unstoppable, self-propelled logic, this music assumes the role of a terrifying monstrous *presence*, oblivious, self-absorbed, and beyond reach." When absolute music is evoked negatively as a topic, the very strengths it exhibits as a practice—its reliance on what is somewhat loosely termed "musical logic"—provide the core indicators; to the above descriptions we may thus add counterpoint and its various devices and constructs, including canon and fugue. Somewhat paradoxically, however, the topic also requires that the apparatus of musical logic manifest itself in a somewhat skewed or exaggerated fashion, so that its logic is somehow also illogical— undercut, perhaps, by an unbalanced application or by other lapses in basic coherence. Something like parody thus provides the aesthetic distance necessary to objectify the practices of absolute music and to make them seem sufficiently "other" so as to function in this way. In this sense, musical parodies such as Mozart's "A Musical Joke" (or virtually the entire corpus of P. D. Q. Bach "discoveries" by Peter Schikele) treat absolute music topically. Indeed, when "A Musical Joke" appears in the 1998 film *Life Is Beautiful*, as background music for a gala social event for the German personnel of a concentration camp, we are for a moment transplanted into the world of Mahler's "Fischpredigt," for in both, a parody of absolute-music procedures is taken for the real thing by listeners whose sensibilities we are implicitly encouraged to judge accordingly.

Representing Alienation

These lapses in coherence help establish a perspective in Mahler's scherzo from which absolute music can appear alienating or alienated, but Mahler employs other devices as well. The opening timpani strokes link the absolutist strand directly to the disruption of the "sad dream" of the previous movement; programmatically, we are wrenched back to the real world while, musically, we are pulled directly by that gesture into an evolving world of absolutist motivic work, with the timpani strokes providing the initiating motivic germ. The extreme gesture of the opening, calculated to disorient, so as to disengage us from the world of the previous movement, also provides an enduring connection to that movement, ensuring that we retain the sensibilities of that earlier world as the vantage point from which we experience the scherzo.[35] As noted, the satiric tone of the E♭ clarinet solos (marked "mit Humor"; r29.22–r30.1 [0:55]) helps establish perspective by attaching a grotesque surface to the evolving processes. The prolonged absence of the vocal melody at the beginning and its abrupt curtailment when it does appear (Example 15; cf. Example 13) expose more nakedly the motivic underpinnings of the melody, an effect enhanced through knowledge of the song but also somewhat independent of it. Even those who have not heard the song will find the inversion of the motivic dynamic of its melody and accompaniment disorienting, as the angular eighth-note figure prepared by the exaggeratedly evolving introduction takes a back seat to the obsessive

Example 15. Mahler, Symphony No. 2, third movement, r30.12–19 (1:11)

circling motion of the running sixteenth-note figures, which accompany in the song but in the scherzo assume the role of principal melody. However, the central assertions of an independent vantage point in the scherzo occur in those extended moments of escape, within the loosely defined "trios"[36] that first leave the scherzo behind through a dreamlike reverie in a remote key (see especially r40–r43; 4:45) and then attempt to reject it outright through the orchestral scream (r50–r51; 8:05–8:28).

Although Mahler's procedures seem to represent a radically new departure, many processes of absolute music had, even before Mahler, a pronounced habit of calling attention to themselves, especially within a symphonic context. This circumstance allowed Mahler to ground his own procedures, however newly conceived, securely within earlier traditions. Two aspects of the scherzo, in particular—its use of musical "perpetual motion" and its occasional evocation of fugal procedures—are thus grounded. In Beethoven's symphonies, for example, a sense of perpetual motion, in which a relatively short melodic "loop" threatens to replicate itself indefinitely, presents and sometimes sustains the possibility that musical process might disengage itself from its background and proliferate endlessly; to some extent, this is a trivialization of the closely allied practice of ostinato, traditionally used to represent obsessional mental states. With Beethoven's perpetual-motion effects, the apparent possibility of unstoppable self-replication is rarely threatening[37] and may be controlled through an overlaying of more dynamic processes, such as crescendo or instrumental exchange. Both of the latter allow Beethoven, in the first movement of his Symphony No. 6 (*Pastoral*), to indulge in extravagantly brazen repetitions of simple motives without either comic effect or tedium, all the while projecting, as a metaphor for nature, a potentially endless sonic landscape that is both static and engaging (thus, mm. 16–26 in the first group and long stretches of the development section, especially mm. 151–186 and 197–232). More common for Beethoven is his comic use of perpetual-motion effects, as in the finale of his Fourth Symphony, or in the scherzo of his Second (just before the reprise in the second part, mm. 50–59).

Fugal processes, too, have a way of calling attention to themselves as musically absolute, even if our recognition of a fugue as such is often swamped by the dramatic gesture in which it participates. Such is the case in the finale of Mozart's Symphony No. 41 (*Jupiter*), where fugue provides a vehicle for bringing together the diverse themes of the movement within a single culminating statement. As symphonic discourse became more overtly narrative with Beethoven, fugue seemed increasingly difficult to integrate, however—a tendency well illustrated by Beethoven's use of fugue in his Symphony No. 3 (*Eroica*). In the first movement, the developmental fugue (mm. 236–248) is short-lived and might seem in itself fairly innocuous, but its disruptive power is nevertheless tremendous. Thus, as if to stop the fugue's absolute processes of self-generating activity, Beethoven gives vent to what was then the most violently dissonant passage in all instrumental music (extending through m. 284, when the passage finally resolves into the notorious "new" theme in E minor); one can only conclude from this disproportionately harsh response that the fugue posed—or at least seemed to pose—a threat so virulent that it had to be stopped dead in its tracks. In the second movement, when the central fugue is allowed to unfold at some length (mm. 114–150), it does indeed overwhelm, both structurally and expressively. It appears, however, not as an intruder, but rather as a subjectively placed ex-

pression of intense grief, confirming a much-exploited association of absolute musical processes with obsessive inwardness that will help shape the
absolute-music topic as Mahler develops it. By contrast, the fugues in the
"Eroica" finale (mm. 117–174 and 277–328) seem fairly complacent affairs.
In their objectified manipulation of derived motives, they seem more a matter of performance (of earlier conflicts? of composing virtuosity?) than of
unfolding drama; their artificiality turns them into quasi-courtly emblems
of a success already achieved. While the "Eroica" fugues might reasonably be
interpreted along somewhat different lines (a lot depends, after all, on performance), there is no denying that they appear in each case *as fugues*, carrying with them an inner compulsion to elaborate themselves as such. Thus,
each in its way threatens to preempt more basic symphonic processes.[38]

The element of perpetual motion has often been identified as a defining
feature of both Mahler's scherzo and the song from which it derives,[39] but
only the scherzo makes overtly fugal gestures; these play a significant role in
the interplay of the absolute-music topic and an ongoing attempt to escape
or reject its compulsive energy. Thus, while perpetual motion is basic, even
definitive for the topic of absolute music as it is deployed in the scherzo, fugal gestures have a specifically narrative role, appearing as tokens of absolutist process to reinscribe the topic when it has been threatened or temporarily displaced (r34f, r36f, and r38–r39 [2:40, 3:23, and 4:09]; in the last
case, Mahler carries fugal processes to an even more absolutist level by playing the subject against its melodic inversion).

There are, however, sections in the scherzo that seem ambivalent about
both the absolute-music topic and the sensibilities mapped to the independent vantage point. The first major-mode section (r32f; see Example 16) seems
in some respects to be an extension of the absolute-music topic, with its
resumption of the running sixteenth notes and its tendency to allow its
melodic lines only a severely limited trajectory (typically four bars). Yet, the
section also seems sympathetic, offering warmth and the most persuasively
dancelike rhythms in the movement; moreover, it emerges through a decep-
tion of sorts, displacing an arrival on C with the sudden assertion of F major
as tonic. So, too, the major-mode outbursts beginning at r37 and r39 seem to
involve a mixed perspective, continuing the absolutist motivic work beneath
a loud intrusive surface, which might reasonably be heard, alternatively, as
either a temporary displacement of the topic or another dimension of it.
Specifically, the affinity between these passages and the passage leading to
the culminating orchestral scream (r49–r51; 7:51–8:28) urges the former identification, so that the passages might be understood to represent outright

rejections of the absolute-music topic. Yet, from the perspective of Mahler's programmatic explanations, these sudden outbursts might also, and perhaps even more reasonably, be understood as part of the irrational bustle of the "dance of life" whose music and rationale cannot be heard. It is scarcely necessary for us to make sense of every detail in the movement in order to understand it as playing out a conflict between absolute music and an outside perspective that finds something grotesque in its detached *moto perpetuo*; Mahler must, after all, project this conflict within the recognizable structure of a symphonic scherzo, which imposes its own demands concerning contrast and overall coherence. Yet, a more nuanced reading of Mahler's deployment of his absolute-music topic might accommodate these ambiguous sections within a three-part scenario of near-seduction by, attempted (but unsuccessful) escape from, and ultimate rejection of the absolutist element.

Absolute music seems by its nature to be highly seductive, so that even when it appears as a negative presence—as a topic of alienation—its repulsive aspect is ineluctably mixed with an attractiveness of nearly equal power. This alliance of polar opposites is basic to the scenario of the scherzo, informing its conflicted subjectivity, which is to say, the vantage point from which its grotesquerie nevertheless holds an almost irresistible fascination. Even without its repulsive aspect, the seductive capacity of absolute music entails a striking paradox: it seduces even though it appears supremely indifferent to any potential objects of seduction. Indeed, it seduces precisely through its own self-absorption, its oblivious machinations providing something analogous to the hypnotist's twirling sphere or methodically oscillating pendulum. A model for this kind of hypnotic seduction is projected early on in Mahler's scherzo, seemingly within the topic itself, as melodic phrases from the vocal line of "Fischpredigt" appear and are absorbed easily and almost immediately into the flow of absolute music. The first instance of this involves no less than the signature vocal melody of "Fischpredigt," which appears briefly (and for the first time) in 130.12, only to become utterly lost within the subsequent sequencing (cf. Examples 13 and 15 above); something similar then immediately happens with a vocal phrase taken from later in "Fischpredigt" ("Auch jene Phantasten"), as shown in Example 17.[40]

The initial turn to F major (Example 16), which occurs shortly thereafter, is similarly embedded within the topic of absolute music, so that its principal dancelike tune emerges only briefly and inconclusively, alternating with a variety of other melodic phrases that develop its warmth into something less congenial. Thus, the oboe and bassoon phrase that gives temporary focus to the dance topic (Example 16, 132.10–14; 1:59) is first extended

Example 16. Mahler, Symphony No. 2, third movement, r32.1–r34.1 (1:50)

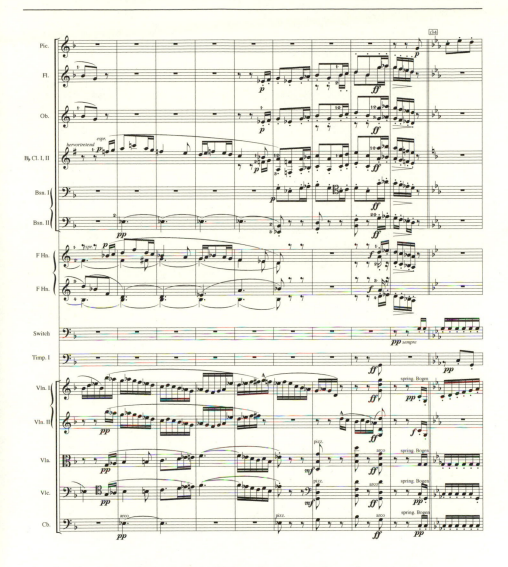

by the clarinets, which carry its lilting rhythms back to the pedantic staccato eighth notes of the Fischpredigt while settling harmonically into the minor (r32.14–r33.1; 2:04–2:08). With its second appearance, the dance topic is extended in the low strings, this time with an insistent chromatic movement upward that eventually propels a second shift in affect, once again to the minor mode and away from the flowing dance rhythms (r33.9–18; 2:17). With its third and final appearance, when it combines vertically

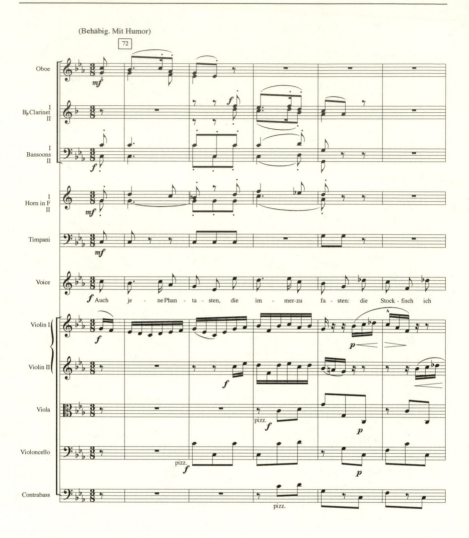

with the chromatic motive, the dance topic loses its harmonic and instrumental moorings; now in E♭ and given to the clarinets and horns, it yields
almost immediately to a staccato eighth-note continuation and a seemingly
inevitable return to C minor (r33.21–29; 2:31).

Despite the distinctly negative direction in which these processes take the
dance topic, the persuasive warmth of the instruments throughout, especially the lower strings, make this episode seem like a nearly successful

seduction. The seduction is interrupted, however, by the abrupt *fortissimo* outburst in r33.28 (2:38), which leads directly back into the signal theme of "Fischpredigt"; the coldness of the return is emphasized through a new stac-cato articulation of the running sixteenth notes and the introduction of fu-gal processes (r34f; 2:40). One might reasonably take the initial interruptive gesture to be a shudder of revulsion, even though it, too, seems embedded in absolute motivic work. Precisely this ambiguity will mark each subse-quent eruption in the movement, albeit on an increasingly more elaborate scale, until the culminating "cry of disgust" caps the final "absolutist" cre-scendo, as the first unambiguous assertion of a perspective at odds with the absolute-music topic.

The fugal processes in the scherzo, which never progress beyond being merely fugal to the extent of elaborating a full fugal exposition, come in three main spans, all within the part of the movement that lies between the failed seduction and the attempted escape represented in the E major trio-like section.[41] The first fugal passage (beginning at r34; 2:40) is based on the vocal melody from "Fischpredigt" and quickly collapses into simple motivic reiter-ation. The second (beginning at r36; see Example 18) begins with a sudden

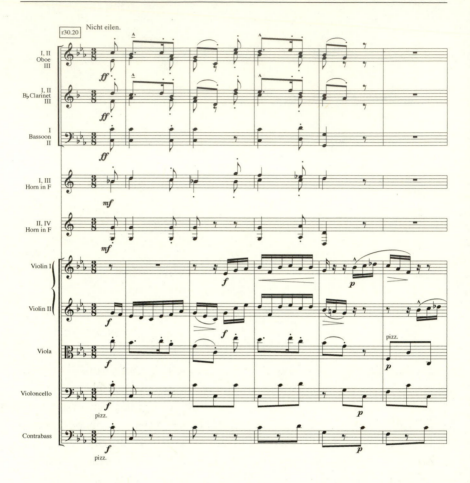

break into C major and takes as its staccato subject a refashioned version of the dance topic, extended in running sixteenth notes that derive audibly from the opening section. Two signs of resistance accompany this passage, however. From the outset, the stasis of a high tonic pedal, anticipating extended moments of repose in the trio to come, stands in sharp relief to the obsessive activity in the low strings. Then, after the pedal has evaporated, the first extended major-mode outburst, in D major, interrupts the *pianissimo* figurations of the fugue. But the absolute-music topic persists throughout the outburst, so that when the it subsides, the fugue simply resumes, this time with a distinctive new counterpoint that will become central for the absolute-music topic in its later phases (r38.1–4; see Example 18). Here, contrapuntal abstraction is at its

furthest remove, as the dance-derived subject is further manipulated through melodic inversion after the eleventh bar.

The major-mode outburst that interrupts this fugal passage is in E major, signaling a newly determined resistance by extending the ascent from C to D that launched the earlier outburst. This time, a seeming escape from the scherzo's obsessions will indeed result, achieved (after a final wrenching gesture of defiance) in the songlike trumpet solo accompanied by harp ("Sehr getragen und gesangvoll"; see Example 19). The effect of escape here is managed in part through a sense of surreal distortion, combining the benediction of two harps with a four-part trumpet choir reeking of nostalgia, through which a small-town rusticity is all the more vividly evoked by way of Mahler's instructions that they "sing" very expressively with bells in the air ("sehr ausdrucksvoll gesungen" and "Schalltrichter in die Höhe"). As if this were not enough, Mahler indicates that nearly every melodic note should be inflected with a swelling dynamic effect; moreover, even after the trumpets

have yielded to other instruments, birdlike trills in the flute punctuate the melody (after r41), so that, metaphorically, the rustic retreat from a citylike bustle seems complete.[42] Yet, escape is never total. While (at first) bending to the demands of the song, the running sixteenth notes continue throughout in the strings, ready to resurface when the time is ripe. The second fugal subject reappears, *pianississimo,* under the birdcalls, providing another reminder of what has not been entirely left behind. With the protracted cadences of the song melody (r41.17; 5:24), the running sixteenth notes emerge *fortissimo* at the top of the instrumental texture, and the harps temporarily

disappear; then, when the harps do return to accompany a final retrospective reprise by the solo trumpet, they do so with staccato eighth notes rather than arpeggiated sixteenth notes as before, overlaying the closing gesture with a clear reminder of the scherzo, whose return is imminent.

The return to the material of the scherzo seems more a resumption than a return (a typical Mahlerian effect). Thus, we hear the interrupted fugal processes resume, simultaneously with the final recessionary cadences of the trumpets from the trio. These are marked initially by a more forceful return of the second fugal subject and continue with melodically inverted counterpoint in the strings (r43; 5:53). Yet fugal processes are quickly layered over, then displaced, by developmental processes, which will take us more clearly back to a fully realized recapitulative gesture. First, the simultaneous melodic inversions are organized into a rising sequence, led initially by the distinctive new counterpoint that appeared with the third fugal span. The actual reprise is then clearly marked by harmonic arrival in C minor, a partial

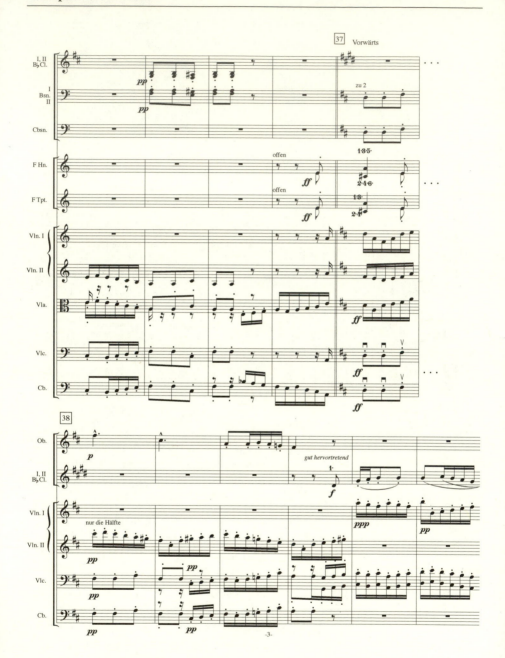

-3-

return of the introductory bars of the scherzo, and a contrapuntal fusion of the most distinctive melodic gestures from the first span of the scherzo, including the running sixteenth notes, the signature tune from "Fischpredigt," and the new counterpoint associated with the later phases of the fugue.

The central effect of these manipulations is that neither the protesting outbursts nor the seeming escape of the trio has truly mattered. After each interruption, the scherzo has simply continued where it left off, almost as if nothing had happened: fugal processes are directed into teleological development, and the permanence of the opening condition is affirmed through an enhanced return. Nothing in this larger pattern is disturbed by the interruptions, only delayed, so that all subjectivity is apparently lost in the oblivious machination of absolute-musical processes. But the reality is even worse, for subjectivity is not simply lost, but rather absorbed and managed: protesting outbursts are replotted as process, and the rising large-scale se-

quence that articulates their fury and determination (from C to D to E) is simply taken over as the central marker for teleological development. If, earlier, one might have reasonably asked what musical events could possibly motivate an orchestral scream of the kind Mahler describes in his programmatic accounts of the movement, the more pressing question at this point is not why the return of the scherzo is followed by mounting hysteria and a culminating scream, but whether even that can have any effect against the absolutist machinery.

Yes, and no. Eventually, the conclusion of "Fischpredigt," bypassed earlier through the formally expanding gestures of fugal process, will return to close the movement, imparting a sense of abiding control to the absolute-music topic. More immediately, however, the scream asserts a subjectivity that can be neither denied nor absorbed, opening and sustaining a renewed space of escape through the calming, sustained harmonies in the upper reg-

Example 19. Mahler, Symphony No. 2, third movement, r40.1–5 (4:45)

ister, the audible residue of the scream. Remarkably, this escape is managed in the very presence of the ongoing absolute-music topic, which churns away in the subdivided lower strings (after r51; 8:28), indicating through its empty symmetries and repetitive passagework that palpable if not lasting damage has been done to it. And, when the topic does return on its own (from r54 [9:36] to the end), it seems incomplete, absent the signature melody from "Fischpredigt," the E♭ clarinet grotesqueries, and the sanguinities embodied in the dance topic and Bruckner allusions, so that the weeping of the angels at the end (in the Schumann allusion) seems also to represent the whimpering of the topic in full retreat. But something else beyond this partial victory, and ultimately more significant, is accomplished by the emetic purge of the orchestral scream: the scream articulates with uncompromising force an irrevocable gesture of denial, of refusing to take part. Thus, no indicators of subjective dismay remain in the fairly brief concluding section—only a sense of psychic detachment, and of waiting. Then, with the calm opening of the next movement, a much less troubled subjectivity is immediately established as the center of our concern, through the sound of a human voice entering without instrumental accompaniment.

Mahler was a little vague about the specific source for the overall scenario of his Second Symphony, perhaps because his apparent literary source, at least in the first movement, lay too close to home in its depiction of an adulterous relationship.[43] The most plausible programmatic explanation for the work is one that recounts the anguish of a soul caught between heaven and hell, forced to wander the earth because his business among the living is not yet finished, who recounts and relives traumatic events in his life, revisiting what led him to suicide in the first movement, dreaming of a lost love in the second, and recoiling in disgust in the scherzo, when, from the vantage point of a soul whose body no longer lives, he contemplates the empty pursuits of the living world. In the end, in the resurrection finale, the wandering soul enters heaven and is forgiven. This overall scenario explains more specifically why, in the scherzo, the "hero" cannot hear the music that the living dance to.

More broadly, this scenario of a wandering outsider bears an uncanny resemblance to the perspective of a late-nineteenth-century converted Jew in the German lands, caught between two worlds, unable to leave the one behind, incapable of fully embracing the other in part because he fears—knows—he will not be welcome. More precisely, this was Mahler's perspective, as a Jew contemplating conversion, extended through melodramatically romantic sensibilities to project the experiences of someone forced to wander the world without a home of his own, disgusted by the emptiness he sees around him. And so we may perhaps see more clearly why the resurrection Mahler details in the finale proves unexpectedly forgiving and nonjudgmental: in the alternative world that Mahler creates for himself in the Second

Symphony, the penitent is offered a blanket forgiveness, one that might absolve, as we may assume, even the most grievous sin of being born a Jew.

But this program has an odd ambivalence, particularly with regard to the scherzo, for the direction in which the symphony as a whole points is diametrically opposed to the orientation of the musical and cultural markers in this movement. Within the program of the symphony, the haunted subjectivity of the scherzo that rejects the empty bustle of living humanity is immediately displaced, in the calm opening of the next movement, by a human voice seeking and eventually finding Christian redemption. From the perspective of the Christian redemption to come, then, the grotesque bustle of the scherzo recalls nothing so vividly as the streets in New York City that Mahler would encounter some years later, whose chaotic Jewishness, according to Alma, he would soundly reject.[44] Yet, taken on its own, the scherzo suggests even more vitally a perspective that is indelibly Jewish, in which a resisting outsider fights against the tide of absorption into the dominant flow of a hostile culture.

Mahler thus presents here a familiar enigma in the form of a double image: a Jewish composer who gives an overwhelmingly convincing performance of conversion to Christianity, but within a narrative inflected indelibly with the perspective of Jewish resistance, almost as if the conscious self cannot escape unconscious affinities. Perhaps the workings of Mahler's music are not so different from the universe that his contemporary Freud did so much to open up to us, the world behind the conscious self (even given Freud's avowed aversion to music). For those who may be concerned to find Mahler's essential Jewishness, this seems to be a particularly vivid manifestation of just that: a Jewishness stubbornly unconverted and unassimilated, deeply embedded in what we might term his music's unconscious.

Chapter 4

The Autonomy of Musical Presence (I)

"Ablösung im Sommer" and the Third Symphony

Songs into Symphonies

In his Second and Third Symphonies, Mahler introduces the human voice in remarkably similar ways, through relatively slow orchestral songs for alto solo at mostly subdued dynamic levels. Both songs attempt, fairly conspicuously, to merge voice with supporting instruments in terms of both timbre and gesture, so that the text, especially in the beginning stages, is as much intoned as sung; thus, significantly, the vocal melody in each case begins with an initial repeated note. Each song communicates a strong sense of suspended time by beginning without clear metrical definition and thereafter lapsing into stretches of inactivity of varying duration. This sense of suspension relates to a dramatic situation common to both songs: despite their very different poetic sources, each articulates and extends a moment of crossroads, in which something of tremendous import hangs in the balance. Each song resolves its dramatic tension through a central denial of pain, and uses almost identical melodic phrases to articulate a starting condition for this denial: "Der Mensch liegt in grösster Noth! Der Mensch liegt in grösster Pein!" in "Urlicht," and "Tief is ihr Weh! Tief ist ihr Weh!" in "O Mensch! Gib Acht!" (see Example 20).[1] This central dramatic focus in each case justifies Mahler's recourse to the human voice and defines its function, since the act of denying pain seems both to require vocal expression and to enable its extension into a more elaborate vocal idiom; thus, it is with the denial itself that mere intoning gives way, in each song, to a more fluid vocality. Finally, each song ends in prayerful quietude after an affirmatory—and affirmation-seeking—gaze into eternity ("Der liebe Gott wird mir ein Lichtchen geben, wird leuchten mir bis in das ewig selig Leben!" in "Urlicht"; "Doch alle Lust will Ewigkeit, will tiefe, teife Ewigkeit!" in "O Mensch! Gib Acht!").[2] Significantly, as well, the movement that follows in each case involves a narrative in which a sinner seeks and receives heavenly redemption.

A less evident but equally striking parallel between the two transitions from instrumental music to song occurs in the movements that immediately precede "Urlicht" and "O Mensch! Gib Acht!" Like the "Fischpredigt" scherzo, which precedes "Urlicht" in the Second Symphony, the corresponding movement in the Third Symphony is an elaborate scherzo derived from a *Wunderhorn* song. In problematizing the topic of absolute music, Mahler creates a need for direct vocal expression. Like its sibling in the Second Symphony, the scherzo in the Third takes as its starting point a song from which Mahler has stripped not only the words, but also the melodic line that carried those words in his original setting, which is hinted at without being fully realized. Thus, each scherzo is not only, literally, a song without words, but also a song without a clearly defined instrumental "singer." By removing all traces of vocality from a preexisting song, Mahler produces a semblance of absolute music in the conventional sense and deepens the need for vocal expression. Even without reference to an original vocal setting, moreover, each scherzo problematizes its absolutist, *Wunderhorn*-derived component by projecting an incompatible perspective alongside it, and by investing that contrasting perspective with sympathetic subjectivity. These then interact within similar narrative structures mapped to a vaguely defined format of scherzo with double trio, in which a compatibility be-

tween the contrasting perspectives is first suggested, then proven untenable, and, in the end, forcefully denied in a purging orchestral outcry.

That Mahler's strategy for adding voices to his Second and Third Symphonies has many parallels to Beethoven's Ninth should be obvious. Thus, Beethoven's finale moves through a series of events quite similar to those described here, elaborating a "song without words" (the instrumental treatment of the *Freudenthema*), whose abstract development provokes an orchestral "cry of pain" (the *Schreckensfanfare* from the opening of the finale, returning in an intensified form), which is succeeded by an actual song that first affirms joy as an alternative to a preceding condition of pain and eventually proceeds to a contemplation of eternity. With Beethoven as with Mahler, the central concern, particularly in the early stages, is to problematize purely instrumental music as incapable of articulating satisfactorily either the denial of pain or a more joyful alternative. Thus, Beethoven first enacts his denial musically, but then verbalizes it when that approach proves inadequate ("nicht diese Töne! sondern . . ."). Meanwhile, the instrumental form of the *Freudenthema*, though initially embraced as a viable solution, seems unable either to sustain itself beyond a few variations or to prevent its own dissolution during a brief developmental extension; it is this failure that precipitates the intensified return of the *Schreckensfanfare*.[3]

Mahler, by spreading these stages across separate movements, but without changing their basic functions or ordering, creates an opportunity to explore more fully than Beethoven the initial stages, in which purely instrumental expression proves inadequate, and to define with increasing subtlety the subjectivities that justify a vocal continuation. In the latter respect—that is, in terms of his sophistication in implementing anew Beethoven's basic strategy—Mahler's Third Symphony represents an advance of sorts over the Second. Thus, despite his continued reliance on Beethoven's procedural apparatus, and despite his retention in his Third Symphony of the basic structures that supported his introduction of voices in his Second Symphony, Mahler's procedures in the scherzo of the Third lead him into surprising variations on his various models—in particular, his own previous symphonic scherzo and the *Wunderhorn* song on which he bases the opening of the movement.

"Ablösung im Sommer"

"Ablösung im Sommer" is, to begin with, a very different source for a symphonic movement than "Des Antonius von Padua Fischpredigt." Most obviously, its narrative is considerably more oblique, and its perspective more sympathetically disposed toward its subject matter. Particularly telling in the latter regard is Mahler's conjoining of naiveté with traditional tokens of grief in the first section of the song; while the grief is thereby layered over with a patina of gentle irony, it is nonetheless marked as genuine, demanding our sympathy if not our empathy. Accordingly, Mahler sets the opening vocal line, "Kukuk hat sich zu Tode gefallen" (Cuckoo has fallen to his death), to the well-worn lamenting gesture of a descending minor-mode tetrachord, but following a completely mechanical declamation, in which naturally accented syllables ("Ku-," "hat," "Tod-," and "fall-") fall squarely on the heads of the four pitches of the tetrachord, with the intervening syllables filling out each beat in precisely even increments, in progressive diminution (see Example 21).[4] In the continuation (mm. 7f), Mahler repeats with pathetic emphasis the word "Weiden" (willow, a word traditionally associated with mourning), setting its repeated wailing motive against an augmented version of the descending tetrachord from the opening phrase. The effect of pathos is undermined by the contrived naiveté of the parallel fifths between melody and bass across mm. 8–10, by the sprightly staccato bass, and by an aspect of affectionate caricature that Mahler layers onto the gesture by repeating the "wailing" motive literally within a melodic sequence, so that it is closely regulated by the brisk and well-marked tempo and meter. Lest we miss these subtle inflections, Mahler proceeds immediately to submit each of the latter structures to processes of exaggeration that, rather grotesquely, fail to increase even slightly the level of pathos. Thus, a chromatic burlesque of the vocal wail (piano interlude, mm. 22–25) leads to a repetition of the concluding phrase of the first strophe, "Wer soll uns denn den Sommer lang die Zeit und Weil' vertreiben?" (Who then shall while away the time for us during the long summer?), against which the descending tetrachord is extended with mechanical simplicity into a plaintive descending scale that now "laments" through a full octave, but that declaims the text with unwavering eighth notes against more starkly stated parallel triads (mm. 28–31; see Example 21).[5]

In addition to these deliberate expressive misfires based on traditional lamenting gestures, we may count many related effects. The major mode that follows the lament of the opening strophe emerges without transition, as nonchalantly as if a switch has been thrown and without even a backward glance at the "grief-stricken" tone of the preceding bars. The resulting effect of affective distraction, reminiscent of a child's lapses in attention, is subtly reinforced by the musical derivation of the sweet trilling of the nightingale from the preceding scalar descents and wailing motive (mm. 32f [0:42]; see Example 21). Given that this is the titular point of the song—the "Ablösung" in question, articulated harmonically as a transition from minor to major—we might reasonably expect more drama. In similar fashion, the absurdly literal combination of the cuckoo motive with an augmented triad— the latter symbolizing death here as it will in the scherzo of Mahler's next symphony—sets the phrase "Kukuk ist todt! Kukuk ist todt!" with a pat economy that completely undermines its simulated cry of pain (mm. 10–11 [0:12]; see Example 21). While this rendering may perhaps be understood as a distracted version of the characteristic instrumental motive that opens the song, with the arrival skewed both melodically and harmonically, the effect of distraction is mostly canceled both by the declamation in even triplets, which dulls the rhythmic piquancy of the head motive, and by the matter-of-fact repetition of the phrase.

Example 21. Mahler, "Ablösung im Sommer," mm. 1–13 and 21–33 (0:28)

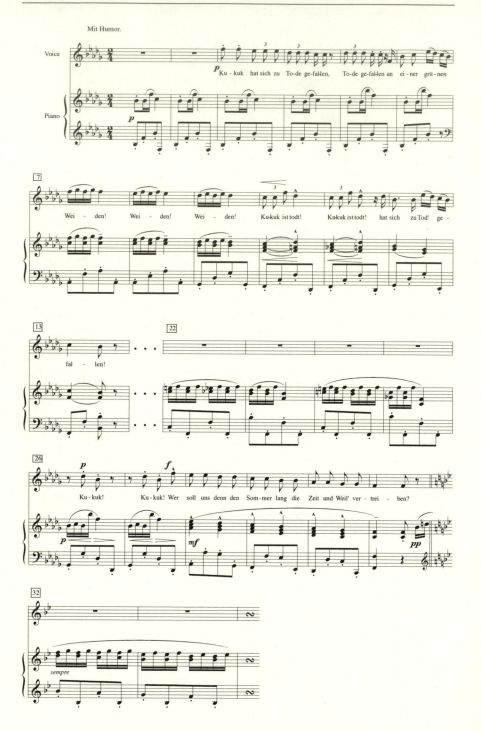

Mahler's textual changes—mostly additions—also contribute to the sense of an affectionately rendered naiveté, along the lines of nursery rhyme. Outwardly, these changes seem calculated specifically to accomplish three separate goals: to emphasize the naiveté of the song's "voice"; to augment the two-verse structure of the original through repetition, expansion, and extension; and to confuse the narrative. While these goals are to some extent independently pursued, they are also intricately intertwined; in particular, the latter two may be construed as yet additional means to accomplish the former, so that, at the very least, we may note as important by-products of the narrative confusions and other material that Mahler adds to the poem both an enhanced naiveté and a subtle encouragement for us to regard that naiveté with kindly condescension. The following shows Mahler's text, with the original *Wunderhorn* text in boldface:

Ablösung im Sommer[6]	**Replacement** in Summer
Kukuk hat sich zu Tode gefallen,	**Cuckoo has fallen to his death,**
Tode gefallen **an einer grünen Weiden!**	Fallen to death **on a green willow!**
Weiden! Weiden!	Willow! Willow!
Kukuk ist todt! Kukuk ist todt!	Cuckoo is dead! Cuckoo is dead!
Hat sich zu Tod' gefallen!	Has fallen to his death!
Wer soll uns denn den Sommer lang	**Who then shall while away the time for us**
Die Zeit und Weil' vertreiben?	**During the long summer?**
Kukuk! Kukuk!	Cuckoo! Cuckoo!
Wer soll uns denn den Sommer lang	Who then shall while away the time for us
Die Zeit und Weil' vertreiben?	During the long summer?
Ei! Das soll thun Frau Nachtigall!	**Why! Frau Nightingale should do it!**
Die sitzt auf grünen Zweige!	**She sits on a green branch!**
Die kleine, feine Nachtigall,	The little, delicate nightingale,
[Die liebe, süsse Nachtigall!]	[The dear, sweet nightingale!]
Sie singt und springt, ist all'zeit froh,	**She sings and springs, is always happy,**
Wenn andre Vögel schweigen!	**When other birds are silent!**
Wir warten auf Frau Nachtigall;	We await Frau Nightingale;
Die wohnt im grünen Hage,	She lives in the green grove,
Und wenn der Kukuk zu Ende ist,	And when the end comes for Cuckoo,
Dann fängt sie an zu schlagen!	Then she begins to sing!

Many of Mahler's additions fall easily in line with the manipulations of musical topics discussed earlier. The addition of infantilizing phrases such as "Die kleine, feine Nachtigall" and the optional "Die liebe, süsse Nachtigall"[7] reinforces the element of condescension already noted. More complex is the repetition of the words "Tode gefallen" after the first line, which in itself adds a note of pathos through textual emphasis and through its immediate return to the first clear indicator that we are, in fact, in the minor mode (the D♭ on the word "Tode"). But the repetition also involves two additional layers of nuance that work in somewhat opposing directions, first through the literalness of the repetition, which undermines its pathetic effect, and second through Mahler's manipulation of the phrase structure so as to make the repeated segment both conclude the antecedent phrase and open the consequent. The profile of this nested manipulation, in which subtleties on one level mitigate an exaggerated naiveté on another, closely approximates some of the procedures already noted; in particular, the sequential repetition of the word "Weiden," with its initial cadential elision, also embeds its trivialization of a straightforward affective device within a more complex phrase manipulation. In fact, because the repetition of "Weiden" follows so closely on that of "Tode gefallen," the two elided effects (along with the subsequent elision on the added text, "Kukuk ist todt") combine to produce a single phrase structure of especially intricate design.

Repetition and re-elaboration of text are, to be sure, staples of song, fulfilling the dual tasks of providing sufficient words for the singer to sing and of emphasizing some words and phrases over others. More surprising here is the way many of Mahler's additions may be seen to be doing much more than this, particularly when the full musical setting is taken into account. Thus, in the first strophe, the interpolation of "Kukuk! Kukuk!," which is set to the characteristic cuckoo motive as if by default,[8] introduces an important note of ambiguity that the final added lines will extend. Is the cuckoo actually dead? If so, how is it that we will miss its cry, when that cry is so easily mimicked by the "voice" of the song—in what is, ostensibly, an outcry of grief in the manner of Gluck's Orfeo calling out to the dead Euridice? On one level, Mahler is using the fact that the cuckoo's name is identical to its call in order to generate yet another undermined affective gesture, as Orfeo's gesture appears here in the guise of the most trivial of musical literalisms. On another level, however, the very point of the gesture thus evaporates with its enactment, since what is being mourned is specifically the diversion offered by the cuckoo's song. The piano overlay provides further clarification that the cuckoo's cry has apparently outlived the cuckoo itself by highlighting the close relationship between that cry and the much-repeated headmotive of the song. Thus, since the former is embedded, in diminution, within the latter, the dead cuckoo is heard throughout the song as an integral part of its characteristic "voice."[9] But even if these echoes may be taken as no more than an afterlife of the cuckoo, the final lines reawaken the possibility that the cuckoo is, after all, not yet dead, and that the entire song has been a rehearsal of what might transpire *if* it should die. Whatever we make of this confusion (not forgetting the possibility that the confusion was Mahler's), it meshes easily with both the folkish element (since narrative confusions of this kind are typical of folksong, where they are generated and perpetuated through oral transmission) and an attitude of condescension toward the song's "voice," for which the central events of concern in the song are apparently open to question. If it is no longer clear, with these final lines, that the cuckoo is actually dead, there seems to be no less confusion about the presence of "Frau Nachtigall," for whom we are now "waiting" even though we have seemingly been hearing her melodic voice throughout the second half of the song.

Confusions of this kind do much to enhance the sense of distractibility that Mahler's additions impart to the "voice" of the song; thus, his frequent repetitions, and especially his sometimes contradictory re-elaborations, ground the early effects of pathetic distraction, ostensibly motivated by grief, within a more general inability to focus. Distractibility, like confusion more generally, thus reaffirms naiveté, while its representation necessitates precisely the kinds of otherwise superfluous additions to the text provided by Mahler. Moreover, distractibility and confusion together augment a dimension of the song that will become central in its symphonic reincarnation, for its "voice" (a designation that has until now been placed within quotation marks) is less a single voice than a multitude of voices, a heteroglossia that articulates a generalized perspective—the spirit of the forest, perhaps, or at least of its collective creatures—through a free intermingling of constituent points of awareness, echoing, interrupting, and reinterpreting each other continuously. While this explanation accounts well for much of the textual manipulation being considered here, the paradox remains that this heteroglossia is being presented *as song*, sung by a single voice with no indication of separate individual personae along the way. Even if we cannot decide between explanations that take the song to be a single confused voice on the one hand, or heteroglossia on the other, these alternatives have at least one aspect in common: from both perspectives, the song represents a scattering of consciousness.

Even the ostensible subject matter of the poem, the "replacement" referred to in its title, is bedeviled by obscurities. Mahler's source for the poem, *Des Knaben Wunderhorn*, includes only the first two verses of a much longer poem in which the supplanting of cuckoo with nightingale is explicitly connected to the (projected?) replacement of one beloved with another, who will, it is hoped, "sing" more sweetly than his or her predecessor. Thus, in the original extended version, the nature-based metaphor of the poem is overtly linked to the vicissitudes of fickle young love.[10] Even had Mahler been aware of this earlier version (which he probably was not), the extension represents a narrowing of perspective so clearly opposed to nineteenth-century romantic sensibilities that it would scarcely be surprising for him to choose not to include the clarifying verses, following Schubert's setting of "Die Forelle."[11] By confining himself to the first two verses, however, Mahler does not thereby put aside more general associations that could support either this or another metaphoric interpretation, associations such as the contrast between the simple, repetitive song of the cuckoo and that of the more elaborate nightingale (a contrast even more explicitly invoked in another of Mahler's *Wunderhorn* settings, "Lob des hohen Verstands"), or the general sentiment that every improvement also entails significant loss. Yet, without the connections spelled out in the extended version of the poem, the contrast between cuckoo and nightingale is perhaps less important in Mahler's version than the sense that both represent nature; even so, the contrast between the two is significant, since, by the later nineteenth century, "nature" would have been understood to be in constant evolutionary flux, the "primitive" necessarily yielding to the more sophisticated. (It is undoubtedly this aspect of the poem that dictated and informed Mahler's adaptation of his setting for inclusion in his Third Symphony, with its post-Darwinian program of an aggressively evolving nature.)

Mahler's own removal from the traditions associated with the *Wunderhorn* poems allows him to remain somewhat aloof from this kind of reductive interpretation, however integral it might have been at one time, either because he was simply ignorant of it or its pedigree, or because he felt that it no longer had sufficient resonance for late-nineteenth-century audiences for it to impose earlier meanings on those he chose to develop in his setting. Yet, these earlier meanings do not simply evaporate: rather, their trace remains subtly and evocatively present—such is, after all, a central premise behind the modes of preservation first fashioned by Arnim and Brentano, and refashioned by Mahler. Thus, while Mahler may have imposed a later evolutionary perspective on the "Ablösung" referred to in the title, something prosaic in the folklike simplicity of the verse pulls the focus back to a rather patronizing perspective on those who are consoling themselves for the loss of the childish cuckoo or cheering the arrival of the more adult nightingale. Indeed, the focal length remains utterly compatible with the earlier, extended version of the poem. At the same time, however, Mahler adds another layer of confusion to the issue by appending the words "im Sommer" to the title, implying that the events described are part of a closed natural cycle and thus seemingly incompatible with the linear narratives of either evolving nature or transient love. Within Mahler's reconfiguration of these various potential meanings, the song may perhaps best be understood as a ritualistic reenactment of evolutionary processes, with cuckoo and nightingale respectively symbolizing simpler and more advanced stages of development at roughly mid-course (thus "im Sommer"). What remains less than clear is how self-conscious this reenactment is.

Some confusion also surrounds the symbolic significance of the two birds in Mahler's treatment, although this confusion is more easily clarified. In the pre-*Wunderhorn* extended version, the cuckoo represents the childish, the immature, and the banal, compared to the more adult and beautiful nightingale; these meanings correspond, as well, to those operating in "Lob des hohen Verstands," with its song contest between the two birds judged by the "impartial" braying ass, who is implicitly understood to be the spiritual and intellectual cousin of the cuckoo. A related focus of contrast centers on the distinction between day and night, with the daytime cuckoo yielding to the more complex beauties of the nightingale; if this distinction seems not quite so disparaging of the cuckoo, the more privileged position in the hierarchy is clearly retained by the nightingale, whose associations with the nighttime have always made it a favorite emblem of the romantics. Yet, the cuckoo has a myriad more clearly positive associations, many of which Mahler evoked in his First Symphony, wherein the cuckoo was allied alternately with the mysteries of primordial nature, the exuberance of benevolent nature, and by extension, the joyful triumph of religious feeling, as its call is overtly embedded within the allusion to the "Hallelujah" Chorus from Handel's *Messiah* in the closing chorale. These associations, in turn, have a substantial history. Most important, the cuckoo provides the closing gesture for the trio of birds at the end of the "Scene am Bach" in Beethoven's *Pastoral* Symphony, where it is grounded in a depiction of nature at its most delightful but seems also to carry a warning from God.[12] In "Ablösung im Sommer," the brittle, daytime cuckoo seems to represent primitive nature, which yields ritualistically to a warmer and more complex (nocturnal) nature represented by the nightingale; in the scherzo of the Third Symphony, this evolutionary process will be extended, through a leap considerably more traumatic, all the way to humanity (or, as early explanations would have it, to "man").

"Der Postillion"

In the scherzo of the Second Symphony, the trio is defined primarily by absence, through its prolongation of a sense of escape from the absolute-music topic that prevails in the scherzo proper. In this respect, the scherzo of the Third Symphony represents a departure, for its trio is defined primarily by a new presence—specifically, by the extended solos for the posthorn. Several other reversals help to clarify the relationship between the two scherzos, which is otherwise remarkably close. In the Second Symphony, subjective awareness finds its center in the trio, through its rejection of the scherzo, while in the Third Symphony, the intruding presence in the trio seems (mostly) oblivious to the sensibilities of the scherzo. In the Second Symphony, the scherzo is something to be abhorred; in the Third Symphony, both scherzo and trio are presented sympathetically, in delicately balanced opposition, so that, while the center of awareness (the scherzo) will eventually protest violently against the intruding presence of the alien "other" (the posthorn trio), the latter lays claim to our long-term sympathies. And in the Second Symphony, the central core of obliviousness (the scherzo) remains the exclusive locus for the absolute-music topic, while in the Third Symphony, the topic is deployed to some extent in both scherzo and trio, if to different ends.

Like the scherzo proper, the trio in the Third Symphony is a song without words: albeit in significantly different ways, it, too, stems from a poetic source, and involves a sense of a poignantly recalled past, obliquely rendered.[13] Outwardly, the posthorn melody is, if anything, more conventionally songlike than the scherzo, since it represents more clearly than the scherzo a single voice. The probable source for the trio is Lenau's "Der Postillion," which describes a postilion (the rider of the lead horse in a team of horses drawing a carriage) who stops at a churchside cemetery at night to play "Wandersänge" (songs of wandering) for his fallen comrade. As he explains it to the poem's narrator:

> Hier ich immer halten muß,
> Dem dort unterm Rasen
> Zum getreuen Brudergruß
> Sein Leiblied zu blasen![14]

> (Here I must always stop to play,
> As a faithful brother's greeting to him
> [Who lies] yonder under the grass,
> His favorite songs!)

While the melody of the posthorn, with its consistent use of anacrusis gestures, was most likely not derived from an actual setting of Lenau's poem, we can be reasonably sure that it was inspired by the scenario the poem relates, for Mahler wrote "Der Postillion!" at this point in the autograph score and later reacted with consternation when someone guessed his poetic source correctly.[15] Critical to Mahler in Lenau's narrative would have been its evocative projection of the posthorn heard through the woods at night, and the quality of nostalgic loneliness associated with the sound. In Lenau's poem, the stillness at the graveside follows a tumultuous ride through the forest and haunts the resumption of that ride; these circumstances, too, find their parallel in Mahler's setting.

The differences between the posthorn solos and the primary scherzo material, derived from "Ablösung im Sommer," are vividly marked, all the more so for the oddly configured parallels between their respective sources. "Ablösung," despite its obscurities, is quite definite, even fussy in its prose style, qualities Mahler augments through both his textual additions and his musical setting. The posthorn solos Lenau describes are, on the other hand, wordless and indefinite, drifting across distance and time. Thus, in Mahler's treatment, we hear the posthorn's melody not as a continuous, closed unit, but fitfully, without clear beginnings and endings, blended with fanfare-like material (or is he, perhaps, just warming up?), given to irregular metrical turns and at times resuming unexpectedly after long pauses. If "Ablösung im Sommer," like Lenau's postilion, also fondly recalls an irretrievable past, it does so unselfconsciously and only for its audience; its various voices remain forever in their own present, seemingly oblivious to what they might represent to an outside, more sophisticated perspective. Lenau's postilion, however, is entirely absorbed in the past; for him, the urgencies of the present are secondary.[16] Thus, and above all else, the critical difference between the two lies in their perspective on time: the voices in "Ablösung im Sommer" seem oblivious to temporality (hence the confusions explored above), while temporality is precisely the point in Lenau's nighttime vigil. Yet, paradoxically, the very subject matter of the former is, precisely, temporal, its fundamental preoccupation being transience, while the latter seeks to efface temporality, to invoke the timelessness of spiritual connectedness through song.[17]

"What the Creatures of the Forest Tell Me"

"Ablösung im Sommer," as a starting point for Mahler's scherzo, already holds within it the fundamental idea—and even the larger structure—of both the movement and (*in nuce*) the symphony as a whole. The fundamental idea, of course, is that of transition and replacement, of an evolving sensibility that defines a need for mankind and a context in which mankind's introduction will seem "natural." As a song, "Ablösung im Sommer" presents an evolutionary transition that might serve as an emblem and model for larger processes. The song's musical structure, however, backs away from any sense of an open-ended evolving structure, or even a simple goal-directed narrative, asserting instead a complacent cyclicism that turns the process into something safe and unthreatening, to be rehearsed as a reassuring ritual that affirms an overarching stability. Thus, the music for the nightingale's verse, while much different from that for the cuckoo's, is nevertheless mostly a variation on it. Even more subtle is the ending, which brings back a variation of the first two bars of the song before it segues into the close of the first extended vocal phrase. While this ending is formulaic, collapsing the first opening and closing gestures into a single, more emphatic closing gesture, it may also be taken as a recasting of a longer segment of the first cadential phrase, which had set the words "Kukuk ist todt! Kukuk ist todt! hat sich zu Tod' gefallen!" This rather macabre recollection is, however, now rendered oddly cheerful, first by Mahler's reversion in its first half to a simply diatonic version of the headmotive (on which "Kukuk ist todt!" is modeled), and second by the way that the disquieting minor third in the tonic triad gradually dissipates by the end (see Example 22). The ending thus well encapsulates the naive sensibility of the song; like the various forms of the headmotive—the most frequently heard adaptation of the cuckoo's cry—the ending simulates carefree simplicity in part by deemphasizing the third of the (minor-mode) tonic triad.

For the scherzo, Mahler opens up the closed cycle of the song in a variety of ways. First, emergence is made part of the trajectory even for the opening section, so that the sense of heteroglossia already present in the song is even more pronounced. Thus, over the first strophe (before the turn to major), there are ten distinct changes in lead instrumental groupings, including six different combinations of instruments (nine, if accompaniments are taken into consideration): after two bars of accompaniment, we hear two bars of the B♭ clarinet playing the headmotive; then four bars of the piccolo playing a varied form of the vocal melody; three additional bars of the piccolo, now joined by the oboe in a high register; two bars of the E♭ clarinet ("Kukuk ist todt!"); two bars of the piccolo (to close the first vocal phrase); four bars of the B♭ clarinet; four bars of the trumpets; four bars of the flutes and oboes; two bars of the B♭ clarinets; and four bars of the trumpets (to close the section; only with the return of the trumpets is a complete instrumental configuration repeated, including both lead instruments and accompaniment).

Example 22. Mahler, "Ablösung im Sommer," mm. 10–13 (0:12) and 63–67 (1:25)

A similar approach governs the major-mode section, where the initial arrival in the major is softened by the texture of fluid strings accompanied by unison harps, and five other new instrumental textures are introduced along the way at, typically, four-bar intervals. With the postlude (Example 23), this gradual accumulation of instruments occasions three important events that will push the discourse beyond the original ending: the full choir of instruments in the first genuine tutti; the "braying ass" motive from "Lob des hohen Verstands" (in the first violins), which extends the identifiable menagerie and brings it to a more raucous level; and a new triplet figure that will lead directly into the next section.[18]

The contrasting section that follows presents itself as a rowdy, sometimes cacophonous trio, a striking contrast to the opening *scherzando*. Narratively, it is the arrival point toward which the ever-emergent adaptation of "Ablösung im Sommer" has been heading, an explosion of activity that seems to represent the full exuberance of the forest. In terms of traditional formal designs, we might surmise, therefore, that the narrative for the movement is essentially over at this point, and that the movement will complete itself either as a straightforward ternary structure or as an extended ternary (with repeated trio). Thus, despite the expanded structure and extended scenario of emergence, the possibility of reverting to yet another cyclical structure seems at this point to be the most likely outcome. Such is not, of course,

Example 23. Mahler, Symphony No. 3, third movement, r3.9–16 (1:22)

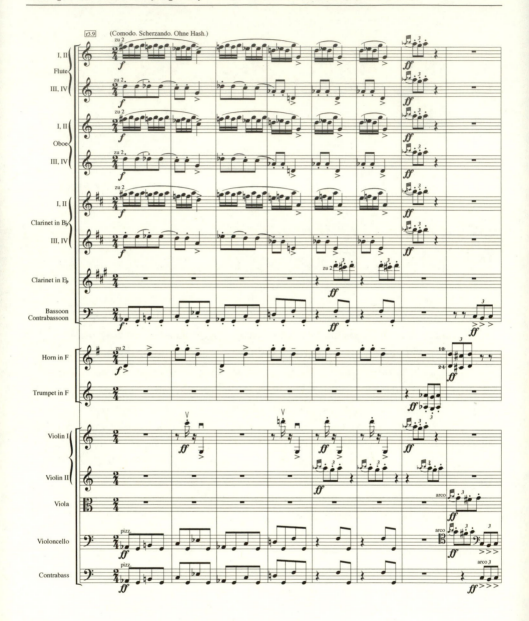

how the movement will actually unfold. Dramatically, however, the possibility that it might do so is precisely what Mahler needs to project at this point; in order for the introduction of "man" to the forest to have its full effect, it has to seem somewhat alien to the processes of emergence that have, with this apparent trio, reached their fullness. "Man" must appear not simply as another creature of the forest, but rather as something wholly different, as an intruder. Yet, he must also function within the forest and interact persuasively with its ongoing dynamic. In order to meet these somewhat conflicting demands, Mahler allows the scherzo to unfold *as though* it will work out to be a closed ternary cycle, but with many indications along the way that such could not be an adequate result. The structural function of "man," therefore, will be to provide a more satisfactory dramatic curve; moreover, through his very presence he will dominate the forest and thus subdue the chaos that otherwise governs its unhierarchical heteroglossia.

The overall shape of the (apparent) trio is the first indication that the ternary shape will be problematic, for it does not provide a balanced structure to stabilize its initial arrival. Rather, after a boisterous extension, it simply winds down gradually, setting up a return to the opening. The "trio" is thus considerably more narrative than architectural. Specifically, and more subtly, the return it prepares has a suspended quality quite unlike the opening, initially absent the headmotive, with a new, strangely pensive octave motive in the bass and a disquieting countermelody played *pianississississimo* by half the first violins, without mutes (see Example 24; 16.1–12 [2:36]). This unsettling return is consistent with the words, if not the music, of "Ablösung im Sommer": the cuckoo is silent with the onset of evening, and we pensively await the nightingale. But arrival is problematic; developmental processes forestall the first cadence, and the major mode is reached only after increasingly disruptive gestures finally generate a *fortissimo* tutti explosion (18.23–24 [3:48], not shown here). Nor does the arrival in the major offer respite from the preceding difficulties. While keeping more or less to the original structure—the highly profiled cadential bars arrive right on time and lead directly into the music of the piano postlude (110.10–12; 4:23)—the major-mode section gives way to a new element, as discussed earlier in connection with "Das himmlische Leben," as four-bar exchanges of dactylic chorale phrases drift into an allusion to the plaintive opening lines of "Das irdische Leben" (see chapter 2, Example 11a). The allusion foretells catastrophe but yields to an unconvincing show of bravado, the latter taking the form of a downsized return of the "trio" music, introduced by clarinets playing the braying-ass motive with bells in the air ("Schalltrichter in die Höhe"; 111.2). But all this evaporates at the first sign of real trouble, that is, at the first sound of the muted trumpet calls, heard as if in the distance (r*11*.23; 4:54).

What the Creatures of the Forest Hear

The interactions between the foregrounded forest world and the more distant human sounds (muted trumpets and, later, posthorn) are described below, with the latter in boldface:

Figure 4-1. Interactions between man and the forest creatures in Mahler, Symphony No. 3, third movement

1. **First muted trumpet call (two trumpets fading to one)** (r*11*.23; 4:54)
2. Subdued response in F minor, blending the dactylic plaint into the suspended reprise (r*12*f; 5:00); in a further reduction of forces, this time the solo violin plays the countermelody, with forces added for the second phrase, which is interrupted by:
3. **Return of the muted trumpet, "somewhat stronger than before" (etwas stärker als vorher;** r*13*.5 [5:28])
4. Brief attempt to assimilate, as head motive echoes trumpet figure (r*13*.9; 5:35)
5. **Extended posthorn solo in F major, beginning with fanfare** (r*14*; 5:41)
6. Tentative echoes of the posthorn in the flutes, as a variation of the opening (r*15*; 7:16)
7. **Interruption: posthorn resumes, joined by supportive horn duet** (r*15*.8 [7:32] and r*15*.12 [7:48]; see Example 25a below)
8. Nervous, repetitive figures in flutes and divided upper strings (r*16*; 8:36)
9. **Interruption: posthorn resumes, joined by supportive horn duet, closing** (r*16*.12 [8:50] and r*16*.18 [9:13]; see Example 25b below)
10. **Abrupt interjection of muted trumpet fanfare** (r*16*.36; 10:13)
11. Extended, developmental reprise of the scherzo in F minor, beginning "with mysterious haste" *(Mit geheimnisvoller Hast!;* r*17* [10:16]), incorporating dactylic plaint (r*17*.12 [10:27]; Example 11b above), but gradually gaining strength and momentum in polka-like section with C major arrival-climax that recalls the original "trio," marked "Crude!" (*Grab!;* r*23* [11:53]), becoming increasingly frenetic and unstable until it is interrupted by:
12. **Sudden trumpet call (three trumpets fading to one)** (r*26*.3; 12:34)
13. Nervous response, imitating trumpet with head motive (r*26*.12; 12:48)

Example 24. Mahler, Symphony No. 3, third movement, r5.24–r6.12 (2:33)

14. **Posthorn solo, beginning with fanfare/head motive, slowing**
    (r27 [13:00]; see Example 25c below)

15. Posthorn melody in divided first violins, slowing (r28 [13:47]; see
    Example 25c below)

16. **Horn duet** (r28.12; 14:19) **joined by posthorn, closing** (r29 [14:23];
    see Example 25c below)

17. Coda, built on a descending minor-mode tetrachord: panicked, highly
    repetitive response on F with huge crescendo (15:28); Eb minor "cry of
    terror" (15:40; horn fanfare shifting to Db while strings fade to *ppppp*;
    fall to C, closing after second huge crescendo.

As may be seen from the above, the "man"-centered events describe a separate narrative that has little or nothing to do with the already established
forest world, which nevertheless retains the foreground. This separate narrative is, in fact, completely compatible with Lenau's as it might appear from

the perspective of those who inhabit Mahler's forest: the postilion is heard from a distance (1), draws near (3), and, as the carriage stops by the grave-yard, gives way to nostalgic song, heard intermittently (5, 7, 9); abruptly, the postilion announces the continuation of the journey (10), but eventually re-turns once again as a haunting presence (12, 14, 16). The postilion seems, through all of this, to take little if any notice of its effect on the forest world. Even if, ambiguously, there is imitative play with the birdcalls, which are sometimes echoed in both the trumpet calls and the posthorn solos (see es-pecially 14), the manifest anxieties it provokes do not register with the pos-tilion, who seems to hear and respond to the bird calls only as sound, never as voices with a legitimate perspective of their own.

Yet, just as clearly, the postilion does interact with the forest, and on a level much deeper than could even have been imagined by its foregrounded

inhabitants. As noted in Figure 4-1, two horns join the posthorn during its second solo (7), supporting it with a warm lyricism; unmistakably, in line with longstanding Germanic associations with the horn, this is the sound of the *Waldhorn,* the eternal spirit of the forest, which enters to make an affirming, comforting connection to the posthorn and, by extension, to man.[19] And, moreover, the posthorn clearly *hears* the horns, pausing to trill for over two bars before resuming its cadential phrase (see Example 25a). But the connection does not achieve identity between posthorn and *Waldhorn,* for they are oddly disjunct as they approach the cadence (Example 25a; r15.21). In their next passage, as shown, there is more separation at the beginning, but also more familiarity, as the posthorn rejoins sooner than before; similarly, while there is a longer period of rhythmic disjuncture (Example 25b; r16.26–29), there is also an extended cadential passage in perfect alignment. With the second group of posthorn solos (Example 25c), negotiations between the two are on a different basis. This time, the initial solo is stretched out, with written-out ritardandi in r27.3–4, r27.8–9, and r27.12–13, perhaps to betoken its more ethereal nature at this point, or perhaps its pensiveness as it awaits the *Waldhorn.* Instead, as shown, half the first violins answer in kind until they, too, drift into a pensive waiting. When the horns do enter, the posthorn immediately answers them, yet their alignment, even more

imperfect than before, now spans six bars (r*29*.6–11). By the end, the horns
alone are left to close, in a clear gesture of affectionate leave-taking.

   There are, as well, significant class-based differences implicit in the two
poetic sources, which may be seen to play themselves out in Mahler's setting.
Thus, the horns, with their *Jäger* (hunting-horn) associations, support the sen-
timentality of the posthorn, much as the aristocratic subjectivity of Lenau's
poem respects and even marvels at the elevated sensibilities of the (presumed)
lower-class postilion. In contrast, the folk basis for the forest animisms of
"Ablösung" project a peasant sensibility that is necessarily excluded by this
elevation; nevertheless, the cultural prestige of "the folk," which provides a conduit to a mythic past and thereby serves as a central marker for authenticity,
also serves to endow these "peasants" with enormous sympathy. This paradox of class relations parallels that projected in the finale of Beethoven's

Pastoral Symphony, wherein the simple yet devout *Landleute* provide a
model of appropriate religious devotion for their more aristocratic guest. In
Mahler, however, this societal structure undergirds an evolutionary model of
entitlement, as the lower-class postilion proves himself worthy of elevation
to a higher status than that normally accessible to the peasants/animals, be-

coming a true *Mensch* through his ritualistic acceptance by the eternal spirit of the forest.

It is this deeper spirit's final gesture of leave-taking that sends the forest world into a state of panic, and it is not hard to see why. What ultimately panics the forest's inhabitants is not the mere presence of an intruder, but rather his ability to disenfranchise them, for he not only has awakened a deeper response from the forest than they have, but is also more at ease in the forest than they are. He has, indeed, made the forest his own by bonding with its spirit and demonstrating his capacity to leave a meaningful trace behind him, and, thus, he has moved beyond mere existence to meaningful existence. The forest's inhabitants must thereafter view their home as much different than they imagined it, and no longer truly theirs. Moreover, and perhaps unkindest of all, they are left out of the loop, unable to connect either to man or to the spirit he has awakened. And it is not for want of trying: their initial response, overcoming all fears and premonitions, is to welcome the intruder, to assimilate him into the forest as they know it (4 and 6 above). Only after this failure to connect do they try, in vain, to act as if the event had not happened (11 above).[20] Even without the return of the posthorn, however, the encounter has had a palpably disastrous effect on the forest creatures, who are even less able than before, as they act out their denial, to control their own exuberant cacophony, due in large part to the note of incipient panic that constantly surfaces, overwhelming the rest. Their (spiritual) flight, then, is what the final bars of the coda represent, as they abandon the forest to man, who is left to face the deep midnight alone.[21]

Incompatible Visions of the Forest

The inspiration for Mahler's scherzo was probably the disparity between the visions of the forest world presented by his setting of "Ablösung," on the one hand, and Lenau's postilion, on the other, the latter resonating with a long tradition of romanticized images of the forest, both in music and in the other arts. At stake as well are alternative views of twilight—remembering that one of the alternative titles Mahler considered for this movement was "Was mir die Dämmerung erzäht" (What the Twilight Tells Me)—which for the forest creatures betokens fearful changes and an occasion for panic, but which for man provides an opportunity for establishing spiritual connection. What is perhaps most remarkable about the result is how separately (and yet sympathetically) each of these visions is maintained, despite the application of all manner of integrative devices and procedures. And, while

Mahler had planned for much of the forest's energy to resurface and assimilate itself within the finale—that is, in "Das himmlische Leben," whose dotted neighbor-note figures would have recalled and grounded the more boisterous moments of the scherzo—it does not do so in the eventual six-movement version of the symphony. No matter our sympathies for the intruded upon, their defeat is, as it turns out, final and irrevocable.

We may well note how important narrative is to an understanding of this movement. It would be all too easy, without a sense of narrative, to be content to note its variety and invention, its outwardly coherent (that is, conventional) treatment of contrasting material within a segmented form resembling either scherzo-trio or rondo, and to consider outer signs of accommodation to be affirmations of a deeper unity. Contrariwise, we might question whether such a deeper unity exists or whether its form is coherent, and thus find the movement disjointed and illogical. Indeed, it is easy enough to play either side of this game: on one side (we might say), there are sufficient motivic links between the posthorn solos and the scherzo proper to achieve a unity beneath their surface disjunctures, but on the other, the returns to the scherzo idiom do not really offer formal stability. And so on. There is no room within the structure of the analytical game as it is usually played for understanding music that questions the premises of the game or finds them irrelevant.[22] Nor is it just a matter of formal paradigms. We may indeed find formal principles more relevant to this movement than conventional scherzo or rondo structures—for example, Adorno's concept of "breakthrough," in which a momentous event overwhelms the working out of an ongoing formal procedure.[23] Yet, even that insight does not fully apply in this case, for the posthorn episodes do not formally preempt the established foreground, even if they do negate its dramatic position and function. Only narrative can adequately explain a movement whose very point is to demonstrate the incompatibility of its constituent components, conceived (in part) as characteristic personae.

As Mahler constructs his two visions of the forest, they are not simply different; they have different modes of being, and they conceive of the world—that is, the forest—in fundamentally different ways. For the forest creatures, all is surface; for man, all depth. This kind of incompatibility—even, specifically, concerning the relationship between creatures of the forest and man—had been explored by Mahler before, in the funeral march of the First Symphony. In that case, the dynamic between hunter and hunted was reversed for purposes of satire, and the attempt to merge the music of the two was comically disastrous. Beneath the comedy were serious issues: Francesca

Draughon has shown how deliberately Mahler devised specifically Catholic and Jewish musical tropes to represent hunter and hunted.[24] In the scherzo of the Third Symphony, however, the failures to mesh are more gently recounted, and the explosion comes only in reaction. While it, too, combines comedy and tragedy in a typical Mahlerian "Humoresque," the tragedy here is not so obviously undercut by comedy, for our sympathies are too heavily invested in the victims of the tragic denouement.

"Absolute Music" and Narrative Identity

Underwriting Mahler's ability to present, sympathetically, two antithetical musical personalities is an aspect of absolute music that was downplayed in the scherzo of the Second Symphony, in which absolute music was evoked, negatively, as a topic—that is, its capacity to project a sense of autonomous unity. Even in the scherzo of the Second Symphony, this feature was critical to the sense of alienation associated with the topic. There, however, the focus was on the mechanical aspects of generating a facsimile of absolute music for the purpose of caricature. For more sympathetic treatments of subjects who will be defined as autonomous presences, absolute music, with its focus on internal unity, again provides an effective means; indeed, this is one of the purposes for which the techniques and procedures characteristic of absolute music were developed.

The task for Mahler in this movement is to project two incompatible unities, each fully developed and sympathetic, within one musical structure. To do so, Mahler cannot rely on a conventional articulation of formal boundaries, which is often construed as the central criterion for establishing a unified musical whole. He must, instead, create a clear sense of an autonomous, internally unified musical presence, whose limits and bounds can be defined more flexibly but no less clearly and rigidly. Moreover, in the "forest" scherzo, the two autonomous musical constructs must be understood to be present at the same time, within a single movement-span and, by projection, within the same physical space. Consistent alignment within a variety of musical parameters (particularly regarding texture) contributes to Mahler's success: a heteroglossic approach to instrumentation and motivic work in the scherzo proper, for example, and the use of specific instruments and styles to establish and elaborate the posthorn episodes. But this by itself is not enough, since defining simultaneity must also involve some acknowledgment by one of the other, which may involve (as it does here) either imitation or reaction. Either of these may be either layered or allowed to unfold in temporal sequence, or some combination of the two. However all this is to be managed, the critical element is, once again, narrative.

Thus, in his "forest" scherzo, Mahler creates two autonomous musical presences and devises for them intersecting narratives. The narrative line established at the beginning is the more complex, and ultimately the more problematic. Mahler borrows from "Ablösung im Sommer" not only a musical structure replete with motives to develop further, but also the spectacle—and charm—of nontemporal creatures coming to terms with temporality.[25] The first narrative strand, then, deals with the attempt to establish and control a static temporality, an oxymoronic project that must necessarily fail, but leaves behind an insecurely established ternary structure, as noted. On one level, the posthorn episodes, with their temporal preoccupations, may be seen to respond to the failure of the opening narrative, but at this point the master narrative bifurcates into two separate strands aligned with the two autonomous presences, with their mutually incompatible perspectives on the forest. In one strand, the solution offered by man swamps whatever problems he was meant to solve, presenting a puzzle that cannot be solved in dramatic-musical terms precisely because the prerogatives of absolute music do not allow it. Thus, the solution implied by the posthorn episodes would entail a loss of musical identity and, if carried forward, would destroy the subject of the opening narrative. Put another way, the posthorn episodes would solve the problem of the scherzo only by, literally, changing the subject. Within the posthorn narrative strand, on the other hand, no notice is taken whatsoever of the opening narrative, in part because it, too, is fully defined by its own independent narrative, based on Lenau as discussed. The later narrative is witnessed with growing horror from the perspective of the earlier; the projected activities of watching it unfold and reacting to it actually become the dominant narrative for the remainder of the movement.

To a large extent, then, narrative establishes and reinforces the autonomous and unified nature of the two separate musical presences that inhabit the movement. Perhaps ironically, even though the "watching" narrative dominates, only the posthorn narrative reaches a satisfying conclusion. But this is, after all, implicit in the opening condition, since the very ability to complete a narrative depends on a sense of temporality. No wonder, then, that it is upon the completion of the posthorn narrative that the forest creatures produce their crescendo of horror.

Can we, with all the differences between the scherzos of the Second and Third Symphonies, continue to see both as evoking absolute music as a topic? In terms of the threefold absoluteness identified in the earlier discussion of

Sybil, we may indeed so identify the posthorn music, adducing its "inaccessible remove from outside control" and "unassailable power to impose itself on its listeners," even while acknowledging that it cannot (without the assent of the *Waldhorn*, the spirit of the forest) "generate indefinitely its own continuation." For the scherzo proper, we are on less certain ground. In Mahler's re-elaboration of the music from "Ablösung im Sommer," we may see him responding to imperatives within the music, both in his drawing out and elaborating more fully its essence and in his fidelity to that essence, his refusal to submerge its personality within the machinations of conventional plot. To the extent that we construe the latter to be a resistance of the music itself to such treatment, then it, too, may be considered absolute in this sense—but not, perhaps, as we have more rigidly defined the topic, for there is no sense that the posthorn music or any other defined perspective in the movement has any stake whatever in the forest creatures' activities and anxieties. Accordingly, and to a somewhat lesser extent than in the "Fischpredigt" scherzo, the topic of absolute music is present only in the posthorn episodes of the "forest" scherzo. Nevertheless, in the latter movement we can see even more clearly the impulse behind Mahler's use of the topic, an impulse that centers on two elements: a sense of musical "character" as an essential component of narrative and a fascination for the musical representation of alienation. Both are intimately connected to the projection of identity, subjectivity, and selfhood.

Chapter 5

Subjectivity And Selfhood

Lieder eines fahrenden Gesellen
and the First Symphony

Subjectivity. . .

The preceding chapters have routinely invoked the idea of subjectivity in Mahler's music, sometimes (as with the scherzo of the Third Symphony) detailing multiple subjectivities within particular movements or songs. But these, so far at least, have not been specifically Mahler's subjectivity, but rather newly constructed subjectivities that may—but also may not—have much in common with Mahler himself. The default assumption, probably, would be that they do reflect Mahler's own subjectivity in significant ways. On the face of it, however, if they are truly subjective, with the kind of musical integrity discussed above, they cannot be *in part* Mahler; it would seem rather that they must either be Mahler or not be him. Even if we accommodate the distinction that a representation (in particular, a self-representation) must be constructed, and thus fundamentally different from the thing itself (in particular, the self, which is also constructed in some sense), it is hard to construe any of the subjectivities discussed so far as, simply or intentionally, Mahler's own. Certainly, if any of them are Mahler, he is hiding behind a wide variety of guises.[1]

On the other hand, the larger concerns in all four symphonies are so clearly derived from Mahler's most personal concerns—for his place in the world and in the cosmos—that not to find Mahler in these symphonies would border on the bizarre. Not only do we have Mahler's own testimony, detailed above, that these four symphonies represent his own life story, "everything [he has] experienced and endured," forming along the way a "Passion trilogy" and finally "a definite unified tetralogy." But we can also see, quite plainly—in the way that each symphony grapples with the nature of Christian belief, and with issues of alienation and what must ultimately be understood as, metaphorically and allegorically, cultural struggles of the kind that engulfed

Mahler himself—that these symphonies are, indeed, about him. And they have always been understood that way, for any number of reasons: first, because of a predilection to see romantic art as being about its creator; second, because of Mahler's career as a conductor, in which he seemed to impose his absolute will on both the orchestra and the music he conducted; third, because of a perceived grandiosity in his personality and manner that could be appeased only through his presenting large-scale symphonies about himself to the public; fourth, because that same grandiosity led him to glorify his own songs, sometimes the slightest of them, by setting them to elaborate orchestral accompaniment and even building his symphonies around them, as if they were vital flakes chipped from his very soul; and fifth, because he never denied it.

A more subtle reason for finding Mahler's subjectivity in his symphonies involves some version of the claim that the ability to create an effective illusion of subjectivity in art, one that will register as "authentic," stems in part from a process of identification in which the artist merges somehow with the locus of constructed subjectivity. Claims of this nature are often made —to take the most pertinent example—regarding the tradition of the German *Lied*, which is widely understood to represent, above all, the composer's subjectivity even though the persona of the song has been established preemptively by the poet, who has presumably already imprinted his or her subjectivity on the persona in question. It is thus to some extent part of the tradition and ethos of (post-Schubert) German romanticism that folklike *Lieder* will project a sense of the composer's self. Thus, even if the situation in a symphonic movement does not involve a subjectivity we can understand as Mahler's, his process of deriving many such movements from his own *Lieder* carries with it a sense of the personal, presumptively more than would the process of composing new, more conventionally symphonic material.

On the other hand, as noted, the "Fischpredigt" scherzo locates its subjectivity in opposition to the *Lied*-derived material that dominates the movement, even if that subjectivity does align with another species of folklike song, in the schmaltzy trumpet trio. This counterexample to the intuitively credible tracking of Mahler's subjectivity through his reuse of his own songs points to a critical issue: the presence or absence of a clearly defined sense of "I" in the original song. Thus, "Des Antonius von Padua Fischpredigt" presents a narrative from an objective viewpoint, and it is partly this objectivity that allows Mahler to derive a negatively evoked absolute-music topic from it (notwithstanding the personal element many hear in the "Bohemian" cast of the song).[2] "Ablösung im Sommer," on the other hand, presents its (somewhat confused) narrative subjectively; the "I" in this case is naive, to be sure, but if we did not sense Mahler's own (at least partial) identification with its perspective, the balance of sympathies in the movement would not work as well as it does. In the "forest" scherzo, then, we may indeed track Mahler's subjectivity from *Lied* to symphony, but only by virtue of and according to the subjectivity of the *Lied* in question.

More promising in this regard is Mahler's reuse of song material from his most conventionally subjective songs: those of his early cycle, *Lieder eines fahrenden Gesellen*, from which he draws prominently in two movements of his First Symphony. The poetic cycle in this case is generally understood to be Mahler's own text, and about himself, even though the first poem of the cycle was derived in much the same way as "Ablösung im Sommer," by elaborating on a poem from *Des knaben Wunderhorn*.[3] Since Mahler never acknowledged this derivation, and since, apart from the first poem, there is no other known source for the poetic cycle, autobiographical intent has been presumed. And quite reasonably so: the cycle was inspired by Mahler's unhappily progressing love affair with the singer Johanna Richter, and the sentiment and some aspects of the situation described in the cycle reflect this association. Mahler takes obvious pains to project, as the narrating persona of the cycle, a version of his own subjective identity, drawing as fully as possible on his own sensibilities and life circumstances (which may be why he was reticent about acknowledging an exterior source for the first poem).

In fact, one might claim that Mahler projected onto this persona a deeper sense of his own subjectivity than his life circumstances allowed him to actualize, so that, in some sense, the persona of the cycle is more Mahler than Mahler, even with the imperfect fit between composer and persona, and even given the derivative nature of the latter. Certainly, the persona accommodates easily to the "wandering" topos shared by Mahler's carefully cultivated identities as a romantic outsider, a struggling musician, and a Jew; moreover, the title's "fahrenden Gesellen" is doubly self-representative, for when he wrote the cycle he was both Johanna Richter's "traveling companion" and a "traveling journeyman" (it should be noted that either of these is a better translation than "Wayfarer," as the phrase is usually given in English translations—although neither alternative by itself captures Mahler's multiple meanings of a companion/lover who is obliged to move on, and whose traveling companions in the final song are (unreturned) love and sorrow ["Lieb' und Leide"]). Certainly, the poems speak with Mahler's voice about romantic attachment and nature, the latter serving alternately as inspiration, tormenter, and solace. But the circumstances of his affair with Johanna Rich-

ter do not really fit those of the cycle, either in the invented fact of her mar-
rying someone else or even in the nature of their fluctuating relationship, so
far as we know it; rather, Mahler seems to have taken particularly dark moments along the way (characteristically centered on failures of communication)[4] and elaborated them into the scenario of the cycle. And here we may
also note that his scenario is much closer to Schubert's two Müller cycles
and to the Schumann/Heine cycle *Dichterliebe* than to Mahler's own circumstances, and that, however well Mahler situates himself within the persona of the "fahrenden Gesellen," by the mid-1880s, that role amounts to
an easily recognized musicopoetic topic.[5] Nevertheless, and even if Mahler
seems never to have been close to the suicidal sentiments of the final song,
nor to have faced the specific causes of the despair he articulates, these extreme modes of expression become tokens of deep subjectivity within the
specific tradition of the song cycle centered around unreciprocated love.

Song Cycle into Symphony

For his First Symphony, Mahler borrows material from the second and
fourth songs of the cycle, taking much of the former as the basic material for
the exposition in the first movement, and using the final part of the fourth
(and thus the final part of the cycle) as an episode within the funeral-march
movement. Positioning is vital in both cases. For the first movement as for
the cycle, the "Ging heut' Morgen übers Feld" material emerges after an extended span of fitful activity (albeit quite differently conceived in terms of
portent) and so seems a flowering contrast, a vibrant emergence, compared
to what has come before. On a broader level, both song and sonata-form exposition are conceived as extended moments of enthusiastic youth, energet-
ically embracing nature before the inevitable disillusionments of adulthood.
In the case of the symphony, this youthfulness is spread over the first two
movements of the symphony (labeled "Aus den Tagen der Jugend" in early
performances, this part once included the discarded "Blumine" movement,
sandwiched between the opening movement and the scherzo).[6] In the cycle,
the youthful vigor of "Ging heut' Morgen" represents a dislocation, a revisiting of earlier enthusiasms that now affront the established self-pitying lan-
guor of the first song in the cycle, "Wenn mein Schatz Hochzeit macht." A
twist of sorts also accompanies the second borrowing: by absorbing the
concluding section of the cycle into the late stages of the funeral march—
the first component of the "Commedia humana" that forms the second half
of the symphony—Mahler is able to project a revision to the narrative of

Lieder eines fahrenden Gesellen, so that the tumultuous and ultimately triumphant finale of the symphony may be seen as an extension of the cycle.
This apparently peripheral quotation, even more than the much longer use
of "Ging heut' Morgen" in the first movement, thus contributes markedly
to our sense that the subjectivity of the symphony, no less than that of the
song cycle, is to be understood as Mahler's, notwithstanding the extent to
which specific musical events and associations may have been reformulated
or altered.

"Spring and No End"

The exposition of the first movement consists entirely of material either
taken directly or obviously derived from "Ging heut' Morgen," elaborated,
however, within a somewhat different narrative arc and standing in a somewhat different relationship to its surroundings. The song is in a varied
strophic form, with two dramatic events: the shift to B major (from D)[7] for
the more expansive third verse about sunshine (after more exuberant verses
about birds and flowers, respectively), and the shift to a slower tempo for
the final abortive verse, which dies away in an unfulfilled half cadence
("Nein! Nein! [Glück] ich mein', mir nimmer, nimmer blühen kann" [No!
No! (happiness) I feel, can never, never bloom for me]). For the symphonic
exposition, the emergence that occurs in the second half of each of the first
two verses of the song (see Example 26a) is spread more gradually across the
full span of the exposition and has little to do with harmonic shifts (the shift
to the dominant happens almost immediately and is fairly perfunctory). Accordingly, Mahler begins with the more relaxed material of the third verse,
saving the more urgent rhythmic and chromatic impulses of the first two
verses until later (beginning at r8; see Example 26b), to generate the celebratory closing section (beginning r9.5; 5:19).[8]

Even more critical than this manipulation of internal structure is Mahler's manipulation of context. With "Ging heut' Morgen," we retain the
subjectivity of the first song of the cycle, "Wenn mein Schatz Hochzeit
macht" (When My Beloved Marries), in which the cuckoo's call has become
a taunt, representing the merriment of others from which the singer is estranged. Throughout the main sections of the song, the vocal line is a melancholy echo of the merriment, or the merriment a burlesque of the vocal
line (see Example 27). More explicitly, the words of the final verse will tell us
that "Lenz ist ja vorbei!" (spring is truly past!). With the following song,
"Ging heut' Morgen," this principle of opposed sensibilities is raised to a

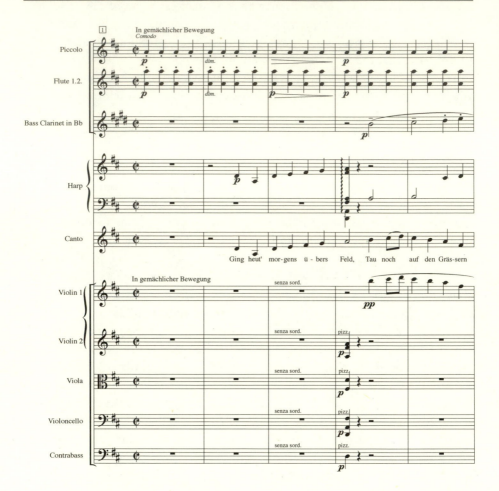

higher structural level: the song as a whole mocks with blithe indifference the perspective of the singer, who wants to recover the joys of nature in spring but cannot, and rejoins with (his) considerably bleaker perspective in the following song. In the symphony, however, we begin with the extended moment of rebirth; spring here is also past, but it is about to come again, as part of a natural cycle. Thus, Mahler explains in early programmatic descriptions that the introduction represents the awakening of nature either from a long winter's sleep or in the earliest morning; more consistently, he calls the movement as a whole "Frühling und kein Ende" (Spring and No End).[9] The cyclic aspect of spring's (or morning's) arrival finds an echo in

the evocation of a life cycle in Mahler's designation for the first half of the symphony, with spring (or morning) mapped to Mahler's "days of youth." The emergence, then, of the music borrowed from "Ging heut' Morgen" follows a familiar trope of (re)birth familiar from countless musical settings, typical for both depictions of spring's arrival and sunrise; even the key scheme (D minor to D major) is a familiar one for this trope.

But Mahler problematizes the cyclic aspect of spring's (morning's, youth's) arrival, which, while rescuing us from the pastness of spring, emphasizes as well its transience. Indeed, one of the projects of the symphony will be to transmute transience into a projection of permanence, to render linear and

self-perpetuating what presents itself initially as part of a cycle, emerging only to disappear again according to a preordained pattern. On a larger scale, this transmutation is set up by the abrupt shift from "Days of Youth" to the funeral march of the third movement, which seems, however absurdly it is configured, to close all too abruptly life's cycle from birth to death. But the finale will articulate the possibility of an afterlife and of (Christian-inflected) redemption, moving—according to its manipulation of familiar musical tropes and allusions, as well as to its earlier programmatic titles— "Dall' Inferno al Paradiso." In the first movement, Mahler manipulates cy-

Schön und flink! Wie mir doch die Welt ge - fällt!"

clic aspects and other conventions of sonata form so as to underscore the limiting nature of cycles and to suggest a possible solution, a way to escape their tyranny. In particular, the conclusion of the exposition represents a pivotal moment of crisis.

Conventionally understood, first-movement sonata-form expositions present a "problem" that will require both a developmental elaboration and a "resolution" that can be represented by an altered restatement (recapitulation) of the exposition. In many cases, however, especially with Beethoven and after, sonata-form expositions actually solve an opening problem, if falsely. Thus, for example, in Beethoven's Fifth Symphony, the close of the exposition in the first movement produces a new version of the opening motive, shed of its dire, fore-

boding quality and couched safely in the major mode. In movements like this, a steep price is exacted for such an easy resolution, for the task of the development becomes, typically, to re-elaborate the problem in such a way that it becomes unsolvable within the confines of sonata form; it will be reckoned solution enough just to restore the opening condition. In a somewhat earlier variation of this pattern—also by Beethoven and also in C minor—in the first movement of the "Pathétique" Sonata (Op. 13), the two returns of the slow introduction, both after the exposition and in the coda, serve emblematically to remind us that the initial problem has not been solved. The convention that operates in the latter case is that the slow introduction represents the first "problem" of the movement, which is "solved" the moment that the sonata-form allegro is successfully launched; thus, in the "Pathétique," a problem

even more basic than that presented in the sonata-form exposition haunts the movement, as if on a more metaphysical level.[10]

Similarly, in Mahler's First Symphony, with the arrival of the Allegro (r4.5; 3:41), spring "solves" winter simply by arriving. Yet, the solution itself has a dramatic shape and thus a clearly mapped life span that is over with

the end of the exposition (in no small part, additionally, because the material from "Ging heut' Morgen" has been exhausted by then). Mahler had originally planned not to repeat the exposition, but rather to fade directly into a recollection of the introduction. In view of the specific trajectory of the exposition, however, the repeat (which Mahler instituted only after the symphony was published)[11] serves to make an important point, both in line with the conventions sketched above and with regard to the particulars of this movement. First, if Mahler's model was Beethoven, at least in part, then

there would have been a compelling reason for him to follow Beethoven's structure as well, not only to complete the structural allusion, but also because Beethoven habitually found ways to make his expositional repeats count dramatically. In Beethoven's Fifth Symphony, for example, the repeat of the first-movement exposition is the first of many wrenching assertions that the initial problem is far from solved. Mahler's repeat makes a different kind of

Example 27. "Wenn mein Schatz Hochzeit macht," mm. 1–9

point, since the situation he creates is fundamentally different from Beetho-ven's; specifically, his exposition offers a solution, not through the series of events it presents (which are not given much weight beyond the move to a celebratory conclusion; as noted, the change of key is almost immediate, and perfunctory), but rather through the contrast its arrival offers to the in-troduction. More important for Mahler is to reinforce the *topic* of symphonic sonata form: by repeating the exposition, he brings more forcefully into play a set of dramatic conventions that, in very specific terms, much of the rest of the movement will actively deny. By its very oddness, Mahler's repeat of the exposition—a section that in this case completes rather than initiates a dramatic process and shape—calls attention to itself as a marker of sonata form.

The conventions of sonata form provide the same kind of reassurances that evocations of many other cycles do, in that they follow familiar patterns that experience has taught us will result in a successful outcome: winter yields to spring, development to recapitulation, conflict to resolution. Mahler's repeat carries precisely that kind of reassurance. But we should be warned here by a number of circumstances that this reassurance is not fully to be trusted: first, because it seems extraneous (why make a point of reassurance when success has already been so well articulated?); second, because Mahler's aesthetic should make us extremely wary of extended literal repetitions in his music ("every repetition is already a lie");[12] and third, because of a slight oddness in his title, which retains its precise profile even as other details in the program change with each version (that is, up until publication, when all titles are finally dropped). Mahler calls this movement "Frühling und kein Ende," which is usually translated "spring without end" but literally means "spring and no end"; critical here is the conjunction "und," which makes the second half of the title an equal dramatic partner: the movement, if we take its title seriously, is about both the emergence of spring and the failure to move beyond it.

An oft-cited "weakness" of this movement is the peculiar configuration of the development section, which not only begins by recalling the slow introduction at considerable length, but also cycles through a harmonic replay of the exposition, with D major yielding quickly to an extended section in A major, all based on new material.[13] Rightly, this is seen to cancel the forward momentum of the exposition (which is largely the point). Less cogently, the D major–A major section is frequently seen as a gross miscalculation, whether as inappropriately conceived development or as some species of false recapitulation; in either case, many have seen this section as an embarrassing lapse forgivable only because of Mahler's relative youth. Yet it is neither development nor recapitulation, but rather exposition in both the formal and material sense, which only a narrative account that accommodates some degree of metaphysics, or perhaps cosmology, can account for adequately.

The crisis engendered by the full arrival of "spring" at the end of the exposition extends to all levels of musical, programmatic, and narrative logic.

Musically, the shape of the exposition is generated by the trope of developmental processes leading to a climax, to such an extent that further development of this material would seem redundant. While, too, the return to the "wintry" introduction seems abrupt and harsh—and Mahler emphasizes this by the rather nervous twitterings of the first flute and piccolo that continue as the octave A's return and we fade back to minor (r12.1–r13.1; see Example 28)—the device allows at least the sense of a new beginning. Programmatically, the movement has already apparently fulfilled its task with the exposition—especially if we take the title seriously, for we have precisely the arrival of spring and no satisfactory continuation or conclusion beyond the "lie" of repetition. Narratively—and this is the crux of the matter—we have completed a segment of one cycle while at the same time articulating another kind of cyclic structure (sonata form) that compels an entirely different mode of continuation. Thus, on the one hand, the cyclic emergence of spring is complete, so that continuation must somehow enforce the principle of cyclicism. To do so programmatically would be to continue with summer (or perhaps high noon);[14] however, not only would this to some extent "change the subject," but it would also create even greater interference patterns with sonata-form structures to come. More abstractly, Mahler could cycle through part or all of what has already happened—which amounts to the choice of repeating the exposition or returning all the way back to the introduction (the very choices he makes, one after the other). On the other hand, sonata-form expectations of a development followed by a reifying recapitulation cannot simply be put aside, especially if the exposition is to be repeated.

Mahler's solution to the crisis, which to some extent honors each of the conflicting orientations, is to stage a new emergence, but one fraught with a significance and portent missing from the opening. Early on in the return of the introduction, Mahler introduces a new figure in the cello that will form the first of two distinctively new thematic elements in the second exposition,[15] deriving audibly from the bird calls in the piccolo and first flute (cf. Example 28: the piccolo in r12.4–5 and the cello in r12.5; the flute in r12.5–7 and the cello in r12.7–9). What marks this derivation as profoundly different from that of the "Ging heut' Morgen" melody, which is also derived audibly from the cuckoo calls and seems to respond in kind to other birdcalls as it goes along, is that here we have a more deliberately traced thought process, involving a seemingly more purposeful, if much less spontaneous, process of modeling, different in kind from the simple exuberance of feeling heard earlier. Thus, while both the "Ging heut' Morgen" melody and the new ma-

Example 28. Mahler, Symphony No. 1, first movement, r12.1–r13.2 (7:54)

terial are tokens of subjectivity, there is a critical difference between them: if the former registers as a kind of oblivious cheerfulness, taking delight in nature as a reflection—an extension, really—of its own psychic energy, subjectivity in the latter case seems to pay attention to nature as something different from it, and begins a process of selective appropriation that will give

pointed articulation to differences between the careless exuberance of spring/
youth and the (presumed? potential?) thoughtfulness of human adulthood.
Central to those differences will be a sense of directional, linear process
peculiar to the human realm, resisting the cyclic patterns of found nature
even as its fundamental gestures are taken over and recast. It is only from the
human—more specifically, the romantic—perspective, after all, that cyclic
repetitions "lie."

Two further associations are strongly evoked by the return to the introduction, the one topical, the other founded in allusion. Topically, the return
seems to represent the presence of death, both because it stills the activity of
the exposition and because it underscores implicitly the cyclic dimension of
life, necessarily including death as part of its cycle. Death's presence is felt
even more definitively as the new thematic element develops, drooping chromatically into the minor mode as the more elaborate birdcalls are absorbed
into the stillness of the octave A's (Example 28, r12.12–15). Allusively, Mah-

ler's introduction invokes, even at the outset, a number of musical fore-
runners, most obviously Beethoven's Fourth and Ninth Symphonies.[16] With
the return to the introduction, particularly after the return to the minor mode
(8:40), Mahler dramatically underscores the latter connection through the
presence of a disturbing third (F♮; 8:55) in the bass, suggesting a major-mode

alternative (in this case, F major, ♭VI/A or III/d) with, however, a fatal instability, as in Beethoven. Notable, too, is how Mahler's open sonorities are given disturbing emphasis through the persistence and manipulation of his cuckoo calls, and how their motivic relationship to the falling fourth at the opening of Beethoven's Ninth is thus additionally underscored. Mahler's passage specifically recalls two related moments in the Ninth when Beethoven recasts his opening as an unstable D major with F♯ in the bass, at the opening of the development when the configuration moves on to G minor, and at the beginning of the recapitulation, when the moment is extended with ferocious energy before the F♯ falls to F♮. Mahler's return to the opening most immediately recalls the earlier passage in the Ninth with its formal parallel, but then more definitively the later with its extended moment of terrifying uneasiness, rendered even more so in Mahler by the quiet dynamic and alternation of open fifths on A and D, the former occasioning a chilling conflict between E and F. What gives these passages their terrifying effect is not so much the threat posed by the persistent presence of the disturbing bass—although in both Beethoven and Mahler, this can be felt to pose a substantial threat—as the sense that there is something tremendously important at stake. The key to this feeling—again, in both Beethoven and Mahler —is the alignment of this disturbing musical difference between the opening and its return with a difference in perspective, for both composers invest the return with an element of subjectivity absent from the opening. The added note in the bass stakes a vested claim in what will happen, insisting on an outcome much different from what had happened earlier.[17] This investiture, coupled with an extended prolongation of its unanswered insistence, produces the stock elements of Hitchcockian suspense, encouraging us to identify all the more with the subjective perspective.

Difference also marks the concluding passage of the introduction on its return, beyond the continued presence of F♮ in the bass. In the introduction itself, the nested descending fourths (alluding to Beethoven's Fourth Symphony and forecasting the triumphant chorale of the finale, with its allusion to Handel's "Hallelujah" Chorus) enter against a mysterious chromatic figure in the bass, rising sequentially and becoming gradually more diatonic as the incipient chorale is given in diminution and overlapped entries. The mysterious sequential figure, like the nested fourths/chorale, has multiple associations, anticipating not only the "Bruder Martin" funeral march of the third movement, but also melodic figures critical to the sense of directed energy introduced in the first movement and taken up again in the finale to effect a sense of triumphant breakthrough. Thus, with the return of this configuration (r14; see Example 29), the sequential rising figure is altered at its third statement to produce a simpler, more direct three-note ascent that more forcefully emphasizes the arrival pitch. Combined with the rising sequence, the figure thus transmutes from a mysterious seething to an incipient marker of heroic—which is to say human—struggle. With this fairly subtle change, however fraught it may be with future significance, come two much more immediately significant changes: the new, subjectively laden thematic material, entering as the rising figure changes, and an inverted form of the latter figure in the horns, which follows and then alternates with the combination of the other two (in addition, the horns effectively displace the nested fourths/chorale).

The horn choir, which appeared early in the first introduction to mark with their solemn song the first cadential arrival in D, was absent during the exposition, except as it contributed occasionally to the general contrapuntal din of the closing group. If the horns, here as in the "forest" scherzo from the Third Symphony, represent the deep spirit of nature (the forest), their response and subsequent dialogue with the subjective human component in the return of the introduction seems to acknowledge the latter's deepened, more thoughtful subjectivity, only now worthy of acknowledgment from this deeper voice of nature. Accordingly, in the new exposition that follows, the first group consists of two main spans: an introductory invocation by the horn choir (r15.1–12; 10:36) and a more substantial elaboration of the new melody that cycles back to material from the first exposition (r15.14–r16; 10:58). Moreover, the new secondary thematic component, derived from the rising sequential theme, occasions a symbolic partnership between the "human" cellos and the "natural" horns (r16.7–18; 11:13).

While most of the ensuing development remains in the major mode, the larger key scheme stands in a remote relationship to D major and points, if somewhat vaguely, to an eventual outcome of F minor, sliding downward from D♭ (r17f; 11:29) to a thematic arrival in C (r19.4f; 12:09). When F minor duly arrives (r21.8f; 12:50), and along with it the rising sequential figure from the introduction, the first of the new themes combines with an augmented version of this figure to set up a dramatic reemergence into D major for the recapitulation, which then blends thematic elements from both earlier expositions. The retransition, with its heroic recovery from the remote key of F minor, will provide a direct model for the second of two breakthroughs to D major in the F minor finale, helping to realize Mahler's desire, as he explained in a letter to Richard Strauss, that the ultimate arrival in D major should feel "earned."[18] But the achievement of the tonic in the first move-

ment occasions a different sort of celebration, considerably less reverent and taking the actual arrival in D rather more for granted, so that the initial horn choir concludes with a series of raucous whoops, and comic exchanges between the timpani and the rest of the orchestra interrupt the closing section; in Mahler's apt description of the movement's final bars, "[his] hero bursts out laughing and runs away."[19]

In a sense, the recapitulation represents a reversion to youth after approaching the brink of maturity, a callow embrace of the cyclic just after demonstrating the possibility of breaking free and pursuing a more linear course. Two things prompt such an outcome. First, Mahler's title, and implicitly his desire for the movement's "spring" to have "no end," demands ei-

ther a basic cyclicism or the projection of an unbounded linear narrative. The latter possibility is, however, not a real alternative, since it lies outside the sensibilities projected by the movement and would in any case entail a progression beyond spring. Second, the movement's subjectivity—its "youth"— cannot fully disentangle itself from exuberant nature and its cycles, something that only a more overt confrontation with death could bring about. Knowledge of death within cyclic processes leads eventually and inevitably to the desire that one's own death not be thus absorbed, nor the deaths of those most firmly inscribed on one's own subjectivity. Full knowledge of death, then, pushes subjectivity away from nature to something beyond it, away from closed cycles to something at least potentially infinite, projected

in geometric terms as either linear or a non-closed curve such as a spiral. While Mahler's larger narrative indeed produces just such a confrontation with death, this confrontation does not occur in the first movement (despite the foretaste offered with the returning introduction), or indeed in Part One of the symphony, which is given over to "Days of Youth."

Mahler's reuse of "Ging heut' Morgen" in the first movement allows both a more complex setting for his evocation of a youthful, exuberant response to nature and a different mode of problematizing that response. In both cases, that response is rendered with tremendous subjective sympathy but judged

inadequate for adult humanity. But, whereas in the song cycle the perspective of youthful naiveté returns to mock the self-pitying protagonist, the symphony permits—indeed, demands—a more sophisticated engagement with the naive perspective, resolving its simply stated contradiction between exuberant nature and human unhappiness on another, higher level. If subjectivity transmutes spring into youth and eventually occasions a sense of the whole that finds automatic, unearned cyclic processes inadequate, it cannot by itself envision a narrative path to escape the tyranny of cycles, nor, indeed, will it evidence much desire to give up youthfulness for the sake of such concerns. Yet, two things happen in the first movement that do not or could not happen in the song cycle: first, because subjectively felt difference is not articulated in the symphony, youthful responses to nature are

not turned aside (thus, the second exposition and recapitulation retain essential material from the first exposition), and second, a distinctly human ability to overcome obstacles is demonstrated, founded in determined, goal-directed activity (but allied as well with nature), even if full narrative urgencies for such energies have yet to be projected.

In the funeral march that launches part 2 of the symphony, Mahler takes the next decisive step in his narrative, not so much through the cultural conflict this movement stages between hunter and animals—represented musically by markers for Catholics and Jews, respectively, as Francesca Draughon has shown[20]—but in the more subjectively rendered central episode. As in the scherzo movements of his next two symphonies, Mahler reserves a trio-like section for his most intensely subjective moment, although here it is actually material from his own song that registers most subjectively, rather than, as in his two later scherzos, merely a projected song that stands in opposition to the song-derived material in the outer sections of the movement. Nor does this episode represent a clearly stated opposition to either side of the already stated conflict of the funeral march. Rather, it seems a moment apart from that conflict, independent even of perplexing issues regarding which of the projected antagonists—hunter or hunted, Catholic or Jew—is to be regarded most sympathetically (for here, as in the scherzo of the Third Symphony, both sides are accorded some degree of sympathetic presentation).

The two *Gesellen* songs that Mahler borrows for his First Symphony frame the cycle's psychological chronology, in that "Ging heut' Morgen" confronts the present with a lost youthful exuberance and "Die zwei blauen Augen" ends with a projection of a future blissfully free from the pains of the present (i.e., within the sleep of death). As a song, "Die zwei blauen Augen" is oddly configured, comprising three stages of decidedly different character, each in its own key and with its own characteristic motivic basis. Mahler sets these three stages with some degree of irony: only the last stage overtly embraces death as an alternative, but it is also the only one to offer sustained comfort, while the earlier stages, each in its turn, project a funereal tone with a distinctive, obsessive motive derived from the general topic of funeral march (repeated-note dotted figures and the slow, steady beat of the timpani, respectively; see mm. 1 and 17 in Example 30).[21] Mahler manages this linear narrative with seemingly token concessions to the conventions of cyclic musical form, involving nested recollections at the end of each of the later two stages and linear processes in which characteristic material for each stage derives from material first heard in the previous stage. But the separate character of each section is maintained despite these concessions and, indeed, is largely articulated by them. Thus, the dotted figure from the opening becomes the focal point of an ambivalent shifting between the major and minor modes that marks the second stage (Example 30, mm. 17–19); in specifically musical terms, this modal ambivalence registers as an equivocal response to a fundamental problem triggered by the shift at the beginning of this stage to the ♭VI (Example 30, mm. 17), an orientation incompatible with the minor-mode dotted figure.[22] Moreover, the resolute tread of the timpani strokes seems all the more regimented after the motivic displacements and added beats of the opening section. The final stage (beginning in m. 37 [2:40]; see Example 30) takes as its characteristic motive the rising major-mode figure that blossoms briefly midway through the second stage; already with this derivation we are warned not to trust its major-mode serenity, and indeed, the recollection is eventually made more literal, with the return of the chromatic descents of "Ade!" (cf. mm. 26–28 [1:56] and 52–55 [3:39] in Example 30). The final stage may well be understood as an expanded form of the second half of the second stage without the timpani strokes (now at rest, and hence more expansive). The implicit (and well-worn) ironies of the final stage are subtly reinforced by this derivation, since it not only undercuts the projected serenity of the opening, but also maps leave-taking ("Ade!") to the notion that, under the linden tree, "da wüßt ich nicht, wie das Leben tut, war alles, alles wieder gut!" (there I knew not how life fared, [there] all was good again!); even more immediately striking is the setting of the latter claim that "all was good again" against the chromatic plaints from the previous verse. Mahler's other major expansion during the final stage, after this phrase but before the final recollection of the opening dotted figure, also projects leave-taking even as the text simply repeats part of the previous phrase; this particular effect, which depends largely on the horn calls that accompany the voice after m. 59 (4:13; see Example 30), is greatly enhanced in the funeral-march movement, where the words are absent.

Long before the trio-like episode that directly recalls the final section of "Die zwei blauen Augen" in the later stages of the movement, the funeral march itself installs the most distinctive funereal elements of the song—the dotted figure and the timpani strokes—but with two crucial differences: not only have the timpani strokes become the primary marker for the funeral march, but also the dotted figure has been given an oddly nuanced secondary role, entering originally as part of a stately counterpoint to the ongoing "Bruder Martin" canon, which develops an untowardly festive lilt along the way (see Example 31, beginning at r3). Moreover, while the conclusion to the phrase reverts to a stately demeanor in keeping with—in fact, modeled on—the conclusion of "Bruder Martin," it slyly mocks the latter as well through the parallel seconds it creates in combination with it (r3.4 [1:27]; this clichéd device for creating the effect in music of satirical laughter is here

Example 30. Mahler, "Die zwei blauen Augen," mm. 1–2, 15–19 (1:09), 25–42 (1:51), and 51–67 (3:33)

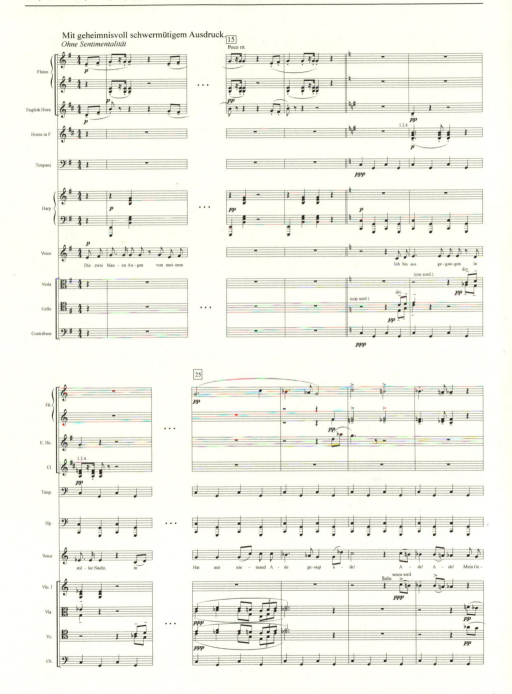

partly muted through the layering of instrumental lines in counterpoint). The ambivalent relationship between this counterpoint and the main theme is never adequately resolved; while all its central elements derive audibly from the "Bruder Martin" tune as Mahler presents it, including the dotted figure itself and the upper-fourth lick (which literally doubles the timpani strokes), it dances rather than marches, and seems to have more affinity with the Jewish klezmer music to come than with the Catholic "Bruder Martin" tune.[23] Yet, in the conclusion of the movement, during the last bars of the funeral march proper, remnants of this tune are at least equal partners with, and seemingly fused to, "Bruder Martin." Inevitably, this ambivalence will affect associative meaning within and around the song quotation, even if the quotation does not include more than a vestige of the more obviously funereal sections of the song.

To some extent, Mahler manages the ambivalent position of the dotted-figure counterpoint to "Bruder Martin" by evoking absolute music as a topic to carry the canonic funeral march, albeit less threateningly than in the "Fischpredigt" scherzo of the Second Symphony. However mocking the counterpoint may be, it shadows the funeral march too closely to avoid getting caught up in its obsessively absolutist flow. In fact, its absorption into the march becomes so complete that from the moment the counterpoint enters, its association with the funeral-march topic gradually becomes closer even than the "Bruder Martin" tune itself. Thus, unlike the latter, the dotted-figure counterpoint plays out intact with every recurrence of the topic. Even during the fragmented conclusion of the movement, the dotted-figure tune gets a full hearing; indeed, its mockery is by then so muted that it can simply substitute for the "Bruder Martin" tune, which, aside from the harp's

playing of the cadential bar in diminution, is not heard at all.[24] Perhaps this can be construed as the triumph of the dance lick over the funeral march; given the more basic presence of the funeral-march topic, however, it seems more the reverse.[25]

Mahler's use of only the third stage of "Die zwei blauen Augen" in the symphony, even apart from the added ambivalence surrounding the dotted figure, takes away substantially from the self-referential meanings generated within the song, which do not transfer to the movement. There is nothing native to the movement to make us mistrust the major-mode serenity in the first bars. Rather, this quality, through being so anomalous to both the material and the tone of the movement up to that point, seems all the more authentic and contributes substantially to the episode's sense of subjectivity. What the quotation seems to do, somewhat differently from the song, is to

establish subjectivity in terms of its separation from previously established realities, a separation based here on memory rather than on the projection of an oblivious future in the dreamless sleep of death. Thus, the serenity of the opening part of the quotation, which clearly could not have come from anything we have heard thus far in the movement, seems activated rather by

Example 31. Mahler, Symphony No. 1, third movement, r3.1–5 (1:13)

memory: it stems from a subjectivity that has removed itself from the present, and that possesses an intimacy and familiarity that betoken remembered past rather than projected future. Then, in the second part of the quotation, with its sagging chromatic lines and "farewell" horn calls, the temporal status of this serenity—its pastness—is clarified, as is its relationship to the larger funereal setting. At the end of the quotation, when the dotted figure returns, it is inflected with a tone of mockery more pronounced than in the song, a foretaste of the return to the objective present and the funeral-march rhythms that immediately follow. Despite these critical differences, it is nevertheless the instrumental part of the song that continues to "speak" in all of this, for serenity, pastness, intense subjectivity, leave-taking, even the exteriority of the dotted figure are all present in some form during the third stage of the song, if sometimes in a kind of musical counterpoint to the words. In particular, the recollection of the dotted figure at the end of the song takes on a quality fundamentally different from the opening, when it seemed directly expressive of the song's subjectivity. By the end it represents something clearly exterior to the song's subjectivity, dying away as an emblem of the cares that earlier seemed inextricably entwined with that subjectivity but which are by that point being denied. Thus, while in the funeral-march movement the exteriority of the dotted figure acquires an added element of mockery, the exteriority itself is already present in the song.

Structurally, too, Mahler exploits relationships already given in the song, but he applies them toward somewhat different ends. Built into the stages of the song is an implicit circularity, as the recollection of the fundamental motive from the first stage at the end of each of the later stages makes feasible (if only abstractly) all possible orderings of the three sections. In the song, this potential circularity is suggested for the sake of denying it; neither the "progressive" key scheme nor the psychological journey is in any way circular. Thus, the middle, more marchlike section wrests us from the moribund first stage by shifting harmonically to a modally ambivalent ♭VI. The march topic here is both funereal and—in part because of the energizing harmonic shift at the opening, in part through the words—a manifestation of a journey undertaken with a sense of resignation and, perhaps, penitence. The recollection of the dotted figure at the end of the march already points to something left behind, and the subsequent stage confirms this as it settles into a comforting, major-mode subdominant specifically as an alternative to harmonic and psychological return. Mahler borrows the latter move, to the major subdominant from the minor tonic, for the opening of the song quotation in the funeral-march movement, converting what was a transport to a comforting oblivion into an escape to subjectivity and memory. At the end, however, he exploits the potential for circularity by borrowing, from the end of the first stage in the song, the move from dotted figure to timpani strokes, which enter in the ♭VI. Within the movement, this represents a structural thematic return (to be expected after a trio-like episode), but, unexpectedly, a half-step removed from the tonic—just as, in the song, the concluding key is F minor after an opening in E minor.[26] But here there is a much greater impact, since the timpani strokes in the funeral-march movement have been more centrally installed as a marker of harmonic stability, fully in line with the traditional symphonic deployment of timpani to reinforce the tonic. Within the extended narrative of the trio, however, the move makes perfect sense, as a reaction of the subjective presence to the mocking entry of the dotted figure. Oddly, then, and for the first time in the movement, the funeral march is thus invested with a disconcerting subjectivity on its return, as if the observed funeral procession has now been joined, with the incremental rise in pitch registering as a correspondingly heightened sense of reality.[27] Odd, too, is how readily the absolute-music topic seems thus to acquiesce to the established subjectivity of the trio. The lack of protest may be seen as either a token of irresistible strength on the part of the trio's subjectivity or the continued weakened state of the funeral-march topic after the klezmer episode, or both. Or perhaps its oblivious detachment—programmatically, the self-absorbed unconcern of the mourners for the world beyond the funeral march—now extends to the matter of its own key.

For the remainder of the movement, the subjective element invests briefly first in one side of the conflict and then the other. As the E♭ minor section winds down, the timpani drop out and the violins take us back to D minor, playing *col legno* as a group but with interspersed solos in what is clearly a gesture of withdrawal (see Example 32a). Almost immediately, the klezmer group enters in direct opposition to the "Bruder Martin" canon, brutally imposing a faster tempo and more raucous sensibility on the sedate funeral march. The implicit violence of the passage makes it a clear precursor for the outcries that mark the later stages of the scherzo movements of the Second and Third Symphonies (discussed above), although here the subjective element has withdrawn temporarily and is neither the complainant (as in the Second Symphony) nor the impugned (as in the Third). As in both later movements, however, the violence that results from the confrontation makes it clear that reconciliation is impossible.[28] Yet this is not the only drama of the movement. As the music slows to the original march tempo, we hear a distinct echo of the song quotation in one of the closing phrases of the klezmer episode (see Example 32b). Although the phrase does not depart musically from the earlier episode (notwithstanding a somewhat different instrumental profile), the similar melodic contour in a suddenly more intimate environment involving unusual string textures (earlier, solo violin duet; now, violins doubled by cellos) enforces the connection. Also, the brief splash of the Neapolitan (E♭) serves as a striking marker of difference against the pedal D–A, recalling the key of the subjectively inflected version of the funeral march just heard. In this brief moment of enhanced subjectivity, with its easy blending of klezmer elements with the "Bruder Martin" canon so soon after their recently demonstrated incompatibility, and with its easy

resolution of the dissonant tonality of E♭ back into the D minor of the funeral march, we may find psychological closure for the movement. The resolution this passage provides is wholly subjective, however, leaving the uneasy worldly tensions to play out to an indecisive conclusion.

. . . And Selfhood (Subjectivity Objectified)

But are the subjectivities I have traced in the first and third movements of the First Symphony truly Mahler's? Not, surely, in the sense that the persona of *Lieder eines fahrenden Gesellen* may be construed as Mahler himself. Mostly, there is the difference in medium; the default assumption with a song or song cycle, especially one involving a first-person narrative in the *Lied* tradition, is that the persona projected therein corresponds closely to the self of someone in the creative hierarchy, whether the poet, composer, singer, or some combination of the three. But the orchestra, as a medium, objectifies. While we may find in Mahler's use of the orchestra a projection of the subjective, even of multiple subjectivities, and while we can trace some of these to constructs (i.e., the *Gesellen* cycle) in which that subjectivity maps easily to Mahler himself, the larger perspective of the symphony objectifies those subjectivities.[29] Moreover, the "I" in this symphony, and in any Mahler symphony, cannot be mapped to a fairly localized subjectivity, however continuously maintained, for a variety of reasons. The "world" that a symphony creates, as Mahler famously decreed it must, is too diverse for us to accept it as encompassed by a single subjective view, particularly since the devices for creating the sense of a diverse world are specifically designed to dispel the illusion of such a focused view.[30] More to the point, the symphony imposes a perspective on its dominant subjectivity or subjectivities—its protagonist(s)—that obviates a simple mapping of creative persona to that subjectivity; rather, in some sense, the creative persona is either coextensive with the larger perspective or split between it and whatever subjectivities it encompasses.[31] And this larger perspective is manifold: the "world" of a Mahler symphony has spatial, temporal, and psychological dimensions that deny the Aristotelian unities required of straightforward subjective mapping—unities that are much easier to maintain in song cycles.

We may note, then, that when Mahler describes the conclusion of the first movement of his First Symphony, it is "the hero" who is heard to run away, not Mahler himself, however close the subjectivity of the movement lies to his own. And this is no subterfuge, for when actions of this kind are presented with such comic effect, they abandon all pretense of subjectivity;

rather, Mahler is at most looking back at his youth, somewhat patronizingly, and constructing his world so as both to challenge his "hero" and to preserve him when the challenge is initially not fully met. Within the First Symphony, Mahler projects a strong sense of his present-tense subjectivity—arguably the only secure mode for projecting selfhood in art—only in the finale. As he put it with regard to the finale of his Second Symphony (but in a formulation that applies here and perhaps to the Third Symphony as well): "Whereas the first three movements are narrative, the last is altogether dramatic; here, all is motion and occurrence."[32] Thus, the finale takes place in the present, as drama; the earlier movements in the past, as narrative.[33] In the Second Symphony, Mahler's subjectivity may be found as well in the fourth movement, "Urlicht," which is left out of Mahler's summation;[34] perhaps, in the First Symphony, moments within the late stages of the funeral march may also have enough of the first-person singular to be construed as Mahler. Significantly, though, for the intense sense of the present self that we have in the finales of both works, Mahler must resort to more "objective" material, newly composed, whose past, if it has one, is universalized. From this perspective, his dropping of "Das himmlische Leben" from the Third Symphony seems entirely appropriate, since, if a symphony is to maintain the illusion of a personal journey, it must end with a sense of "I" either in the present or projected into the future. While "Das himmlische Leben" may perhaps be construed as projecting the self into the future, its objectifying narrative tone continuously denies that it does.

In general terms, while Mahler depends heavily on his own songs to simulate subjectivity in his early symphonies, and especially to project troubled subjectivity or even warring subjectivities, his re-cyclings do not directly produce the sense that his symphonies are specifically about *him* and in fact may cast doubt on the notion that they are. Indirectly, however, they contribute significantly to this impression, for if his symphonies mean to project a world, and more particularly a world that reflects his own past and his own experiences, however objectively rendered, then his songs figure prominently on a number of levels. To the extent that they register as folklike songs, or as song-derived, they establish a vital trace of an authentic cultural voice. To the extent that they register as Mahler's own songs, they establish a sense of his experience of the culture that is being represented within them. And to the extent that they register as specific songs with specific meanings, Mahler is able to map a deeply evocative interactive nexus of meanings while leaving aside the most specifically meaningful surface of the song (i.e., its text). The result will thus seem more purely musical than in the song, but will nevertheless channel a strongly felt associative dimension. On this level, Mahler seems to assert that the text is but a single possible reading of the music, a single look at Mozhukhin's face. In the act of reusing the music of a song, however, of reading it differently or simply more generally, Mahler moves from reality to image in the Bazinian sense, sacrificing one dimension of authenticity—the music's sense of "I"—only to restore this dimension on a more fully embracive level.

Chapter 6

Beyond Selfhood:
The Autonomy of Musical Presence (II)

> Without knowing at first where it's leading, you find your-
> self pushed further and further beyond the bounds of the
> original form, whose potentialities lay hidden within it like
> the plant within the seed. . . . The inception and creation of
> a work are mystical from beginning to end; unconsciously,
> as if in the grip of command from outside oneself one is
> compelled to create something whose origin one can scarcely
> comprehend afterwards.
>
> —GUSTAV MAHLER, in Natalie Bauer-Lechner,
> *Recollections of Gustav Mahler*

Mahler's ambivalence about absolute music connected to his many religious, cultural, and aesthetic ambivalences, all of which combined to form something akin to Multiple Personality Disorder whose effects reached into every corner of his adult activities. In each of these realms, Mahler was effectively (as he himself put it) homeless: a Jew who could embrace neither Judaism nor his people;[1] a Catholic who was not wholly a Catholic, nor ever really accepted as such;[2] a pan-Germanist who was neither German nor Austrian, but a displaced Germanic-assimilated Jew from the Bohemian provinces, and thus triply an outsider even there;[3] a Wagnerian who failed to produce any staged musical works beyond his completion of Weber's *Die drei Pintos*, and who was habitually at odds with Richard Strauss, Wagner's most successful acolyte and the supreme German nationalist of that generation of composers; the presumptive heir to the Germanic symphonic tradition who was attacked virulently for his performances of Beethoven symphonies and for his apparent failure to produce works recognizably within that tradition.[4] And yet, he was unquestionably Jewish, Catholic, Bohemian, Austrian, German, a dramatist, and a symphonist. He was one of the most famous and successful Jews of his generation—the composer of the widely beloved *Resurrection* Symphony, accepted by many as the most effective aesthetic representation of Christian belief on offer; a composer who "spoke" musical dialects and composed in idioms directly reflective of his diverse Bohemian, Austrian, and German musical roots; a practicing musical dramatist of the first order, whose performances of Mozart and Wagner reportedly affected profoundly the likes of both Brahms and Hitler and permitted his survival as director of the Vienna State Opera in the face of anti-Semitic attacks in that city that were both constant and intense; and, without serious question, the most important symphonist of his generation, one whose star is still in the ascendant a century later. So, too, with the traditions of absolute music, for not only was Mahler singularly adept at evoking absolute music in order to denounce implicitly its potential for oppression, but he was also fully capable, as in the finales of his Third and Ninth Symphonies, of harnessing its hypnotically persuasive power in the service of deeply sympathetic ends. It may be too easy to map his ambivalent relationship to late-nineteenth-century Germanic culture generally, with its unhealthy combination of oppressive beauties and particularly ugly forms of oppression, directly to this specific ambivalence regarding what is often seen as the highest form of achievement in German music—too easy, perhaps, but surely not wrong.

On the other hand, there is much more to Mahler's engagement with the absoluteness of music than exploring its potential, as a topic or in conventional practice, to either express or oppress through its seeming autonomy and overwhelming sense of presence, or to project this potential in terms either positive or negative. The capacity for music to project absoluteness was indispensable to him for the delineation of separate and even alienated personae and identities to represent individual and multiple subjectivities as well as autonomously oppressive forces. And, beyond these uses that Mahler found or developed for absolute music as it could be deployed topically—in two senses of the word, that is, both as a topic and on a relatively local level within his sprawling, heterogeneous musical structures—Mahler encountered and responded to a different kind of absoluteness in the music he chose for his re-cyclings as he negotiated between the previously established meanings for his borrowed material and the demands of whatever new contexture he was devising for it. This kind of absoluteness, a sense of deep intrinsic character somehow embedded or embodied in a musical structure—

almost, we might say, the music's own subjectivity, or even its selfhood—seems to have figured prominently both in Mahler's choice of material to reuse and in the nature of the difficulties he sometimes had in reusing it. Specifically, and perhaps surprisingly, it is this peculiar kind of musical self-hood that interfered with his attempts to transfer personal subjectivities directly from songs to symphonies, for notwithstanding the ease with which Mahler projected his own subjectivity in songs, that dimension seemingly became hermetically sealed off from him when he took over and recast the same music for use in his symphonies, for it had by then been assimilated into the music's autonomous nature. As a result, Mahler became consistently alienated from his own music, an experience sufficiently troubling to him that he would try to articulate it to Natalie Bauer-Lechner, as quoted above.[5]

To be sure, this manner of understanding the situation is largely artificial, since music has no actual self in this sense beyond what its composer, performers, and audiences bring to it—although the same kind of objection may be made against the concept of absolute music as it has generally been understood, for both formulations identify a set of beliefs surrounding musical practice rather than something inherent in the music itself.[6] But, artificially or not, Mahler was virtually forced into this estranged relationship with his own creations by two constraining structures, no matter how closely allied those creations might have been to his own sense of self. Within the Germanic musical traditions of the late nineteenth century, "good" music had to embody a particular kind of musical integrity, such that every musical detail could seem to be determined and animated completely by its place and function within an organically unified work and, moreover, be seen to hold within it, implicitly, the whole of the work. Within this tradition, one could not casually reuse material, for to be convincing in different contexts, music had itself to be different. Since Mahler was not, in most cases, revising his songs into symphonies according to a sense of the music's unique manifest destiny—thus, for example, he did not withdraw *Lieder eines fahrenden Gesellen* after composing the First Symphony, but rather returned to it and even orchestrated it in the mid-1890s[7]—he had to find a way to preserve the identity of the reused material while also changing it in fundamental ways. In the organic metaphor, Mahler's process could be understood as elaborating a somehow deeper sense of the music's identity as he took it over for use in one of his symphonies; moreover, going for a deeper sense of the music's "self" was quite possibly the only way to justify reusing it at all. Even so, the enterprise was extremely risky.

One would be hard pressed to find a novelist transplanting large chunks of prose from one novel into another and still harder pressed to find a positive critical response to such a procedure. The situation in German music during Mahler's lifetime was no less stringent.

But Mahler was caught as well in a more specific bind, even apart from issues of reception within his specific cultural setting. Had he tried to penetrate the hermetic seal that protected the identity of the music he was reusing, he would have destroyed the very set of meanings that mattered most to him in the first place, and there would then have been no real point to his re-cycling ventures. Thus, for Mahler, re-cycling music was not a matter of convenience, but rather of extreme inconvenience; he was, after all, no Handel or Rossini pillaging earlier works for musical structures that could be put to new uses because they were virtually forgotten, but was taking over material he might reasonably expect his audiences to know, and so had to work out musical/narrative/programmatic meanings that could be extended beyond the boundaries of the work in question to merge in some sense with their source works. To be sure, this was not only or even primarily a problem, for Mahler also obviously derived much from the rich associative meanings he was able to tap into by presenting two readings of the same music, one more absolute (and thus deeper) than the other. Perhaps, indeed, it is from the standpoint of these considerations that he felt compelled to drop the "Blumine" movement in the First Symphony. Most have argued that the relevant issue in that case was one of abstract effectiveness; yet, perhaps more important, the disappearance of the source work, owing to Mahler's suppression of his music for *Der Trompeter von Säkkingen*, stripped the movement of the kind of enriched associations every other movement in the symphony taps into. Ironically, then, Mahler may well have dropped the movement specifically because it was not *unoriginal* enough for his aesthetic, and so was less effective in a way that presents itself as abstract simply because the movement is not as fully referential as Mahler had intended it to be.[8]

In the process of composing his songs and thinking about them afterward, Mahler was pulled simultaneously in two directions. On the one hand, he responded with something like reverence to the mystical manner in which the work separated itself not only from him, but also from processes of composition. The passages quoted above can thus be read as a description of the emergence of the work's selfhood during the process of composition, so that by the later stages of composition the process becomes not really creation but rather a form of archaeology or restoration—or perhaps Mahler moves, figuratively, from adding colors to a canvas to chipping away carefully at a marble block to reveal a form that has already taken definitive shape beneath the surface. Yet, on the other hand, as a song took on a definite form and character —and partly because of the definiteness of both its form and its character— Mahler seems to have become acutely aware as well of what the song was *not*, in terms of its greater implications and potential, which could express themselves fully only beyond the confines of the song. The musical component of a song thus became a kind of Frankenstein's monster; while Mahler had given it a "self" that it might better set the specific words of a poem, it thereby developed a will of sorts independent of its creator's (albeit perceptible only to Mahler himself). In this sense, George Bernard Shaw's *Pygmalion* (1912), which may be seen as another version of the Frankenstein story, is also pertinent, for one of the markers of Eliza's selfhood is her resistance of and insubordination to her ostensible creator. Accordingly, Mahler's notion of the involvement of an "outside" force recognizes that his creations no longer answer to him alone. Unlike Mary Shelley's Dr. Frankenstein or Shaw's Henry Higgins, however, Mahler neither abandons his creations nor allows himself to be blindsided by their independence, but rather tries to make them happy, to help them realize their potential in other settings.[9]

In tracing some of Mahler's specific responses to his autonomous, yet unfulfilled creations, I have here progressed mostly in reverse chronological order, starting with the finale of his Fourth Symphony and working back to the First. Earlier I identified as my rationale for this order a wish to move "from least to most complex revisions of actual borrowed material." This was somewhat disingenuous, for something more basic led me to this order: my response to Mahler's own developing sensitivities to the selves of his songs, to the autonomy of their various musical presences. In his first symphonies, Mahler simply uses his songs as starting points, and initially with less concern for their integrity than he would develop by the time he began working with "Das himmlische Leben." With the latter song, Mahler strives hard to honor and preserve the integrity of the song's music, but finds the project extremely frustrating; he thereafter largely abandons the process of working with already formed musical selves, for in none of his later symphonies does he re-cycle his songs as such, even if he does occasionally allude to them. Thus, at the core of Mahler's reversion to absolute musical expression from his Fifth Symphony onward, one may see a response to the absoluteness of the music that prompted and directed his seemingly least absolute musical procedures. And indeed, as an explanation for the shift in Mahler's aesthetic after 1900, this formulation is more compelling than most of the standard ones,[10] which attach exaggerated significance to the absence of either programs or texts and must inevitably puzzle through (that is, explain away) Mahler's "Alma" theme and hammer blows in the Sixth Symphony, or stammer confusedly over aberrations such as the Eighth Symphony or *Das Lied von der Erde*.

In his First Symphony, Mahler borrows song material from his *Lieder eines fahrenden Gesellen* in a manner that clearly indicates that he is finding his way. At times, he seems blithely indifferent to meanings central to his earlier setting: in the first movement, the ironies of the model are largely abandoned even if he does eventually problematize the exaggerated ebullience of its material. And, if irony is indelibly a part of "Ging heut' Morgen" as a song, so too are the progressive steps taken toward the finality of death definitive for "Die zwei blauen Augen"; Mahler's consigning the final stage of the latter song to a subjective episode in the funeral march of the First Symphony in order to supersede it in the finale, then, seems hardly to take the full measure of the song's self even if, again, a deeper dimension of the song is revealed in the process. Perhaps even more troubling is the manner in which Mahler places these borrowings within the larger symphonic statement. Though each movement in the symphony refers to an outside song source (the funeral march doubly), this apparent consistency in approach presents a puzzlingly diverse totality, with the two *Gesellen* borrowings differing markedly from each other and even more so from the other sources. "Hans und Grethe" is scarcely a model for the scherzo in the same sense that any of the other songs considered here are for their respective movements, nor is it particularly easy to find a connection between song and movement except on a very generic level. The funeral march deliberately perverts the sense of the Catholic children's song "Bruder Martin" ("schläftst du schön?" at a funeral!);[11] not even its possible heritage as a taunt directed at Jewish children, relevant as it might be to the politics of the movement, carries over into its presentation, as the self-absorbed funeral march seems mostly oblivious to the klezmer music. And the allusion to Handel's "Hallelujah" Chorus is just that—an allusion—managed much as Brahms might have done, with an overt derivation from yet another allusive theme stemming from Beethoven's Fourth Symphony. Against this diverse pattern of exploitative re-cycling, the *Gesellen* borrowings must inevitably register as either similarly exploitative or aberrational. Even more insidious is the specific way Mahler makes the "Ging heut' Morgen" borrowing matter across the span of the symphony. Having derived the opening phrase of the song directly from the invitational cuckoo calls at the end of the introduction, Mahler later reduces that same phrase to a motivic shape in order to make it serve as part of the "organic" basis for the symphony, *à la* Beethoven. Thus, the phrase dutifully shows up to do its integrative bit in each subsequent movement, giving the scherzo its first splash of exuberance, inscribing the overall contour of the "Bruder Martin" timpani-stroke complex in the third movement, and forming the backbone of the "correction" to the breakthrough passage in the finale (see brackets in Example 33). While this process may be seen to elevate the tune in some sense, it does the reverse for the selfhood of the source song, reducing its music to an abstract collection of notes so as to serve as a marker for the organic wholeness of another work. Significantly, nowhere in the later appearances of the integrative motive do we hear "Ging heut' Morgen" as such.

With the scherzos of his Second and Third Symphonies, Mahler becomes progressively sophisticated and circumspect in the ways that he uses his *Wunderhorn* source songs. In each case, he sacrifices conventional principles of organic unity, even on the level of the movement, but preserves more fully the identity of his source, albeit in a deepened and more generalized mode. In each case, too, he casts his borrowed material in a supporting role even though he also allows it pride of place in launching the movement; thus, he gives up from the start the potential for using his songs to inject his own subjectivity directly into the symphonic movement. In fact, he gives this potential up *before* the start; he had, after all, composed many other songs with a strong sense of first-person subjectivity, but chose instead to work with material that was more objective to begin with. It seems at least plausible that his particular choices of songs and situations reflect some dissatisfaction with how his borrowings played out in the First Symphony, where he achieved some success at injecting his own (past) subjectivity into his re-cycled material only through violating the preexisting sense of the cycle's own subjectivity, despite both works having been essentially autobiographical in conception. Thus, with the First Symphony, the interference patterns between source and symphony argue against considering them too closely together; indeed, however enlightening the process may be, it does not bring the two works together in an aesthetically useful way, serving instead to delineate all too clearly the fact that fundamentally different musical personae are being represented with the same music. Quite the opposite holds true for the scherzos of his Second and Third Symphonies, where revisiting the song sheds crucial light on the symphonic movement and vice versa.

The difference might usefully be put another way. In Mahler's adaptations of *Wunderhorn* songs for the scherzos of his Second and Third Sym-

Example 33b. Mahler, Symphony No. 1, third movement, mm. 1–6

Example 33c. Mahler, Symphony No. 1, fourth movement, r33.3–r34.1 (10:00) and r53.3–5 (18:38)

phonies, the personae of the original songs are encountered as preexisting in the world, in this sense objectified before and throughout the process of adaptation so as to preserve their deeper selves. Thus, in the Third Symphony, both halves of Mahler's (eventually dropped) title for the movement are significant, for the movement is not merely about the "creatures of the forest," but also and first of all about "what [they] told me." Mahler is here not only separating "me" from the ostensible subject of the movement, but also identifying an act of listening, an act that implicitly respects and preserves the sense of identity embodied in the voices being listened to, even as it presumes, perhaps, to make more out of what is being said than might have been intended. And each of Mahler's scenarios for the scherzo of his Second Symphony describes a dysfunctional encounter between a subjective self and a monstrous other representing seemingly pointless activity. Here, too, Mahler objectifies and preserves the identity of the exterior presence, if through much different means, by first presenting it as unassailably and obliviously what it is and then rejecting it. With both borrowings from the *Gesellen* cycle in the First Symphony, on the other hand, Mahler positions the material both objectively and subjectively, with a disturbing double-image effect. In the funeral march, the *Gesellen* quotation is the third "identity" to be presented in the movement (or possibly even the fourth, if we count the dotted-figure counterpoint to "Bruder Martin" as a separate identity); inevitably, the fact that it is one among many helps objectify the "Die zwei blauen Augen" quotation, but this particular identity nevertheless distinguishes itself within the movement by its deeper sense of subjectivity. In the first movement, the situation is even more problematic, since, as the song material first emerges, it is doubly representative of spring and a youthful subjectivity responding to the cuckoo calls at the end of the introduction. In the song, text and context clarify this duality in terms of how the two differ: the governing subjectivity distorts the cheerfulness of nature, attempts vainly to align itself with that cheerfulness, and finally dissociates itself from it. In the song, much of the "accompaniment" may thus be taken to represent nature—at least as experienced by the persona of the song, with perhaps a tinge of mocking exaggeration—but the point of the song lies in the subjective response to nature, not in its depiction. In the symphony, where there are no clarifying words and a quite different context, the principal vocal melody is soon lost in counterpoint, and the opening subjectivity is similarly lost in straightforward depiction, merging with the more objective depiction of nature. Even if this awkward reversal of the very point of the source song is not native to the symphony as such and dissipates to the extent that we can forget what that music represents in the song, it is hard to forget as well that Mahler teaches us elsewhere specifically *not* to drop larger context in this way.

Along the way, while his Second Symphony still remained incomplete, Mahler became particularly enamored of one of his richer *Wunderhorn* settings, "Das himmlische Leben," discussed extensively in chapter 2. While it should not be necessary to revisit the complexities of this song at any length here, certain of its qualities are particularly relevant to the issues at hand. The presentation, as in "Fischpredigt" and "Ablösung," is essentially objective; nevertheless, behind this objectivity lies a great sense of personal stake in its narrative, whichever of the contextures described above applies. Thus, as a lullaby, the song projects adult concern and affection for the child, whereas, paired with "Das irdische Leben," it projects as well a more generalized concern for the vulnerability of children. The combination of objective presentation and personal stake already evident in these two earlier settings for the song makes it, even as a song, more symphonic by far than any of the others; accordingly, Mahler's response to it is also fundamentally different, for "Das himmlische Leben," from the beginning and throughout, remains a song, with effectively no changes made to its internal configuration. Nevertheless, its placement in a symphony, according to Mahler's treatment of the genre to that point, is intensely problematic. In both his first two symphonies, as noted, narration of past events gives way, in the finale, to an enactment of present drama involving a strongly stated personal subjectivity. If "Das himmlische Leben" is by its nature suitable only as a finale —for what could possibly follow and continue its narrative description of heavenly life?—it is also inherently, in Mahler's formulation, a narrative rather than "dramatic occurrence." In order to enable it to function as a symphonic finale, Mahler thus had to realign his symphonic sensibilities.

Mahler's first attempt at such a realignment, for what would become his Third Symphony, was to conceive a symphonic structure of individual narratives in which subjectivity is overtly cast not as a participant, but as a mute listener, with each movement after the first titled "What [. . .] Tells Me." Within this structure, subjectivity is ostensibly everywhere and embracive— a kind of meta-subjectivity—but registering in its details at all points as separate, nested subjectivities. Yet, this pattern breaks down after the scherzo, with the introduction of voices and especially with the more intense subjectivity of "O Mensch! Gib Acht!" At this point, the orientation shifts from *what* is being told to what the *experience* of being told is like, so that the choice between pain and joy in Nietzsche's text (or their projected alignment) is not only articulated but also felt. And this juncture represents, by its nature, a threshold that cannot be recrossed, as the parallels traced at the beginning of chapter 4 regarding the introduction of voices in the Second and Third Symphonies make clear. Despite the objectifying heteroglossia of "Es sungen drei Engel," the return of the alto solo from "O Mensch! Gib Acht!" provides a continuity of voice and of subjectivity that seems designed to convey the feeling of being forgiven. Similarly, in the sixth movement, the thrust of what "love" has to tell us seems to involve what it feels like to be loved as much as what it is to love. After these three movements, "Das himmlische Leben" presents an unsolvable contradiction, for the song articulates an unbridgeable chasm between childhood and adulthood, while, implicitly, the progressive orientations of the previous movements invite us to feel again what it means to be a child. Perhaps such a contradiction is permissible in music, whose business it has long been to project resolutions and reconciliations that we know to be impossible; thus, "Das himmlische Leben" may well have succeeded as the finale to the Third Symphony not in spite but precisely because of the richness of its situational impossibility. But "Das himmlische Leben," as a musical construct, would have been seriously compromised in the process, its basic orientation undercut to make it serve as a foil for the sake of exterior imperatives. And standing behind the potential violence that might have been done to the song's selfhood is, perhaps, a larger concern: the almost blasphemous transgression of attempting to recross the frontier of childhood, of attempting to merge its perspectives with those of adulthood.[12] One of the points of reclaiming and validating the childly perspective of "Das himmlische Leben" is to provide, within that more innocent space, an opportunity to fantasize freely about the nature of heaven, without fear of reproach. How critical this removal from adult perspectives is may be confirmed through the simple mental exercise of trying to derive an alternative view of heaven, suitable for inclusion in the Third Symphony, through a parallel indulgence in *adult* fantasy-fulfillment.

Mahler's eventual solution, for the Fourth Symphony, was to reconceive the symphonic structure yet again, this time in a deliberate reversion to what would be perceived as an archaic style and approach reminiscent of Haydn. Whether or not it was Mahler's intention to evoke Haydn specifically, the linkage is a fortunate one, for the prevailing perception of Haydn in the late nineteenth century and beyond as a musical naif, and his times as more innocent, reinforces both generally and specifically two aspects of the symphony's tone that effectively objectify its every subjectivity: its sense of nostalgia and its evocation of childhood.[13] For the Fourth Symphony, Mahler reverts in all outer respects—if in few inner ones, beyond the form of the first movement—to what is for him a reactionary version of the symphonic cycle of movements, and maintains more consistently than is typical for him a single perspective: that of an adult contemplating childhood. Since, in effect, the persona of "Das himmlische Leben" is thus extended to embrace the symphony as a whole, there is no conflict between symphony and song, no schismatic double-image effect between song and symphonic finale.

It must be stressed that the guiding principle for every decision Mahler made with regard to the fate of "Das himmlische Leben" involved the preservation of the song as such, not only with every note in place but also with its persona and orientation fully realized. Not even the imperatives of his greatest symphony (at least as measured by length) outweighed his allegiance to the song's self, that is, its autonomy and sense of presence. There is really no other way to make adequate sense of either his dropping the song from the Third Symphony or the manner of solution he eventually devised. For Mahler, "Das himmlische Leben" was absolute music.

At the same time, it should be clear that Mahler had also reached a breaking point with his project of allowing his songs to exert their will so forcefully on his symphonies. On some level, he must have shared what is surely the general view that symphonies simply matter more than songs, in terms not only of his own career and legacy, but also of their dramatic possibilities, cultural status, expressive power, and capacity to make a difference. If all that failed to make his songs any less compelling as absolute musical constructs, by the same token it rendered the relationship between song and symphony progressively problematic. Moreover, if part of Mahler's motivation had been to enhance subjectivity in his symphonies by drawing on his songs—and this seems to have been largely the case at least in his First Symphony—the realities worked out much differently: the songs problematized subjectivity more than they enhanced it. While the dividends of this problematic relationship were undoubtedly great, the price Mahler paid for his symphonic re-cyclings was steep and mounting exponentially. Already Mahler had had to compromise his most ambitious work and then virtually reverse the symphonic course he had charted for himself—all for the sake of a mere children's song.

Chapter 7

Epilogue:
Reclaiming Childhood
in the Fourth Symphony

Why Childhood?

The stylistic orientation of Mahler's Fourth Symphony is both unusual and puzzling. Even identifying that orientation has been problematic, partly because we have found it necessary in the twentieth century to either censure or defend extreme accessibility of style within the high-art tradition. Thus, some have identified the "Haydnesque" Fourth Symphony as "neoclassic," referencing a later aesthetic movement that Mahler would seem, however inconveniently, to have had as little to do with as Bach and Mozart had to do with serialism.[1] More insightfully, some have found its defining characteristic to be its projection of an idealized childhood. Adorno, for example, observes that the Fourth's "image-world is that of childhood," and that the entire symphony—Mahler's "fairy-tale symphony"—"shuffles nonexistent children's songs together." More recently, Mark Evan Bonds, who opens and closes his discussion of the finale with telling references to *The Polar Express* (a 1985 children's book in which sleigh bells play a prominent role), underscores the "childlike perspective" of the symphony and identifies its central issues as "childhood, innocence, [and] faith."[2] While this identification is well grounded in Mahler's own comments about the work, it does not dissolve our puzzlement regarding the symphony's orientation so much as give that puzzlement an additional focus. The very features of the symphony that argue against its being labeled neoclassic—at least in the sense in which this designation applies to many works of the next generation, which tend to emphasize more purely musical concerns over expressive content—also call into question the notion that the principal point of the symphony is its projection of images from an idealized childhood. Specifically, there would seem to be little room in such a sentimentalized world for the symphony's many contrasting and often contradictory elements. These therefore appear oddly dissonant, perhaps serving as a somewhat improbable example of Mahler's eclectic mixing of perspectives in his symphonies.

One possible way out of this interpretive quandary—besides playing the "eclectic" wild card—would be to claim that the symphony invokes its childhood images only as a starting point, and that the musical structures of the symphony remain largely dissociated from this content, according to the (often misunderstood!) model of the "characteristic" symphony of a century earlier. Such an approach would emphasize the extraordinary degree of musical integration in the symphony, an emphasis grounded as surely in Mahler's own testimony as is the claim that the symphony's material images childhood.[3] Indeed, Mahler's comments about the symphony bear witness to an extraordinary—and quite prideful—concern for its musical organization, almost as if the symphony's musical sophistication redeemed it from its childish content; accordingly, one might argue that Mahler plays the presumed opposites of childishness and sophistication off against each other, the former serving as a foil for the latter. But this view cannot satisfy, despite how widespread its general features are in the general reception of the symphony, for it construes Mahler as placing the childhood images of the symphony within quotation marks, with an implicit irony that seems foreign both to Mahler's attitudes about childhood and to the force and role of child-based images in the symphony.[4] Moreover, this view reduces the aesthetic function of those images to one of relative simplicity, if not triviality, which seems a singularly inadequate accounting of them.

Nor is this trivialization of the child-oriented content of the symphony negated once we acknowledge the powerful element of nostalgia triggered by its evocations of childhood. Nostalgia might help to explain the substantial and often antagonistic tension in the symphony between childly images and musical sophistication, with the latter perhaps representing an adult perspective that demarcates the object of nostalgic contemplation as unattainably separate. Ultimately, though, this approach is also unsatisfactory, since the symphony does not set childhood apart as an idealized, remembered past; quite the contrary, it instead removes childhood altogether from the possibility of pure idealization. Darker elements are subtly present from the outset of the symphony and pervasive thereafter, constantly inflecting and undermining the idealized content of the childly images; surely, to locate the dominant voice of the symphony in nostalgia is to deny the importance within Mahler's vision of the bleak underside to childhood innocence and vulnerability. Moreover, the nostalgic view of Mahler's Fourth conforms more with current Western attitudes toward childhood than with those of Mahler's generation; for them, the death of children was a more pressing practical concern than it is today, and was treated much differently in art and literature.

Before considering here the contours of the dark vision of childhood's innocence and vulnerability that Mahler presents to us in the Fourth Symphony, we may thus reasonably probe further the rationale for its sophisticated engagement with childly images. Specifically, we may ask: why childhood? why so sophisticated? and, above all, why so dark? We can find answers to all of these questions by locating the symphony both within Mahler's career and within culture more generally, and by extending and elaborating further some of the discussions undertaken in the previous chapters.

Mahler divided his First Symphony into two roughly equal parts of two movements each, beginning with "Aus den Tagen der Jugend"("from the days of youth") and tracing, in general, a progression from relative youthfulness to mature adulthood. Similarly, part 2 of his Third Symphony (the second through the sixth movements) traces an even more elaborate path from relative innocence to elevated sensibilities and higher sophistication. It may seem odd, then, that his Fourth reverts so resolutely to a childly orientation. But throughout Mahler's first three symphonies we can see the seductive appeal of just such a reversion, from the deep nostalgia of the quotation from "Die zwei blauen Augen" in the funeral-march movement of the First Symphony (see chapter 5), to the failed attempt to recapture the past that plays out in the second and third movements of the Second (chapter 3), to the successful "rescue" from Nietzschean gloom in the Third effected by the childlike heteroglossia of "Es sungen drei Engel" (chapter 2). Moreover, as early as one movement beyond his First Symphony—that is, before his Second Symphony had progressed beyond its opening "Todtenfeier" movement—Mahler imagined a symphonic finale that would complete a multisymphonic cycle by reclaiming the childly innocence that the First Symphony bypassed altogether with its "Tagen der Jugend." That Mahler rejected "Das himmlische Leben" as a potential finale to his Second Symphony without relinquishing his desire to install it as the final movement of a multisymphonic cycle may be seen as the single most important factor in his early career as a symphonist, at least from 1892 on. And that Mahler's imagined symphonic pair had first to become a trilogy and even a tetralogy before he could successfully conclude this somewhat bizarre quest speaks not only to the persuasive power that this reversion held for Mahler, but also to the level of sophistication to which he aspires in the work, and to its frequently dark tone.

Two other contexts for understanding Mahler's evocation of childhood in his Fourth Symphony, especially when considered together, shed even more light on the associated imperatives toward darkness and sophistication. The Fourth was the first major work to follow his return to Vienna. It thus appeared at a critical juncture in his life, when both his need and his ability to see his life as an ordered whole would have been significantly heightened. These circumstances are reflected especially vividly in his personal life: nearly coincident with his composition of the Fourth Symphony, his last ties with his former life were broken and the basis for a quite different one established.[5] His familial duties, which had been quite taxing since the death of his parents, were finally discharged in full, a process that had taken a decade to unfold, beginning unhappily with the deaths of his father, sister Leopoldine, and mother—all in 1889—and continuing even more darkly with the suicide of his youngest brother, Otto, in 1895, but concluding well with the marriages of his surviving sisters, Emma and Justine, to his respected colleagues, the brothers Eduard and Arnold Rosé, in 1898 and 1902, respectively. Decisive as well were the mental degeneration and death of his former schoolmate Hugo Wolf after a decade that had seen the deaths of Mahler's principal supporters from the previous generation, von Bülow, Bruckner, and Brahms. Perhaps most significant of all were the termination of his curious relationship with the ever-faithful Natalie Bauer-Lechner and the beginnings of his attachment to Alma Schindler, whom he was shortly to marry and start a family with (although not precisely in that order). If, while his personal house thus resolved into a semblance of harmonic accord, Mahler also sought to close the circle of his spiraling career as a symphonist so as to bring his compositional career into a rounded wholeness that could match the satisfying tidiness wrought by his triumphant return to Vienna, then the Fourth surely filled the bill, completing a series of compositional quests that almost precisely spanned the previous decade of deaths, discharged familial obligations, and professional exile from Vienna. In particular, the Fourth's resolute return to childhood, enacted at the height of Mahler's career, provided the same kind of gestural close as his return to Vienna, superimposing a moment of adult ascendancy onto a revisited past and, moreover, hooking back within an implicit chronology to embrace the "youth" with which his First Symphony begins. In an important sense, Mahler's Fourth thus asserts the organic wholeness of Mahler's own life and career by charting—and apparently reclaiming—a childhood that holds within its purview the whole of humanly existence, from childhood's vulnerability and uncertainty to the smug (if skewed) certainties of "Das himmlische Leben"—the latter representation brought into being and sustained only through the precarious marriage of a childly perspective to adult sophistication.

Notably, however, it is a *Christian* childhood that Mahler projects in the Fourth Symphony, a childhood especially privileged and especially fragile, yet rendered eternally secure through faith and heavenly grace. It is thus *not* Mahler's own childhood that he reclaims in the Fourth Symphony, but rather a projected childhood, one that superimposes Christian redemption on the earthly vulnerabilities of childhood that he knew all too well. If we may thus find a personal basis for the darkness of Mahler's projection, we may also find still deeper roots: arguably, what was at stake in his evocation of a childhood whose orientation was so far removed from his own was more than the coherence of his life, career, and work, for the Fourth addresses even more cogently the coherence of his fragmented cultural heritage.

Prominent among the many personified images within Germanic culture that posed specific mortal threats against childhood, which range from the Erlkönig of Goethe and Schubert to Freund Hein, who makes an appearance in the second movement of Mahler's Fourth, is that of the Talmudic Jew who, according to the infamous blood libel that persisted through centuries of European history, must seek out and kill Christian children in order to use their blood in the preparation of matzoh, the traditional unleavened bread of Passover. But, while the Erlkönig and Freund Hein were understood to be beyond human control, the Jew was eminently available for redress. Indeed, well-publicized trials of Jews accused of ritualistic murder of Christian children in the Austro-Hungarian Empire marked each of Mahler's nineteenth-century Viennese tenures. In a blood-libel case of 1882, a panel of three judges at Nyíregyháza in Hungary found in favor of the accused, concluding that "the charge of murder against Salamon Schwarcz and his companions [was] not proved"; ominously, the decision did little to counteract entrenched popular sentiment or even to deny institutionalized belief in the blood libel itself.[6] Even more damaging, against a background of frequent pogroms in the eastern reaches of the empire throughout the 1890s, the Bohemian Jew Leopold Hilsner was convicted in 1898 of the ritualistic murder of a nineteen-year-old Christian girl despite his manifest innocence and strenuous legal efforts on his behalf; in the wake of the initial verdict (which was confirmed a year later, although the sentence was commuted by Emperor Franz Joseph), there were widespread anti-Semitic riots throughout the east, and Mahler himself was hissed at the podium and subjected to repeated attacks in the press.[7] In the specific context of a series of shocking child-abuse cases that publicized near the turn of the century in Vienna, Larry Wolff suggests that the scandal-mongering reportage in the *Neue Freie Presse* may have been a ploy to deflect attention from the Hilsner case, implicitly locating more likely perpetrators of infanticide within the home.[8] One might perhaps find in Mahler's Fourth Symphony a similar attempt to deflect, focusing attention not on the actual, supposed, and in any case myriad perpetrators of abuse, but instead on the supreme vulnerability of the victims. The coincidence of Hilsner's trial and conviction with Mahler's return to a Vienna of newly intensified anti-Semitism gave a telling focus to the tenuousness of Mahler's cultural position as an especially visible converted Jew in Vienna, especially since Hilsner was a fellow Czech Jew whose background was on several accounts similar to Mahler's. Through the persistence of the blood libel, the fragile purity of the child—specifically the Christian child, who had been rendered even purer through the sacrament of baptism—became the focal point for one of the most virulent forms of anti-Semitism.

In converting to Catholicism, Mahler implicitly accepted the difficult burden of both denying his Jewish heritage and establishing his full alliance with Christianity. The distasteful aspects of the first half of this dual burden were unlikely ever to be successful, for in the perception of Germanic Christendom, or at least of its laity, being born Jewish was a stigma that could not be effaced through conversion; Mahler, like many another, would be caught forever between the two worlds, rejecting one and never fully accepted into the other. As for the second half, Mahler had long since begun a process of articulating, in his symphonies, his acceptance of Christianity, albeit a continually evolving version of Christianity that differed markedly from the Catholicism he embraced officially. The Christian themes of the Fourth Symphony directly reflect the implicitly acknowledged strangeness of his evolving faith, adroitly addressing and to some extent deflecting each of the components of his conversion that could be seen as problematic. Adopting a childly perspective allowed skewed versions of Christian tenets to pass by without challenge, exonerated by their very naiveté; moreover, this particular move served to underscore the principle, most famously articulated by St. Paul with specific analogy to the naiveté of children, that no living human can really know heaven. In making the childly perspective of the symphony supremely vulnerable, Mahler may have risked association with a figure many perceived to be the most noxious threat to Christian children—

the Talmudic Jew—but he also thereby encouraged an identification of his own perspective with that of the child, through a kind of aesthetic baptism. In adopting the symphonic persona of a specifically Christian child, Mahler might thus be seen as cleansed of his inherited Judaism, almost as if he had retroactively submitted to the nefarious Christian practice, long since forbidden, of kidnapping Jewish children for the purpose of baptizing them. Even more subtle is Mahler's evocation in the second movement of Freund Hein, a mythical figure who ought to be seen, in the context of this symphony and fin-de-siècle Vienna, as a substitute for the Jew accused of ritualistic murder; moreover, this substitution manages as well to cast the supreme threat to childhood more benignly than ever before, since Freund Hein fiddles his victims "up to heaven." Within this implicit denial of his own association with Judaism, then, Mahler also manages to present a softer version of the Jew (if never acknowledged as such), one who does no actual violence to his victims and who acts within a Christian hierarchy—serving, indeed, as a conduit to heaven.

Yet, oddly, Mahler's sleight of hand in reconfiguring the "us" of the Fourth Symphony—that is, himself and his audience—as the Christian child seems to be put at extreme risk during the lines dealing with Herod (see chapter 2), which include the text, "*We* lead a meek, innocent, little lamb to its death!" (emphasis added). From the perspective of a Christian child, or within a lullaby directed to such a child, these words betoken innocent fun. But if for only a moment one hears them as coming more directly from Mahler, untransmuted into a Christian child, they could have only one of two connotations, in eerily perfect alignment with the two principal charges that were then being leveled against Jews. If the lamb can reasonably be taken to represent, in this context, only Christ or the child, then Mahler is implicitly evoking not only the blood libel, but also the accusation that Jews were collectively responsible for Christ's death.

In the following reading, my primary concern will be the first two movements of the symphony, which set the terms for the whole. The finale has in any case been much discussed (see especially chapter 2), and it is specifically the task of the opening movements to establish, through sophisticated musical means, a version of childhood both sufficiently innocent and sufficiently beclouded that the manifest destiny Mahler sensed in "Das himmlische Leben" nearly a decade earlier—and at the same stroke his manifest right to his own destiny, so recently achieved—might be realized.

Sleigh Bells

Mahler's Fourth Symphony begins with an intrusion:

Example 34. Mahler, Symphony No. 4, first movement, mm. 1–21

In a technical sense, the opening three bars merely do what one might expect any symphonic opening to do. Functioning in part as thematic exposition, they present one of the central ideas of the symphony in high profile: staccato eighth notes in the winds playing repeated open fifths, inflected with an upper semitone grace note implying the minor mode, augmented by sleigh bells. Moreover, these opening bars serve a conventional function conventionally modified, by providing an introduction for a theme (beginning in m. 3) that cannot convincingly begin a symphony on its own,[9] shaded, à la Beethoven, so as to be harmonically inconclusive regarding both mode and tonic. But the effect here, despite resonances with traditional symphonic discourse, is emphatically one of intrusion on a number of levels.

First and foremost, there is the sound of the opening: sleigh bells deployed so as to make their timbrel foreignness the center of the sound, with the other instruments (initially just the flutes) providing stark support for a motivic figure based on simple staccato reiteration, clearly meant to evoke the sound of functioning sleigh bells. Even the indistinct harmonic environment and the absence of string tone in this opening derive from the sleigh bells and their associations, projecting the coldly resonant emptiness of an open fifth oddly touched by naiveté. This naturalistic deployment of sleigh bells corresponds closely to Mahler's later use of cowbells in his symphonies: with each, both referential meanings and the strangeness of the sound itself

in a symphonic context come into play. In the Fourth Symphony, however, unlike in Mahler's later practice, the intrusion of the nonsymphonic instruments into the symphony is immediate and definitional, presenting us with an initial double image paradoxically combining the roles of intruder and background. And, too, the sleigh bells have an estranging referential effect, for they belong both to a wintry outside and to memory. These two frames of reference combine to produce a tone of nostalgia with a disturbing, potentially chilling undertone.[10]

The dramatic shape of the symphony will revolve around the conflicting tones of remembered childhood as evoked in this opening, involving both the innocence and the mortal vulnerability of youth, rendered indistinct by temporal distance (nostalgic naiveté) and a dreamlike sense of unreality that does not exclude nightmare. Ultimately, the finale of the symphony, "Das himmlische Leben," will blend the nightmarish with a childish vision of Heaven, through which a sometimes malicious play with religious symbols and a bizarre preoccupation with food continue to disturb even as we submit in the end to the warm embrace of E major. We are comforted by this

ending only to the extent that we hear it as ritualistic, as simple lullaby, and forget that in some scenarios of child seduction (such as in "Erlkönig"), it is explicitly death and not sleep to which the child is lulled. And it is not hard to see through the preoccupation with food, even without knowing Mahler had earlier planned to pair this song with "Das irdische Leben," which begins with the pleas of a starving child and ends with its death (see chapter 2). Such preoccupations seem considerably less strange when we project the harsher reality from which this imagined place of ostentatious bounty implicitly offers an escape, a projection that is encouraged by the portentous declamations that punctuate the song, in each case leading to urgent, driving recollections of the sleigh bells from the first movement.[11]

To be sure, irony is not the only viable interpretation here. The major-mode ending leaves open the question of whether these intrusions represent nightmares recalled from the vantage point of an achieved utopia or reality threatening to disturb a blessed dream state. Nevertheless, an ironic reading, in which the child dies of starvation while dreaming of plenty—as in Hans Christian Andersen's "Little Match Girl" (1872)—seems fully justified by

the balance of the symphony.[12] Indeed, we may usefully compare the end of Mahler's Fourth to that of "Erlkönig," in which the mythic intruder seduces the child; Mahler's finale, if taken ironically, is considerably more disturbing, both for being grounded more obviously in the reality of hungry children and for its presentation of escape as the foreground, the abiding and transfiguring setting in which painful reality becomes the resisted intruder.[13]

The finale is thus richly ambivalent. Its alarming recollection of the sleigh bells from the first movement is inflected, no less than its vision of heaven, with a distorting sense of unreality, so that we may choose to regard either side of the opposition—or both—as dream-based, providing a visionary heaven on the one hand, a depiction of nightmare on the other. We may also choose to regard either side—or both—as essentially real, with distortions on either side stemming from either wakeful delirium or an attempt to represent a child's perspective, so that we are shown only what a child might

take in of heaven, or are made to experience the nightmarish distortions that can inform a child's seemingly direct perceptions.

This interpretive richness should lead us to reconsider once again the circumstances that surrounded Mahler's decision to remove "Das himmlische Leben" from its planned position as the finale of his Third Symphony. Discussions of this removal have tended either toward puzzlement, since so much in the Third Symphony anticipates the thematic material of the song, or near indifference, as if one need not wonder that Mahler would cut a movement from what would remain his longest symphony even after this pruning.[14] Taking into account both his subsequent urgency to proceed with a Fourth Symphony that would ground the ironies of his orchestral *Lied* in an opening ambivalence and the fact that "Das himmlische Leben" would have served the Third Symphony primarily through the innocence of its tone (hence Mahler's subtitle, "What the Child Told Me")—and thus by implicitly denying its ironies and ambivalences—it seems likely that Mah-

ler's concern lay more with the song than with the Third Symphony. Arguably, not only has the presumed greater importance of Mahler's longest symphony blinded us to his prevailing concern for the individual imperatives of "Das himmlische Leben," but, in addition, the association of the latter with the Third Symphony has made its projection of childhood innocence seem to matter more than the darker meanings this projection but thinly cloaks.[15]

The First Movement

The dreamlike sense of unreality that pervades the opening movement is maintained by coupling the structures of normality—symphonic discourse based on "organic" motivic work within a clearly articulated sonata form (or, more precisely, sonata-rondo form)—with a fragmented presentation of "naive" material, in which individual gestures and phrases sharply contrast with their neighbors in tone and instrumentation even as they clearly re-cycle a relative handful of basic motives. Within this procedure, naiveté functions both as an agent of sophisticated organicism—defining the basic tone and style of the movement and helping to keep motivic relationships transparent—and as justification for an outwardly unsophisticated cobbling of material, creating a discursive context in which the hierarchy of intruder and intruded-upon seems constantly in jeopardy of being overturned.

Mahler's approach thus offers a fundamental departure from the Beethovenian models it seems to imitate. Beethoven characteristically uses harmonically ambiguous introductory gestures to create an overriding need for clarity, a need sufficiently powerful that we readily accept an extremely harsh opening condition as long as it provides the clarity we need. Most famously in his Fifth and Ninth Symphonies,[16] Beethoven provides this kind of clarity by extending the opening discourse, basing his clarification on further elaborations of his opening materials. In Mahler's Fourth, however, as the first instance of a pervasively fragmented discourse, clarification comes through the introduction of new material that precisely inverts Beethoven's method, creating a singular sense of disturbance through its extreme warmth (major mode, strings, and conventional accompanimental texture) rather than by projecting a harsh reality and a Kantian imperative to engage in heroic struggle against it.

Taken on its own, the violin phrase beginning in m. 3 betokens normality, if nostalgically rendered, based within a pure string texture securely grounded in conventional harmonic and textural practice. Yet it also denies and displaces the most significant tokens of symphonic normalcy that support the introductory sleigh bells, which have been carefully built into the first three bars of the symphony. Thus, notwithstanding the intruding aspects of this opening, it establishes a clearly articulated pulse and delineates a conventional organic process of growth, with accelerating metrical subdivisions (again à la Beethoven)[17] progressing from a full bar of identical eighth-note divisions, to half-bar divisions in m. 2, to quarter-note divisions in the first half of m. 3, arriving full circle with the eighth-note divisions in the second half of m 3, all the while seeming to move toward a clarifying arrival in either B minor (with possible Phrygian inflections) or "natural" E minor. These processes, through which the intruding sleigh bells lay claim to symphonic normalcy, are self-contained and internally coherent; they are also specifically and systematically contradicted, beginning in m. 3, by the theme they ostensibly introduce.

First, the opening anacrusis figure of the violin melody imposes a *ritar-dando* on the clear pulse of the opening, with the continuation establish-ing a more relaxed tempo (*Rechtgemächlich*) as the *Haupttempo* of the move-ment.[18] Next, the organic shaping of the opening (through motivic accu-mulation and metrical acceleration) is replaced by a loosely structured series of fairly independent one-bar melodic units, related to each other mainly through their parallel use of extended anacruses for the downbeats in mm. 4, 5, and 6 (with the first two of these further emphasized through elaborate appoggiatura gestures), shaped rather casually through the extension of this structure across m. 6 to strengthen the arrival in m. 7.[19] This more segmen-ted melodic discourse is supported by a hierarchical accompaniment (simple bass with characteristic arpeggiation in the inner voices), in sharp contrast to the opening accumulation of independent strands; moreover, the har-monic structure replaces the vague stasis of the opening with an utterly con-ventional progression verging on the tautological (I – IV [ii$_6$]–V [I$^6_4$– V$_7$]–I), in a conventionally regular harmonic rhythm.

The most extreme contradiction, however, is the sudden turn to G major, the tonic of the violin melody (and of the movement as a whole), which emerges as if by magic through a sleight-of-hand rearrangement of the opening elements. Thus, at the critical moment of articulation, when new tempo, new homophonic texture, new instrumentation, and the first unam-biguous full harmony are asserted, the hierarchy of the opening neighbor-note figure is inverted, with the grace-note G assuming central melodic importance, suddenly elevated in status from mere melodic inflection to un-equivocal tonic. Significantly, the immediate descent to B after this arrival both confirms a connection to the opening and underscores a vital differ-ence: the defining motivic interval has warmed from open fifth to minor sixth, with the sentimental dip to the pivotal note B providing a focus for this new warmth by underscoring the changed role of B, transformed from the base of an open fifth to the comforting third of a major triad.

Mahler's harmonic legerdemain carries the additional effect that G major, the principal tonic, is first presented as an escape, a ♭VI digression against the background of the opening suggestion of B minor. This effect not only casts the uncomplicated innocence of the opening sleigh bells in further doubt, but also imparts a sense of otherworldliness to the defining key of the first movement, and hence to its main theme and tempo. Moreover, be-yond the first movement, the contingent status of G major in its first ap-pearance helps prepare the more extreme gesture of escape offered in the finale, to E major, which again uses sleigh bells to define the immediate "reality" that is being escaped from. Beyond the symphony, Mahler's device stands midway between an earlier practice, in which the ♭VI often seemed to provide a haven of sorts through its quality of harmonic difference and the typically deceptive mode of its arrival (hence, the exaggerated sleight of hand in Mahler's application),[20] and Mahler's own developing sense of discomfort in resolving straightforwardly to the tonic. The latter discomfort, shared by others in his generation, finds its most elaborate expression in the finale of his Ninth Symphony, in which deceptive resolutions to ♭VI are so completely normalized that traditional resolutions to the tonic are rendered strangely exotic.[21] Mahler's extension of the earlier practice at the beginning of the Fourth Symphony is centrally important to its tone, for his opening places the referential tonic for most of the symphony within large-scale parentheses, marking the symphony (or at least the first movement) as an escape on a large scale without first clearly defining what it is an escape from. And the resonance with his more elaborate procedures in the Ninth Symphony is also significant: in both cases, the escape provided through deceptive resolution supports a sense of overwhelming nostalgia.[22]

While the sense of nostalgia accompanying the shift to G major does help to clarify what is being escaped from—the present and, perhaps, adulthood—nostalgia cannot be the crux of the matter, since a sense of nostalgia is one of the things that links the string theme to, rather than separates it from, the opening passage for sleigh bells. If the sense of nostalgia is nevertheless intensified with the shift, this differentiation in intensity (but not the affect itself) is due to an essential difference between the two passages, which might best be understood in terms of connotative motion. The music for sleigh bells is referentially mobile, reproducing, if abstractly, the sound of a sleigh *in motion*, and layering onto this sound the kind of oscillating motivic work frequently used to suggest regulated movement. Harmonically, too, the opening is dynamic in its implications, if relatively static in a more literal sense: it leads us to anticipate arrival. The passage for strings, in contrast, is at rest, complacent, even indolent in its relaxed unfolding of generic stability; locally, it represents an escape from motion and the anxieties pertaining thereto.

The contrast between the first two passages establishes the first as the central destabilizing presence for the movement—an intruder that facilitates further intrusion—and the second, along with its key, tempo, and theme, as the central stabilizing presence. This polarity depends on a critical difference between the violin theme and the sleigh-bells music. Although the former displaces the latter, its appearance provides relief, warmth, and a sense of normalcy, and imposes no obvious intrusive threat. To the extent that the violin theme represents stability, it is more intruded upon than intruder, and thus feels, paradoxically, remarkably like a return even in its first appearance. This effect is reinforced by its nostalgic allusion to Schubert, its introductory *ritardando*, and the tendency, in most performances, for the sleigh bells not to slow sufficiently to accommodate that *ritardando*. In this way, the violin theme reinscribes the sleigh bells as intruder, despite their priority, and even if the shock value of the opening has been substantially muted by familiarity.

Within a general pattern of negotiation between the opening and the violin theme, both in terms of larger sections of the form and interactive passages in which they confront each other more freely, motivic tokens from the sleigh bells passage generate a sense of motion, while the violin theme attempts, figuratively, to apply the brakes. Interactions of this sort are already subtly present within the G major theme and are used to shape the remainder of the first group. Thus, the dotted rhythms in m. 6, which provide the only sustained propulsive energy in the violin theme as they push beyond the downbeat, borrow their energy from the grace notes of the opening. The connection to the opening is made more explicit immediately following the close in m. 7, as repeated staccato eighth notes in the winds (now without grace notes or sleigh bells, and sounding full triads) accompany the dotted figure, which registers as a questioning intruder despite its immediate derivation from the violin theme itself. Following closely on the heels of this intruder is yet another intruder, as the horn usurps the continuation with its own characteristic motive (m. 10; 0:31), again derived from the repeated eighth notes of the opening, with a triplet inflection adapted from the original grace notes.

Each of these entries appears as an intrusion in part because its principal instrumental sound is being heard for the first time (*arco* cellos and basses, then horns). Significantly, then, when the violins return to answer the rising dotted-rhythm figure in simultaneous inversion (m. 12), they immediately assume the role of restraining the propulsive effect of the intruding figures. The exchanges that follow (mm. 13–17) clearly align the forces of mobility and stasis against each other, with the horn figure (now given to oboes and clarinets with horn support) twice interrupting the anacrusis that follows each appoggiatura in the violins. With the second interruption, the rising dotted-note figure in the lower strings supports the horn figure, and the combination of the two builds as if to prepare a climactic arrival. But the arrival is not organically achieved; rather, the violins' melody returns as yet another interruption at the peak of this build-up (at the end of m. 17; 0:53), its sense of stability enriched through a new imitative counterpoint in the cello.

In an important sense, the first group (Example 34 above) fulfills the principal function of exposition in sonata form, establishing the main sources of harmonic and thematic tension for the movement and reaching a temporary stability. The remainder of the sonata-form exposition, conventional at least to the extent of offering a lyrical second group in the dominant, does, however, provide a few significant surprises. After the bridge elaborates a more extreme version of the digressive exchanges of mm. 7–17 (in mm. 21–32; 1:02), we are given this time a more "organic" climax, an extreme, carnivalesque outburst (mm. 32f; 1:32) instead of the previous retreat to an earlier representation of stability. Even here, however, there is an overriding effect of intrusion, partly because the instruments involved in the last stages of the build-up (first violins, bass, flutes, and oboes) break off without "arriving," displaced for two measures by raucous clarinets playing stark octaves in a high register, after which they begin to reassert themselves (mm. 34f). But the sense of intrusion is more basic, as the tone—established through tempo, key, register, and affect—represents an extreme departure, even for this movement, in which extreme departures are the rule rather than the exception. All that links this passage to the foregoing is its aggressive childishness, which is enthusiastically maintained even after the clarinets drop out. Yet, the outburst has a conventional function within the tradition Mahler is nostalgically invoking, filling in for the celebratory cadential passages that so often close off the first group in a Mozartian sonata form. In fact, it reproduces precisely the late-eighteenth-century structure Robert Winter identifies as a "bifocal close," ending with a strong half-cadence in the original tonic before proceeding, after a pause, in the new key.[23]

Also seemingly conventional in function is the closing group (mm. 58f; 2:58), in which a more relaxed form of the opening material provides a sense of closure while simultaneously preparing for a return to the opening. Yet Mahler's closing group is curiously ambivalent about both closure and the feasibility of return, as he creates the impression of trying unsuccessfully to regenerate a sense of motion after the languorous second group. Twice, rather static transformations of the opening figures are jerked into accelerated motion, first in a *forte* 2/4 bar (m. 62), and then in an expansion of this bar combined with the earlier dotted-note motive (m. 66). Although these attempts fail, so that the exposition closes with the musical equivalent of a slow fade, their very lack of fulfillment leaves us with a sense of expectancy that is well answered by the return of the sleigh bells for the first time since the opening. And yet, the meaning of this return is muddled from the outset, appearing (appropriately enough for this movement) as an intruder before the fade is complete and proceeding as a varied repeat of the opening —close enough to the original to be taken for a genuine return, yet subtly progressive in its narrative implications.

What follows this return corresponds closely to a traditional manipulation of sonata form often referred to as sonata-rondo, in which a return to the opening theme in the tonic leads to a development section and thence to a recapitulation in which the main theme may be withheld until the end or otherwise curtailed. Haydn and especially Mozart used this form frequently in finales, but not until Brahms's Fourth Symphony (1885) is a version of it used for the first movement of a major work. This distinction is crucial, since its use in a finale, in which, typically, a tunelike first theme will emphasize the rondo element of the mixed form, can differ substantially from its use in a first movement, where the return to the opening will inevitably play on our expectation of a repeat of the exposition.[24] Here, despite the evident importance to Mahler of outwardly following convention, there are critical differences between his procedures and more traditional practice. First, as stated, the recollection of the opening quickly veers away from strict repetition, following broadly the structure and strategies of the first group but with significant departures. Second, Mahler introduces several episodes in his development that will have long-range significance for the work as a whole.[25] And, finally, disquieting events in the recapitulation and coda maintain the principle of intrusion through what is traditionally the most stable section of sonata form.

The return to sleigh bells (m. 72; 3:40) expands the opening three bars to four and a half, with a varied treatment of both instrumentation and motivic unfolding; in particular, the expansion brings G major into play earlier, coincident with a new treatment of the repeated eighth notes. Intriguingly, the latter serves to tighten the relationship between Mahler's sleigh-bells motive and the chorus of the familiar carol "Jingle Bells" by adding the third of the chord, deriving a three-note "Jin-gle-Bells" pattern at the beginning of each half bar and emphasizing, like the carol, the three notes of the tonic triad (see Example 35).[26] More important, though, the return functions as neither a rondolike return nor a false repetition of the exposition; instead, we are given, as part of an ongoing narrative, a new negotiation between the two opening ideas, which begins with a more benign form of the sleigh-bells music and continues with a more graceful interweaving of the two as the G major theme enters.

Because of the more accommodating interaction between the previously

Example 35b. Mahler, Symphony No. 4, first movement, mm. 72–76 (3:40)

antagonistic themes, we are easily led to a reconciliation of sorts between them, a reconciliation that relies heavily on an incidental figure introduced as part of the enhanced counterpoint for the G major theme in its second appearance (m. 20 [1:00]; see Example 34). At the time of its introduction, this figure is the first and only contribution of wind sound to the four-bar G major theme, and represents a conciliatory derivation from the opening

Example 35c. "Jingle Bells" (original form of chorus, opening phrase)

dotted rhythms and $\hat{6}$–$\hat{5}$ melodic motion. In the more relaxed atmosphere that follows the exposition, not only are other significant motives from the sleigh-bells theme offered as counterpoint to the violins' theme (in the cellos), but the winds are also allowed significant imitative play with the theme itself (mm. 77f; 3:54). After a considerably less contentious rehearsal of the negotiation that originally followed the four-bar theme (mm. 80f), an extended treatment of the new figure (mm 91f; 4:31), rather than the four-bar violin theme, serves to close this section with a sense of peaceful concord.

Closure at this point (m. 101; 5:13) is more complete than at any point so far in the movement. In a typical movement in this form, however, it is precisely at this point, near the end of the first return to the first thematic group, that stability is most severely undermined, in order to launch and justify a developmental episode. It is important to note how and why this departure from convention occurs.

The how is relatively simple: what we are given between mm. 72 and 101 is the equivalent of a recapitulation of the first group, which in its original form set up the principal thematic conflict of the movement. Functioning as recapitulation, this section presents the original material in much the same structural order, yet considerably stabilized, with formerly antagonistic forces seemingly reconciled. By m. 101, something of import has indeed been accomplished, and it is this dramatic circumstance that makes an elaborate closing gesture seem appropriate.

Why Mahler manipulates his form in this way, on the other hand, involves two interlocking rationales. Working on a remote level, he has derived for this section a motivic shape to convey a satisfying sense of closure, a shape that closely approximates the main theme of the finale in terms of both its contour and its comforting affect: the defining figure in each case begins with a broken arpeggiation of the octave between lower and upper dominants and ends with a characteristic $\hat{6}$–$\hat{5}$ motion to mark a leap to the top of this span (Example 36; note also the varied form of the three-note anacrusis in the violins that emerges in this section, which also anticipates the main theme of the finale). In both movements, the figure is given first to the clarinet; in the finale it serves as a harbinger of the human voice, which enters shortly thereafter with the same figure (see Example 36). Thus, the transcendent apotheosis of the finale is foretold midway through the first movement, accompanied with a strong (if premature) feeling of closure. But also foretold at this point is the problematic persistence of the sleigh bells, which enter immediately thereafter with, as so often in the finale, an effect of devastating estrangement from the security just achieved.

Understood more locally, but again with long-range consequences for the finale, the premature closing gesture compels a new beginning, one whose trajectory will not so easily bend toward comforting closure. Thus, in a pattern to be echoed and amplified in the finale (see chapter 2), local closure is answered with a disruptive passage for sleigh bells, which realizes more fully the disturbing potential of the opening. Following the close in m. 101, then, the sleigh bells are given their most elaborate hearing to this point in the symphony, continuing for seven full bars with a clear minor-mode orientation throughout and inaugurating an extended, often harrowing journey in which the G major theme appears only in a distorted form and closure seems unattainable. In this way, the comforting tone of the close in m. 101 provides the impetus for its antithesis, an extreme reawakening of the disruptive powers of the initial intrusion.

We do well to understand this juncture in the movement as a lullaby leading to an uneasy sleep besieged by nightmare, thus accounting for the vocal qualities of the clarinet figure, the *morendo* conclusion in mm. 100–101, and the subsequent tokens of nightmarish distortion. In extension, the finale carries this scenario further, providing even more explicit tokens of lullaby in its combination of a woman's voice singing a childish lyric in a soothing, folklike manner. (Lullaby was, after all, the originally projected genre for "Das himmlische Leben"; see chapter 2). In this reading, then, it is the adult who creates the fantasy of heavenly bounty, in order to lull the child to sleep; we may, in turn, take the subsequent intrusions of sleigh bells as reality checks, disturbing the child's slumber either directly or through nightmare.

Moreover, a reading of the development of the first movement as nightmare accounts well for its various distortions:

1. the solo violin in mm. 103f (5:20), which anticipates the violin solos of the second movement; more immediately, it draws us abruptly into a more intimate (and subjective) discursive tone;

2. the mocking new theme in mm. 125f (6:17), set for four unison flutes, couched in the unnatural brightness of A major, and supported by "raspberry"-like trills in the lower strings;[27]

3. the collapse in mm. 155f (7:26) to E♭ minor, a wrenching tritone away from A major; here, ironically, Mahler creates a sense of estrangement by leaving sleigh bells out of the instrumental mix, even though he employs all of the motives previously allied with sleigh bells, and sticks mainly with wind tone;

4. the disquieting slip into F minor for an extended treatment of the "Jingle Bells" motive (mm. 167f; 7:53), still without sleigh bells although supported intermittently by the triangle; the passage introduces *col legno* effects in the strings and culminates in grotesque versions of the G major theme;

5. the heroic outburst in C major (mm. 209f; 9:29); here, the supporting pedal on G seems to signal imminent return, apparently to be achieved (as in the first movement of Beethoven's *Pastoral* Symphony) through the subdominant, but a frenzied build-up to a *fortississimo* climax (m. 221; 9:57) simply collapses back onto itself;[28] and

6. the most devastating passage in the movement: after the collapse, low-lying trumpets play a familiar funeral-march figure accompanied by sleigh bells that are now combined, not with an open fifth with grace-note impetus, but with a stark, upper-register tritone played by all four flutes (mm. 225 f; 10:03).

In each of these, familiar material is defamiliarized through instrumental texture—solo violin, isolated unison flutes playing *à 4*, accompanimental trills, absence of sleigh bells, *col legno*, grandiose tutti—but the final section, which belatedly brings back the sleigh bells, is the only one that introduces material that is fundamentally new, for the funereal motive in the trumpets has virtually no motivic background in this movement. Among the many intruders in this movement, this passage stands alone as the real intruder, for it represents death; however disturbing we might find the implications of this movement's nostalgic evocation of childhood, this stark confrontation violates its governing sensibilities. The musical topic here, after all, refers to adult preoccupations with death, in particular resonating with Beethoven's funeral march in his Third Symphony and emphasizing the principal rhythmic motive of Beethoven's Fifth; Mahler's first direct intimation of death in the symphony thus carries with it an intense sense of grief on the one hand and a portentous sense of malevolent fate on the other— neither of which belongs to this child-oriented movement. Yet, this quality of profound discord is precisely what Mahler needs here, to provide a nightmare experience too extreme to be tolerated. As in a nightmare, which according to common wisdom must end before the dreamer dies, we are allowed a respite from this extremity of devastation: we simply wake up, safely in G major, just in time to hear the conclusion of the G major theme (m. 239; 10:40).[29]

If the beginning of the recapitulation thus further supports the development-as-nightmare scenario, the disorientation of the remainder of the first group in the recapitulation may, in extension, be seen as corresponding to the disorientation that follows an awakening from a disturbing dream, in which nightmare and reality must be firmly separated. Significantly, it is the recollection of the grandiose subdominant tutti from the development (no. 5 above) in mm. 251f (11:11) that restores order, for it was this tutti, alone in the development, that held the promise of a positive outcome. Here, there is no collapse; rather, the tutti leads directly into the raucous conclusion of the bridge, projecting a more acceptable reordering of the dream's plot contour, in which funereal intonations are safely bypassed.

The intruders late in the movement follow the final sleigh-bells episode in mm. 297f (13:26) and include most prominently allusions to the scherzo of Mahler's Third Symphony (beginning in m. 300; 13:35) and the emergence of an evocative solo horn passage in mm. 336–338 (15:30) that recalls the intrusion of the posthorn in the scherzo of the Third Symphony and anticipates a similar effect in the scherzo of the Fifth Symphony. While the common source for these intruders (the scherzo of Mahler's previous symphony) suggests a link between them, that link is based not on a direct integration of the two, but rather on their scherzo-based functions. In fact, both intruders are carefully—and independently—grounded in the motivic work of the movement.

Although the return of the sleigh bells in mm. 297 closely resembles their return at the end of the exposition, where they serve to introduce a recapitulatory version of the main theme, they function here quite differently, in two mutually contrasting ways. For the first time in the movement, the sound of the sleigh bells is isolated, as they are heard initially (if briefly) without their wind accompaniment. Allied with this effect, the E minor orientation of the accompaniment in the following bar makes it clear that this is to be a retrospective return, stabilized harmonically and offering a sense of closure through its subdominant relationship to the original; this impression is confirmed with the cadential pizzicato gesture in mm. 299–300. We might reasonably expect a similarly retrospective treatment of the head of the G major theme, which was withheld at the beginning of the recapitulation, but for that we are made to wait.

Conflicting with these emblems of closure, obviously appropriate to a coda, is the new figure that emerges in m. 300, recalling the bustling "creatures of the forest" music from the scherzo of the Third Symphony. Motivically, this figure is an extension of the "motion motive" associated with the sleigh bells. However, its newness is emphasized in several ways: through being accompanied by arpeggiated pizzicato strings in parallel to the G major theme (the expected continuation after the retrospective treatment of the sleigh bells); through its concluding tritone figure, landing on ♯4; and through its ongoing sense of motion, which extends the sleigh-bells topic to over thirteen bars before it links with the thematic "negotiations" that follow each of the earlier statements of the G major theme (m. 311f; 14:01).

Typically for a coda, this passage specifically recalls material from the development in order to negotiate a more satisfying resolution. Untypically, its referentiality reaches well beyond the development to re-create, if briefly, the scenario of the scherzo in Mahler's Third Symphony, in which obsessive, ostinatolike motion is stilled by an intruding solo voice in the trio. In this case, the solo horn phrase beginning in m. 336 completes this dialectic, but the horn phrase itself has an allied function within the movement, serving to resolve, finally, the antagonism between the sleigh bells–inspired dynamic element and the G major theme.

It is, in fact, the horns that apply the brakes to the new episode in m. 311

—even before their arresting solo—with an imposing appoggiatura, and they continue to play an important part in the ensuing negotiation. But their presence is most profoundly felt in the extended resolution after m. 323 (14:31). This resolution first borrows the conciliatory tone of the thematic material that closed off the first return to the opening, then combines this theme with a reductive version of the head of the G major theme, simplified to provide a sense of closure (mm. 330f; 15:00); specifically, instead of dipping down to B after the arrival on G, it rocks gently between tonic and dominant in an uncomplicated imitative texture (see Example 37). Beginning in m. 334 (15:16), the horns take up this oscillating figure and convert it (through retrograde) into a version of its most distinctive sleigh bells–derived motive (first introduced in m. 10; see Example 34). In this form, which fuses the antagonists into a single phrase, the figure is offered up by the horn in its trio-like voice, stilling for good the chaotic motion of the foregoing and providing a calming stability in its stead. All that is required for closure after this moment is the gradual return to the original head motive of the G major theme (mm. 341 and 342; 16:52), which is given a religious and sentimental tone through its slower tempo and plagal emphasis.

In trying to interpret further the role of the culminating horn solo, we may look first to its model in the scherzo of the Third Symphony, where the posthorn intruder is traditionally understood to be man, exerting his sway over the chaotic energy of the forest animals (see chapter 4). And we might look beyond this scherzo to the *Wunderhorn* song on which it is based, "Ablösung im Sommer," in which the death of the cuckoo marks, ambiguously, the transition from day to night or from spring to summer. Thus the solo horn intrudes in order to dominate for a critical moment a world that had previously been peopled only by children and—as may be inferred from Mahler's occasional suggestion of lullaby—their women caretakers. It exerts a specifically adult male presence, calming and ordering the earlier conflicts of the movement[30] and thus, by uniting the opposing thematic gestures, performs the traditionally masculine function of providing a reassuring rationality, offering a closing synthesis to the established thesis-antithesis.[31] But the extended context also applies, for, in leaving the basically optimistic day of the first movement, we are about to enter a very different nighttime world in the second.

In "Ablösung im Sommer," the death of the cuckoo prepares us for the nightingale. Reinterpreted allegorically, within the world established by the first movement of the Fourth Symphony, this scenario suggests that the naive child must die so as to emerge into a more sophisticated adulthood.

Example 37. Mahler, Symphony No. 4, first movement, mm. 330–342 (15:00)

For the scherzo of his Third Symphony, of which "Das himmlische Leben" was originally to have served as finale, Mahler recast this image of inevitable displacement to underscore the loss of innocence caused by the intrusive presence of humanity in nature. Although Mahler recalls this image at the end of the first movement of his Fourth Symphony (in part to provide local closure), however, he leaves the world of the child intact. Thus, the child, unlike the cuckoo, does not die; moreover, man's presence is felt, but briefly and benignly enough that it does not take over.[32] These differences, in themselves, offer further explanation for Mahler's removal of "Das himmlische Leben" from the Third Symphony, which after its scherzo is set to probe the dark complexities of adult humanity. They also help explain why, in the Fourth Symphony, we are given a much different kind of scherzo, one that projects the perspective of innocence with considerably more subjectivity than the scherzo of the Third Symphony.

Freund Hein

Three referential explanations for the scherzo of the Fourth Symphony are particularly relevant here: the original title Mahler gave this movement, "Freund Hein spielt zum Tanz auf; der Tod streicht recht absonderlich die Fiedel und geigt uns in den Himmel hinauf." (Freund Hein [Death] strikes up the dance; Death bows the fiddle quite strangely and fiddles us up to Heaven)[33] and two related pictorial representations of death. The older of these, whose connection to this movement is strongly documented, is the set of forty-one woodcuts by Hans Holbein the Younger (c. 1497–1543) depicting, with strongly moralistic overtones, a skeletal figure of death calling on a wide spectrum of humanity, often privileged and unprepared for his appearance.[34] Less well documented is Alma Mahler's reported claim that Mahler's scherzo was written while he was "under the spell of the self-portrait by Arnold Böcklin, in which Death fiddles into the painter's ear while the latter sits entranced."[35]

Of the latter two, Böcklin's painting (Figure 7-1), despite its weaker documentation, seems the more probable as an inspiration for Mahler's scherzo. It is more easily reconciled with the early subtitle for the movement, as both involve the figure of Death playing the fiddle; the choice of instrument reinforces the traditional association of death with the diabolical. Moreover, a Böcklin connection is entirely plausible on other grounds. We know, after all, that Mahler greatly admired Böcklin[36] and that Böcklin's paintings circulated widely in reproductions, since their success with the public depended not only on his skill as a painter, but also on the power of his evocative images to provoke the imagination of the viewer.[37] There can be little doubt that Mahler would have known this particularly evocative painting. We may be somewhat dubious of the anecdote for reasons of chronology (since Alma's acquaintance with Mahler postdates the composition of the movement), and we may certainly put aside her image of nested enchantment—Mahler by the painting, Böcklin by death—as a mere distraction. Nevertheless, Mahler's penchant for pictorial inspiration, most famously with regard to the funeral march of the First Symphony, but also with regard to the scherzo of the Second, makes the association eminently believable, and there were few contemporary images of this sort to which Mahler would have been more likely to respond in this way.[38]

The connection of Holbein's series of woodcuts to Mahler's scherzo also has much to recommend it, at least on the surface. They are central to the tradition of the *Todtentanz* (dance of death), to which Mahler's scherzo clearly refers.[39] The provenance and medium of Holbein's pictures resonate with the naive nostalgia of the first movement; moreover, Holbein concludes his earthly scenes with Death taking "daß jung Kint" by the hand (Figure 7-2), as the child reaches desperately back to its grieving parents.[40] If the reference is to the collection as a whole, as Mengelberg's note in the score implies, the connection becomes all the more plausible. Holbein offers shifting, episodic representations of Death, who assumes appropriate guises while cheerfully mocking each prospective victim with his skeletal leer, sardonic demeanor, and, at times, direct parody of his prey (tilling the ground

Figure 7-1. Arnold Böcklin, *Selbstbildnis mit fiedelndem Tod* (1872).
Staatliche Museen zu Berlin—Preußischer Kulturbesitz. Nationalgalerie.
Used with permission.

with Adam, marching in procession with the clergyman, holding a skull in imitation of the astronomer's scientific pose, etc.). Thus, Holbein's series offers significant points of congruence with Mahler's ever-evolving episodic structure, in which death seems always present, yet always unexpected and never twice the same.

So, too, would a connection to Holbein's prints help Mahler embed his

Daß Iungkint.

Figure 7-2. Hans Holbein the Younger, "Daß Jung Kint,"
from his *Bilder des Todes*

music in a Germanic-Christian context, in a way analogous to his dependence in each of his first four symphonies on the *Wunderhorn* legacy. Although the skeletal figure of death undoubtedly predates a specifically Christian context, that context is indelibly a part of both the pictorial conceit and the inspirational context of the woodcuts, for they begin with Adam and Eve, whose story allows death a commanding position over humanity, and continue with a series of implicit moral lessons firmly grounded in Christian teachings. This associational nexus well explains why Mahler might have been more ready to cite Holbein's prints as pictorial inspiration than he was Böcklin's portrait, especially since the latter projects, above all else, the self-centered and self-conscious projection of an individual artist, whereas Holbein's series had long since achieved the universalized cultural position of a folk emblem.

Nevertheless, much argues against a direct inspiration. Holbein's moralistic tone has no obvious counterpart in Mahler's music, and his objectively adult attitude seems out of place in Mahler's subjectively child-oriented scherzo. There is little hint of the diabolical in Holbein's portrayal of death, who plays the fiddle in only one scene: "Die Herzoginn" (The Duchess; see Figure 7-3). And, despite the traditional association of Holbein's images with the *Todtentanz*, music and dance are fairly incidental to the series.[41] There is, moreover, a striking difference in emphasis: when Holbein's Death does dance or play music, it is to mock his victims with frivolity rather than to bewitch them or to set them dancing, while in Mahler's scherzo the uncanny, seductive playing of Death—represented, as in Camille Saint-Saëns's *Danse macabre* (1874), by a solo violin playing *scordatura*—hypnotizes his victims with an irresistible desire to join the dance. Thus, while Holbein's series of woodcuts might have provided a useful point of reference for Mahler as an inspiration for performance, to help orient Mengelberg toward the spirit of the movement, it seems less likely to have been as central a compositional inspiration.

As all three points of reference make clear, the focus of this scherzo is somewhat narrower than that of its predecessor in the Third Symphony, specifically highlighting the transaction of death rather than the displacement of a naive spirit with a more sophisticated one; here, the reality of death is reduced to an effect of estrangement in the negotiation between the two. Three questions concerning this "negotiation" are central to our present concerns: For whom is Freund Hein playing? What is the attitude toward death projected by the movement? And to what does death lead (or promise to lead)?

The answer to the first of these questions will embrace the other two. It must be addressed in part because of long-standing ambiguities in the ways these various associations have been understood, and in this regard Böcklin's painting provides a particularly useful point of reference. Böcklin's self-portrait, first of all, is much richer in interpretive possibilities than Alma purportedly suggests. The painter is not sitting, but pausing to listen while in the act of painting, holding his brush in much the same position as Death holds his bow. Death is not in the foreground, as Alma implies, but is mostly obscured by darkness and by the more vividly colored painter, whom he stands closely behind, represented only by a skull-like head with a gaping toothsome grin and by a gnarled hand with skin stretched tight over the bones. The fiddle he plays, although carefully rendered in many respects, has but one string, and that (apparently) the lowest. The expression on the face of the painter, whose head is cocked slightly to one side, may represent his concentration on either the painting before him or the music he hears, or both. Böcklin thus captures a moment more fluid than what Alma describes, an actively engaged moment for both painter and Death; the painter, in particular, is rendered more thoughtful than immobile by the music he hears, although perhaps his attention is torn for a moment between music and painting.

The most peculiar thing about the association of this painting with this symphonic movement is the very different orientation of the latter. The painting is extremely adult in concept—perhaps even more than Holbein's woodcuts—and is hard to transplant directly into the childly world of Mahler's Fourth Symphony. Böcklin presents himself in the painting as a handsome, intelligent artist, presumptively Faustian in his thoughtful appropriation of the diabolical for inspiration; yet the foregrounded painter is mercilessly mocked by the caricatured figure standing behind him, slightly taller than he is, impudently thrusting himself into what we would now call the personal space of the earnest painter (who seems unaware of Death's close proximity), grinning idiotically with apparent contempt for the painting Böcklin is laboring on, seemingly mimicking with his bow hand the affected manner of the painter as he holds his brush. It is widely believed that Böcklin added Death to the painting after the self-portrait was either complete or nearly so; whether or not this is the case, his ghastly presence ferociously undermines the smugly gratifying image Böcklin created of himself.[42] Although it is easy to imagine Mahler's being captivated by this painting, particularly with its simultaneous presentation of two incompatible worlds and its sense of ironic self-mockery, its relevance to this particular movement would not seem to extend beyond its background image of death —an image Mahler moves to the foreground while virtually ignoring not only the actual foreground of the painting, but also much of its richly adult meanings.

Regarding Freund Hein himself, the notion is frequently advanced in English writings that he specifically targets children, in parallel to common

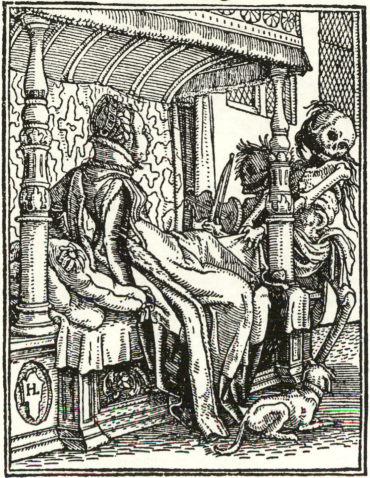

Figure 7-2. Hans Holbein the Younger, "Die Herzoginn," from his *Bilder des Todes*

beliefs about goblins and witches (and Jews). Deryck Cooke, for example, explicitly compares him to the Pied Piper, whose powers of musical seduction led all but one of an entire town's children to their doom.[43] Yet there is no particular association of Freund Hein with children in Germanic culture; on the contrary, Freund Hein is a more universal personification of death, dealing with adults and children alike, roughly equivalent to the expressions "Old Henry" (English) and "Beinheinrich" (Swiss).[44] Even so, Mahler's invocation of Freund Hein here—especially when allied with Böcklin's background image of Death fiddling—does turn out to be disturbingly relevant to the child's world that Mahler has created in the first movement, in a way that a more direct connection to a Pied Piper–like figure might serve to obscure.

Mahler's musical evocation of Freund Hein in the scherzo offers a sharp contrast to the death-related image that occurs at the climax of the development section in the first movement. Instead of images drawn from the political and personal realities of adulthood, projecting defeat and public mourning on a heroic scale, the scherzo conveys an air of fantasy, of seductive intimacy enlivened by dance. It is this aura of fantasy, typically evoked in child seduction (e.g., in "Erlkönig"), that allows Freund Hein a place in this symphony, a place that the trappings of adult grief are pointedly denied in the first movement. The diabolical cheerfulness of Böcklin's Death, drawing like so much of his work on familiar topics of fantasy, combines with the suggestive intimacy of the word "Freund" attached to this character, and with the casual insolence of the phrase, "Freund Hein spielt auf," to convert death into something more playful than threatening.

Perhaps, then, what Mahler saw in Böcklin's painting and sought to re-create in his scherzo was its essentially childish image of Death (allied with the childish impulse that may have driven Böcklin to put him there), which contrasts with and mocks the high seriousness of the handsome painter (allied with Böcklin's own vanity). If so, we may take the symphonic genre in the abstract (allied with Mahler's pretensions as a symphonist) and its most distressing manifestation in the first movement (the funereal topic late in the development) as the "serious painter" that Freund Hein will mock in the scherzo. Death, then, presents himself as an ally to the child, a playful companion and a weapon of sorts against the vain pretensions of adulthood. He plays for the amusement of the child in direct parody of the adult world and offers, ironically, the possibility of eternally prolonging childhood, a possibility that the finale will eventually realize. In a sense, then, the role of death in the symphony is to invert the cuckoo-nightingale allegory, as the child's death allows childhood itself to survive, whereas a surviving child must inevitably enter adulthood.[45]

According to Laurence Lerner, the nineteenth century maintained a uniquely sentimental perspective on the death of children, seldom evident before then and displaced in the twentieth century by a more skeptical attitude. Thus, while interest in the subject of child death arose naturally from a generally more prominent interest during the nineteenth century in childhood and the passage into adulthood and was colored by the growing perception in the nineteenth century that the death of children was increasingly avoidable, the transition into the twentieth was "from a culture that represented [child] death as painless, as being received by God, into one that sees it as departing reluctantly and painfully from the only life we actually know."[46] Mahler's direct focus on the transaction of death shows him to be on the cusp between the two centuries, focusing, if obliquely, on the excruciating pain of death (through starvation), but allowing too for the comfort of being released into a better world. If a diabolical Death leads the child into the unknown, we can at least imagine the consequences to be, not pain leading to oblivion, but the direct opposite: being first released from pain (as the child, seduced by Death, is transported to another world) and then, in the end, "being received by God." Mahler's full subtitle, with its reference to heaven, acknowledges this need for reassurance. But such a perspective is risky in Mahler's world and requires considerable protection from turn-of-the-century realities. Mahler provides that protection in two stages, cloaking us first in the heavy nostalgia of the first movement before offering up a child-oriented fantasy of spectral seduction in the second.[47]

The Second Movement

Even if Freund Hein may thus be seen as accommodated to the sensibilities of the first movement, he is clearly presented as an intruder at the outset of the scherzo. The movement opens with insinuating fragments relating directly to the first movement, all of which are rendered strange in some way (see Example 38). Thus, the principal motive from the closing group (the opening anacrusis for the scherzo, repeated across mm. 2–3) is ambiguously placed in G minor, estranged somewhat from both the G major of the previous movement and the C minor to come. The minor-mode upper-neighbor figure (m. 1, also repeated) is given a new emphasis, disturbingly portentous. The repeated staccato notes in the winds (m. 3) play a diminished fourth (B♭–F♯, with the D of the horn motive completing an augmented triad) that does not resolve properly but slides chromatically down, away from the apparent tonic, after a mocking appoggiatura trill. The "motion" figure that frequently supported the sleigh bells in the first movement, which will provide the basic dance impulse for the scherzo, is manipulated to give unsettling emphasis to the raised fourth (F♯ on the downbeats of mm. 5 and 6) and augmented triad (G–B–E♭ in the clarinet, reinforced by the E♭ in the horns against the B–G of the flutes at the end of m. 5). The source for these estrangements is made clear immediately, as the *scordatura* solo violin, tuned a step above the normal tuning and to be played, as Mahler instructs, "wie eine Fiedel," combines precisely these estranging elements into a supple, chromatically glib dance tune. Thus, the "fiddle" takes up an arpeggiation of the augmented triad as its anacrusis figure (beginning with a diminished fourth), emphasizes a minor-second neighbor-note recalling the horn figure but transplanted to F#, and uses this to initiate a process of chromatic slippage.[48]

The opening creates an introductory atmosphere through which we sense the presence of an intruder even before we hear the intruder himself; we hear his world before we hear him. Or, rather, we hear the world we have grown accustomed to (that of the first movement) altered—fragmented and parodied—by the intruder. When we do hear him, the parody immediately sharpens, first of all through the introduction of an "unnatural" version of a sound we have heard before: the solo violin from the intimate opening paragraph of the first-movement development section, rendered strange through *scordatura*. By the end of the nineteenth century, violin *scordatura* was mostly confined to two possible applications, either heightening the effect of the solo instrument (as in Paganini's First Concerto) or suggesting the supernatural, more specifically the diabolical (as in Saint-Saëns's *Danse macabre*; considering Paganini's reputation, this association may also obtain for his First Concerto). Because Mahler has given us a "normal" foretaste in the first movement as a point of reference, his application has a foot in both realms, marking the solo violin in the scherzo as diabolical other while, on another level, heightening its sense of intrusive, insinuating intimacy. The double effect is also visible in performance: when the concertmaster switches violins, he personalizes the relationship for the audience and alerts it to the quality of difference *scordatura* entails.

In other ways, as well, the entrance of the solo violin parodies the first movement, most pointedly through its completion of a similar opening structure: repeated eighth notes and "motion" motive without string tone leading to a string theme introduced with a three-note anacrusis.[49] Estrangement, and thus parody, is projected by the way the details recall and diverge from the model. Thus, the switch to string tone is retained but modified, not only through the use of scordatura solo violin, but also through employing mutes for the larger choir and beginning with solo textures in the lower strings. The ubiquitous three-note anacrusis figure, altered from a scalar approach to the tonic (as in the first movement) to an arpeggiated augmented triad (in its first and most characteristic form), reproduces the arrival pitches

Example 38. Mahler, Symphony No. 4, second movement, mm. 1–10

NB Der 1. Sologeiger hat sich mit 2 Instrumenten zu versehen, von denen das eine um einen Ganzton höher, das andere normal gestimmt ist.
*) wie eine Fiedel

of the model, but reversed from F♯–G to G–F♯, insouciantly denying the resolution rendered so nostalgically in the first movement by turning us temporarily away from the tonic with a foreign tone. More fundamentally, the string tune here represents motion instead of stasis, displacing the hesitant fragments of the introduction with a propulsive energy, albeit through the circular motion of dance rather than the more directional motion projected by the sleigh bells of the first movement.

Outwardly symmetrical, the movement falls with deceptive neatness into the shape of a scherzo with double trio, with culminating C major interludes in each of the three scherzo sections. Each part of the form, however, is rewritten in both detail and overall shape, so that a sense of fluid narrative obscures the clarity of the formal outlines. Characteristically, for example, Mahler plays continually with the instrumental configuration of repeated material. Thus, with the many returns to the opening dance tune, Mahler provides a counterpart to its chromatic shiftiness by constantly allowing new instrumental colors to intrude, which also gives the impression of a variety of personages stepping up to lead the dance by turn—always, however, presided over by the *Fiedel*. To be sure, Mahler is simply following his proclivity for varying his instrumental presentation as much as possible, but in a movement in which the sense of a distinct supernatural presence is created through direct association with an unusual instrumental timbre, each new alteration potentially acquires significance. Moreover, the sense of ongoing narrative that smaller changes of this kind help foster is confirmed in the ways that Mahler negotiates and renegotiates among the various sections of the movement.

The first scherzo-trio combination takes us through a fiddle dance in three slightly asymmetrical spans to a pastoral trio in the subdominant and a more relaxed tempo. The three spans of the opening scherzo section, each led by the solo fiddle, constitute a loose departure-return framework in which the contrasting middle moves quickly to an extended C major respite from the fiddle dance that may be heard, in part, as advance dominant preparation for the pastoral trio. The third span reproduces the first with a varied instrumentation but does not close off completely. Rather, while a second return to the opening motive prepares yet another round of the fiddle dance (m. 63f [1:32]; cf. m. 22f [0:32] after the first span), this material is abruptly taken over by a horn playing in its brightest register, doubled a tenth below by the clarinet playing in its darkest (m. 68f [1:39])—a stark appropriation that leads us directly into the trio before the scherzo can close properly. In this way, the eventual return of the fiddle dance will appear more as a continuation than a repetition of the opening scherzo section. Mahler's narrative strategy, then, is to impose a sense of interrupted continuity on the schematic scherzo-trio structure, which allows an asymmetrical narrative shape to emerge against the symmetrical formal scheme.

The key to this asymmetrical narrative shape lies in the differing characters of the three types of major-mode episodes: the four brief C major intervals within the fiddle dance sections, the two F major trios, and the D major "breakthrough" before the final fiddle dance. Of these, the repeated episodes —the second trio and the later C major intervals—appear as evolving variants of their predecessors, creating a system of linked narrative strands taking place on several levels in alternation. These separate strata may be best understood in terms of their affective and symbolic distances from the original level, which had been dominated by the C minor diabolical dance. Thus, the C major episodes stand closest to the world of the fiddle dance, appearing as brief visionary images at the same tempo, summarily dispelled; the F major trios, more relaxed in tempo, mark clear removals to another, more pastoral world; and the more ethereal D major episode, at the most relaxed tempo in the movement, appears as an extended moment of transcendence—or, perhaps, an extended foretaste of a transcendence to come. The "plot" of the movement progresses in a generalized outward spiral, propelled (or led) by the dance, and advancing in gradual steps from vision, through pastoral removal, and eventually to transcendence, with what follows the latter serving more as liquidation than as additional narrative. Within the more conventional formal outline of scherzo with double trio, the resulting narrative may be mapped as follows (where H represents Freund Hein's fiddle dance, and major-mode episodes are indicated by key):

Figure 7-4. Formal layout of Mahler's Symphony No. 4, second movement

$Scherzo_1$			$Trio_1$		$Scherzo_2$				$Trio_2$				$Scherzo_3$			
			F_1 retrans.						F_2 retrans.		D retrans.					
	C_1					C_2	C_3								C_4-coda	
H_1 H_2		H_3			H_4 H_5		H_6						H_7 H_8			
No. of bars: 30	3	12	23	33	13	23	7	12	28	18	43	8	20	7	26	7	51
Timing: 0:10	0:44	0:49	1:09	1:39	2:40	3:04	3:38	3:43	4:04	4:42	5:03	6:23	6:37	7:14	7:27	8:03	8:14/8:36

(No. of bars includes transitional material, if any)

The stratified dynamic that regulates the larger narrative progress of this movement—leading us in graduated steps "up to heaven," as Mahler's original subtitle has it—resembles the orbital structure of electrons within the atom as projected by Niels Bohr. A younger contemporary of Mahler, Bohr was similarly concerned with mysterious processes of transmutation, which he, too, rationalized within a mechanistic model of movement between orbital strata, with a corresponding decrease in energy at more removed strata.[50] A more accessible model of stepwise ascent might be found in traditional approaches to education—Fux's *Gradus ad Parnassum* comes readily to mind[51] —but there is a palpable sense in Mahler's scherzo of a spiraling motion outward, and a sense, too, that we are propelled to a higher level at each step in our progress by the centrifugal force generated by Freund Hein's fiddling.

Significantly, Mahler's narrative procedures insulate the various strata from each other to differing degrees. Thus, the trio is particularly well insulated from both the fiddle dance and the D major transcendence, launched in each case by an exaggerated brass declamation and dissolved in a lengthy retransition evocative of a slow cinematic fade (e.g., m. 102f; 2:40). On the other hand, the arrivals in C major seem almost too easy—C major is, after all, the parallel major for the main key of the fiddle dance—and these episodes are easily dispelled with a mocking reintroduction of chromaticism, an abrupt reminder that we have not left the purview of Freund Hein, who, in fact, maintains a presiding presence throughout the second C major episode (mm. 145–156; 3:43) and is represented by horns and winds during the third (mm. 185–199; 4:42). Perhaps the most effective insulation is given to the D major transcendence, which occurs as an extended parenthesis within a transitional passage, appearing and disappearing as if disconnected from the here and now of the movement.

Within each stratum, narrative concerns account for the significant differences from one episode to the next. In each of the two trios, for example, an intensely sweet string-dominated sound eventually displaces a pastorale-inspired wind-dominated sound; but in the second, the move toward a string sound occurs sooner and more decisively and leads eventually to a higher level of sweetness, featuring in its final stages a solo violin rendered all the sweeter by its being played non-*scordatura*.[52] The lead-ins to the two trios are also sharply differentiated. The first, with its distorted horn and clarinet sound, immediately evokes an air of rustic simplicity, displacing the overripe sophistication of the fiddle dance and preparing the pastoral trio. The second, while it relates obviously to the first in its brass tone and rhythmic figure, is both less rustic and less simple, as a midrange solo trumpet (in F) displaces the preceding chromaticism with a dramatic angular figure, broadly diatonic. The rationale for the change is twofold. Mahler is, with the second trio, preempting an expected return to the fiddle dance following the C major episode of mm. 185f, so that the trumpet provides a quasi-military tone of authority to enforce the rupture. Thus, the trumpet appears, as in the trumpet fanfare late in the second movement of Haydn's *Military* Symphony, as a solo voice, initially without other instrumental support. But the trumpet also offers a more polished tone and a more complex motivic figure, in both its contour and its nonsequential deployment, and so helps push the second trio more quickly beyond the more primitive pastorale betokened by pure wind sound to its second, string-dominated phase.

The narrative progress within the two trios enables and justifies the D major breakthrough in two ways. The second trio, in introducing a solo violin in its later stages, bypasses the most characteristic string melody of the first trio (m. 90f), which returns in the D major episode after the initial breakthrough (m. 262f), so that this additional episode acts as closure to the trio in completing its thematic structure on the one hand, and links naturally back to the cadential retransition to the fiddle dance on the other (m. 274 f; cf. m.102 f). More immediately, the retransition following the trio is more intimately scored the second time through (cf. mm. 246f [7:14] and mm. 102f [2:40])[53]—quite naturally so, since the later stages of the second trio are scored for a soli string choir, *pianissimo e morendo*—and so engenders a heightened sense of expectation. A simple return to the fiddle dance at that point would be anticlimactic.

Mahler forges links across the various strata in other ways as well. The C major intervals in the scherzo sections provide dominant preparation for the F major trios, and Mahler makes this harmonic link palpable through the celestial F major explosions that punctuate, *fortissimo,* the placid *pianissimo* arpeggios in the strings. Significantly, it is initially the harp, in its first appearance in the scherzo, that both marks the arrival in C major (in the bass) and points the way to a later stage of arrival with its imposition of an upper-register F (mm. 34–36; 0:49). Throughout the movement, the harp appears as an indicator of transcendence, playing a prominent role in all three of the upper strata; yet it, too, is made to play the fiddle-dance tune when, just after the first trio, it marks a transitional stage as we descend to the lowest stratum (mm. 115–177 [3:01]; note that even in this descent to the level of Freund Hein, the harp fastidiously avoids the augmented triad).

In the second extended climb toward transcendence (the second scherzo-trio span), both C major sections are contaminated throughout by the shadow of Freund Hein. In the first he plays along with the harp; in the second, his supporting cast of menacing, low-lying horns and teasing upper winds frame the registral space. Paradoxically, it is precisely these instrumental enhancements—all intruders from the lower stratum—that propel us more emphatically to a higher level in the second trio, launching a general crescendo of transcendence that will eventually dissipate only in the D major transcendence. We seem here not so much led by Freund Hein as herded, driven by him to seek refuge at an ever greater remove.

Similarly, the D major transcendence, which stands in relation to the F major trio precisely as the E major conclusion to the symphony stands to the G major opening of the finale, influences profoundly the narrative flow of the lower strata despite its affective removal. As already noted, its principal melody completes the trajectory of the preceding trio. Even more important, it severely undermines the authority of Freund Hein for the remainder of the movement. Thus, when the fiddle dance returns, it is led, without tritones, by a normally tuned solo violin, beginning in G major and wandering through a succession of related keys (mm. 280–294; 7:27). Gradually, the diabolical side reemerges, first with the return of the *scordatura* solo violin (m. 298; 7:51) and the augmented-triad anacrusis (m. 307; 8:03), but it remains but a shadowy presence. Although the *scordatura* solo violin and the teasing upper winds again intrude on the C major episode (m. 314f; 8:14), it is with much different effect, for the inverted dynamics and trills in the winds link them more to the trio than to Freund Hein[54] and the harp plays, more warmly, in the middle register. The eerie conclusion of the movement represents Freund Hein in retreat, unable to reassert his authority in the wake of the breakthrough to the D major episode. The last echoes of his fiddle dance evaporate as quickly as they are heard, and the movement ends, if uneasily, in C major.

The scherzo of the Fourth Symphony has much in common with its immediate predecessors in the Third and Second Symphonies, most notably in its double deployment of a pastoral, rustic trio to contrast with the busy scherzo idiom that dominates the opening and intervening sections. The parallel is particularly strong with the "Fischpredigt" scherzo of the Second Symphony, since in both movements a seductive dance idiom dominates the scherzo sections. One might expect, then, that Freund Hein would partake more than he does of the negatively inscribed absolute-music topic, particularly since he, no less than the governing sensibility of the "Fischpredigt" scherzo (or, for that matter, the funeral march of the First Symphony), enforces compliance through seductively obsessive motion. Intriguingly, however, the Fourth Symphony trios are configured not so much as escapes from the scherzo, but as escapes enabled by the scherzo; hence, the trios represent the fulfillment of promises delivered in the scherzo and convey a sense of continuity with the scherzo through the fact that they continue to dance, albeit to a rustic *Ländler* instead of the more sophisticated and seductive undulance of Freund Hein. What makes the crucial difference here is the redemptively human face worn by Freund Hein, who at all times pays attention to his victims/partners, who effects an air of playful interaction, and who in the end honors his promise to conduct them to a better place. Wholly absent from this movement, then, is what is potentially most frightening about the absolute-music topic: its impenetrable air of oblivious self-absorption.

Child Love, Child Death

Mahler composed his Fourth Symphony within a male-dominated artistic environment that found in the idealized innocence of the child—according to Bram Dijkstra—a substitute for the purity its practitioners and patrons sought, but no longer believed they could find, in women. Thus, after tracing the post-Darwin equation of women's intellectual development with that of a child, Dijkstra writes:

> To escape the frighteningly physical and emotional demands grown women tended to place on them, many men who had expected to find in the women of their own age group the same meek, nunlike qualities they had seen in their fathers' wives, began to yearn for the purity of the child. . . . These men seem to have come to the conclusion that if woman's grown body soiled the passive purity of her childlike mind, it was better to seek all the positive qualities, all the passive, compliant qualities of woman, in the child itself. . . . Hence the world of the child came to hold a special fascination for the late nineteenth century. . . . Major developments occurred during this period in the establishment of a literature and art which was supposedly specifically directed toward children but which was actually populated with fantasies about childhood fabricated by the grownups who wrote the narratives and . . . drew the pictures. These fantasies were directly linked to the chivalric dream

and a general longing for the world of the child as a reliable substitute for the perversely untrustworthy dependency of woman on man.[55]

According to this paradigm, Mahler's scherzo, like Lewis Carroll's fantasy tales—an obvious touchstone for Dijkstra's arguments—may well appeal to the imaginative child, but much more to the adult who apprehends the work simultaneously from an imagined perspective of the idealized child who delights in its strangeness, and from a more knowing perspective, one that will, for example, more reliably hear the *scordatura* violin's augmented triad as a distorted version of the familiar. In fact, however, most children will no more take in Mahler's pointedly perverse manipulations of harmony and instrumentation than grasp the satire that pervades much of Carroll's seeming nonsense. Hence, as Dijkstra would have it, the imagined child auditor is at best a figment of self-deception and at worst a fiction designed to camouflage less savory motivations than the desire to give delight to children.

Yet, although adults may misjudge the capacity of actual children to respond on this level—most children would surely prefer, or at least equally enjoy, a more conventional setting of the dance—Dijkstra's construction of a suspiciously convenient (self-)deception is only partly correct. Adults who experience either Mahler's scherzo or Carroll's tales in parallel to a real or imagined child's experience of them, if they are themselves sufficiently knowledgeable, will be acutely aware of a different level of sophistication in their respective responses and cherish the difference as an emblem of the relative innocence of the child—however abstractly or concretely "the child" is construed. The enormous success of Carroll's Alice books has always depended on his facility for hiding the sophistication of his fancy from his ostensible audience (a facility remarkably mirrored in John Tenniel's illustrations), in order to provide a vehicle for the adult to experience, with equal vividness, the child's relative innocence and a sense of his (or her) intellectual superiority to the child.

Something like this happens as well with Mahler's scherzo, with perhaps an added layer of nostalgia, so that the imagined child may be mapped to the remembered innocence of the adult listener's own past, a perspective encouraged by Mahler's earlier indications for the movement: "Death leads us," or, alternatively, "Death . . . fiddles us up to Heaven." Mahler, unlike Carroll, overtly invites us to become the child, or at least to project ourselves into the world of the child. In so doing, Mahler perhaps unconsciously reveals the depth of his conversion to Christianity, for idealizing the innocence of children in this manner—scarcely unique to the nineteenth century

—most vividly recalls Christ's admonition to his disciples: "Suffer the little children to come unto me, and forbid them not: for of such is the kingdom of God. Verily I say unto you, Whosoever shall not receive the kingdom of God as a little child, he shall not enter therein" (see note 45).[56]

The anguished circumstances of Émile Zola's *Abbé Mouret* (*La faute de l'Abbé Mouret*, 1874), which Dijkstra discusses at some length, must ultimately be contrasted with even a literal understanding of Christ's teaching, despite an obvious derivation from the latter. In the course of Zola's passionate indictment of celibacy as unnatural, his "sinful" Abbé prays thus to the Virgin Mary:

> I should like to be a child once more. I should like to be always a child, walking in the shadow of your gown. When I was quite little, I clasped my hands when I uttered the name of Mary. My cradle was white, my body was white, my every thought was white. I could see you distinctly, I could hear you calling me, I went towards you in the light of a smile over scattered rose petals. And nought else did I feel or think, I lived but just enough to be a flower at your feet. No one should grow up. . . . A child alone can say your name without befouling it.[57]

Even if Zola has left out the clarifying quotation marks implied in his title (thus: *The "Sin" of Abbé Mouret*)—which would have destroyed its reflexive duality, its challenge to his readers to recognize both the moralistic force and the unnaturalness of this designation—we must bear in mind that he was here not indicting society as a whole (although that might have been his larger project), nor was his Abbé meant to stand in for Dijkstra's vague "many men." Rather, his target was specifically the unnatural celibacy demanded of priests by the Catholic Church. While there is undoubtedly a vital relationship between this enforced celibacy and the entrenched tendency in Western culture to view sexuality as sinful, the two cannot simply be merged, for church and society are not coextensive. More specific to Dijkstra's argument, Abbé Mouret's revulsion against the urges of his adult body, meant to register as both authentic and grotesque, should not be taken as a more generalized (if overdone) "portrayal of the male's desperate longing for the purity of childhood."[58] Self-hatred in adult males and their (erotic) idealizing of women and/or children may be related phenomena, but they are not the same thing; here, at least, we may distinguish between smoke and fire, and admit to a variety of combinatorial possibilities.

Lewis Carroll, to take up Dijkstra's next exemplar, may be distinguished from both Abbé Mouret and Mahler along precisely these lines. It is clear, from Carroll's photographic predilections and the designated purpose of his "Pillow Problems" (that is, to drive out "impure thoughts" at bedtime), that he was obsessed with the same issues that beset Mouret—childhood innocence and the unwelcome urges of the flesh, understood to be sinful—even if he was considerably less self-conscious and, perhaps, less frank about the nature of his impure thoughts. But Carroll's well-known aversion to boys makes it plain that there was little if any personal nostalgia involved in his attitude toward childhood innocence; his desired escape from adulthood, unlike Mouret's, did not involve the desire to go back himself to a childlike state. Indeed, we can all too easily imagine the relief his own transition into adulthood must have brought him, as the youthful impurity of his thoughts was brought more manageably under adult control. Mahler's idealizing of the child, on the other hand, is at once heavily tinged with nostalgia, yet too heavily invested in adult perspectives to be taken as a Mouret-like denunciation of adulthood, desperately seeking a lost innocence.

The conversion of the idealized child into the eroticized child, however prevalent, and even inevitable, in the literary and pictorial arts, is foreign to both Mahler's apparent intent in the Fourth Symphony and to its reception. It is relatively easy to find sex lurking in the shadows of late-nineteenth-century preoccupations with children. By Carroll's own admission, he concocted his stories in order to prolong his contact with young girls—and perhaps also to gain their confidence and the confidence of their parents, to revel in their rapt attention, and, like his later adult readers, to project their innocence against the backdrop of his own sophistication. While we may well find some of this unsavory, particularly in light of his well-known hobby of photographing young nude girls in sometimes provocatively adult poses,[59] neither Mahler's motivations nor the effects of his music can be similarly faulted. Mahler's Fourth Symphony was intended for an unequivocally adult venue and lacks the literal referentiality of more obviously representational art, which may too easily invite prurient, even pornographic interests to masquerade as pious solicitation.

Hans Christian Andersen's "Little Match Girl," cited above for its possible affinities with Mahler's Symphony, offers as well a pointed contrast that is especially relevant to this issue. Unlike Mahler, who allows a visionary heaven to penetrate the very fabric of his symphony, Andersen saves his moment of redemption for the end, where it appears almost incidentally. For most of "The Little Match Girl," we are invited to gaze, through Andersen's descriptions, at an unnamed, supremely vulnerable little girl: cold, hungry, unloved, half naked, and fearing abuse from her father; even after she is taken by her grandmother to heaven, her frozen body remains behind, to be found and discussed by the curious.[60] Nor is this kind of quasi-pornographic treatment atypical of Andersen's tales: in "The Girl Who Trod on the Loaf," the unfortunate Ingé is made to serve as a living statue beneath the moors, on display in her soiled finery for literally decades, so that "the eyes of all were fixed upon her, and their evil thoughts gleamed forth from their eyes, and they spoke to one another, moving their lips, from which no sound whatever came forth."[61] In "The Little Sea Maid," it is only at the price of extreme continuous pain and the loss of her voice—and the prospect of death without redemption should she fail—that the heroine is given legs and the chance to win the heart of the prince, with the seductive power of mute compliance and visual display her only available means for doing so (indeed, under Andersen's careful stage management, when the prince first sees her in human form, she is unconscious and nude).[62] The possible pornographic value of Mahler's music pales to nothing next to the more graphically perverse of Andersen's tales, however easily one might construe the scherzo movement of the Fourth Symphony as depicting the diabolical seduction of the innocent, quite in line with contemporary, frankly erotic images of ravaged vulnerability.

Yet we may want to back away from the confidence of this conclusion, for music has a long history of cloaking subversive meanings, whether political or sexual, from the uninitiated, of stating the forbidden without noticeable fear of censure. From the militaristic expansion of the phrase "Viva la liberté!" in the first-act finale of Mozart's *Don Giovanni* and Ferrando's musical rape of Fiordiligi in the second act of *Così fan tutte* (where he enforces his will by preempting her aria, already in progress), to the politically charged operas of Giuseppe Verdi and the frankly sexual musical images of Wagner's Venusberg music in *Tannhäuser* and second-act duet in *Tristan und Isolde* (not to mention later imitations in Richard Strauss's *Don Juan* and *Salome*), composers have found myriad ways to communicate in music what could not have been stated in words or depicted on stage. And it has been argued that the private musical codes of such straight-laced musical personalities as Schumann and Brahms hid a private, sexually charged fantasy world from the general public.[63] Indeed, there is some evidence that early audiences found parts of the Fourth sexually suggestive;[64] perhaps, after all, the informed pedophile derives more pleasure than we want to know about from Mahler's Fourth Symphony.

But even if Mahler's fascination with childhood innocence seems, in the reading offered here, not as erotically charged as that of many of his contemporaries, his music exhibits a similar pairing of two contrasting perspectives: those of the innocent, vulnerable child and of the more knowing adult. For Mahler, however, the latter perspective is tinged with an aching nostalgia, for his attempt to fashion a convincing semblance of childish innocence from the materials of worldly adulthood seems only to widen the gulf between the two. Thus, the "uncanny" sound he sought for his scherzo betokens more than an attempt to depict the supernatural presence of Freund Hein; as an adult concoction of sophisticated musical devices within the faux naiveté of his projected child-world, it also serves as a poignant emblem of the irretrievability of youth. It would seem that the vulnerability of childhood extends, as well, to its memory.

Notes

Notes to Preface

1 For this chapter, I have extensively rewritten and expanded the article's introduction but done little to the remainder; the new material offers additional rationales for the unusual perspective of the symphony and places the essay within the ongoing discussion of the book.

2 See Schoenberg, "Gustav Mahler (1912 and 1948)" and "Gustav Mahler: In Memoriam (1912)."

3 Two signal events in the "rediscovery" of Mahler, at least in the United States, were Bernstein's Centennial celebration in 1960 and his recording of the complete symphonies for CBS, completed in 1967. While the centrality of Bernstein's role in the Mahler revival has been disputed, Mahler's central role in Bernstein's career is manifest; see Page, "Leonard Bernstein and the Resurrection of Gustav Mahler."

4 See esp., among other discussions, Schorske, *Fin-de-siècle Vienna.*

5 See Alma Mahler, *Memories and Letters.* Ironically, perhaps, responsibility for the mystification of Mahler must also lie with the famously superstitious Arnold Schoenberg.

6 Adorno's most important writings on Mahler framed the decade of the 1960s; see his "Mahler (Centenary Address, Vienna 1960)," and *Mahler, A Musical Physiognomy* (originally published in 1971). For a useful discussion of Adorno's place in Mahler research, see Franklin, "' . . . His Fractures Are the Script of Truth.'"

Notes to Chapter 1

1 Easily the most indelicate articulation of the problem—and the indelicacy is noticeable even from the title, which is virtually an abstract—is Smith, "Song Is the Basic Element of the Vast Symphonic Structures Mahler Created" (1960): "The term 'song-symphonist' has been applied to composers other than Mahler, but in no case with equal justification. Indeed, if the symphonies, and symphonies so-

called, wherein the vocal element, in either of the two manifestations in which it is here considered, did not exist, there would be little left upon which a substantial reputation could be built. . . . We might easily infer that Mahler's mind was not of true symphonic cast" (p. 10). While Smith goes on to "explain" Mahler's practice in terms of Mahler's "very human" approach to composition, the typical tone of disparagement implicit in the way he and others set up such discussions is surely what provoked Donald Mitchell's claim that "Mahler never composed or attempted to compose [a song-symphony], despite the persistence with which this pernicious and misleading label was at one time affixed to his works" (Mitchell, *Gustav Mahler: The Wunderhorn Years,* p. 32).

2 Tibbe, *Über die Verwendung von Liedern und Liedelementen in instrumentalen Symphoniesätzen Gustav Mahlers* (1971), provides the most extensive discussion of Mahler's practice to date. While her study is undoubtedly more sophisticated than Smith's short essay "Mahler Quotes Mahler"(1954) or his longer "Song Is the Basic Element," both Tibbe and Smith are more concerned with identifying and characterizing what Mahler did than with attempting explanations grounded in musical experience. Typical of the apologists is Cooke, *Gustav Mahler,* pp. 3–18 ("Mahler as Man and Artist"): "But he redeemed any borrowings by imprinting his personality vividly on practically every note" (p. 13); and "Mahler's [symphonies] are like roomy, discursive volumes of autobiography. But though they are 'impure,' they are none the less essentially on the tragic plane" (p. 18).

3 Mahler's enthusiastic embrace of the *Wunderhorn* poems as his most frequent source for song texts during these years involves a curious historical disjuncture. Hoping to stimulate awareness of German *Volk* culture, Achim von Arnim and Clemens Brentano published *Des Knaben Wunderhorn* in two volumes between 1805 and 1808. Despite Goethe's strong endorsement of the collections, however, and his expressed hope that composers would provide new settings for the old folk poems, his challenge went largely unanswered by the mainstream of nineteenth-century *Lieder* composers, with only a few settings from Schumann (six), Mendelssohn (one), and Brahms (three) predating Mahler's. (Among more obscure contributions to the repertory, some settings by Carl Maria von Weber were probably known to Mahler, and perhaps also eight student settings by Hugo Wolf, now lost.) To be sure, the *Wunderhorn* collections exerted a considerable indirect impact on nineteenth-century music, as they established a point of reference for several generations of poets whose poems provided the foundation for the nineteenth-century *Lied* tradition. For general background about Mahler's settings of *Wunderhorn* poems, see Finson, "The Reception of Gustav Mahler's *Wunderhorn-Lieder*"; see also Hamburger, "Mahler and *Des Knaben Wunderhorn.*"

4 This striking change has been ascribed to a variety of rationales (beyond those to be newly offered here): his gradual disenchantment with programmatic explanations, the need for which was greatly encouraged by this practice; his move to Vienna, by which point his first four symphonies were all either complete or

planned; and the influence of Alma and her circle. For a useful discussion of these and other changes that divide Mahler's career around the turn of the century, see Schorske, "Gustav Mahler: Formation and Transformation."

5 As noted in Mitchell, *Gustav Mahler: The Wunderhorn Years,* pp. 62–64.

6 See Mitchell, *Gustav Mahler: The Wunderhorn Years,* pp. 217–224 for his account of this connection, which he was the first to notice. Mitchell makes the case that "Blumine" was simply borrowed from *Trompeter,* although this is largely conjecture. While apparently not a song movement in either of its settings, it is included here as an example because it represents in all other respects the kind of borrowing that is at issue here.

7 See, e.g., Wagner, *Das Kunstwerk der Zukunft* (1849), in which he chides latter-day symphonists for not realizing that, with Beethoven's Ninth, "the *last* symphony already *had been written*" ("die *letzte* Symphonie bereits *geschrieben sei*"). Carl Dahlhaus places Wagner's obituary notice for the symphony slightly later, stating that "in *Oper und Drama* (1851) Wagner pronounced the death of the symphony, viewing the post-Beethovenian efforts as a mere epilogue with nothing substantially new to say"(Dahlhaus, *Nineteenth-Century Music,* p. 265); it is in part 1 of *Oper und Drama* (Wagner VII) where he is most elaborate in his explanations for the failure of the symphony to appropriate the folk element successfully. The general issue of the problems Beethoven's Ninth caused later symphonists has often been taken up, notably and recently by Bonds, *After Beethoven;* see also chapters 2 and 6 of Knapp, *Brahms and the Challenge of the Symphony.*

8 See, e.g., Kramer, "The Harem Threshold."

9 See Dahlhaus, "The Natural World and the 'Folklike Tone.'" Dahlhaus finds "realism" in Mahler's use of folklike material to derive in large part from the very act of quotation (p. 110), and goes on to elaborate and partly challenge a structure of authenticity in folk music based on its being "not once-and-for-all finished, ... but ... in a constant state of becoming" (p. 112; Dahlhaus is here quoting the nineteenth-century sociologist (and anti-Semite) Wilhelm Heinrich Riehl, who had much to do with establishing the close association between German nationalism and nature (especially the forest). A useful discussion of the specific tradition for locating nature in folk materials, and the relationship of that tradition to Mahler, may be found in Monelle, *The Sense of Music* ("Mahler and Gustav," especially pp. 173–176); see also note 22 below.

10 See Solomon, "The Ninth Symphony: A Search for Order"; see also Wagner's arguments in part 1 of *Oper und Drama.*

11 While Mahler spent most of the years in which his first four symphonies were written outside of Vienna, Vienna remained at all times a musical mecca for him, from his childhood on. Moreover, both his involvement in politics and the mix of religious and philosophical speculations that led to his conversion to Catholicism can be well understood only in terms of the continuation of *influences* stemming from his student years in Vienna, especially involving the Wagner Society and the

intellectual circle that included Siegfried Lipiner, Victor Adler, and Engelbert Pernerstorfer. A useful and concise account of the latter associations may be found in Franklin, *The Life of Mahler,* especially chapter 2.

12 Cf. Draughon, "Mahler and the Music of *Fin-de-siècle* Identity," esp. chapter 3, "'As a Jew throughout the World': The Crisis of Religious Identity in the First Symphony"; see also Draughon and Knapp, "Mahler and the Crisis of Jewish Identity." Elizabeth Abbate provides another useful discussion in "Myth, Symbol, and Meaning in Mahler's Early Symphonies," pp. 31–36.

13 Adorno is perhaps most eloquent in describing this aspect of Mahler's music; thus, regarding the opening of the First Symphony (see below), he writes, "The tormenting pedal point . . . presupposes the official ideal of good instrumentation in order to reject it" (Adorno, *Mahler,* p. 15); and, similarly, "Mahler's atmosphere is the illusion of familiarity in which the Other is clothed" (p. 20).

14 Thus, Mitchell writes in *Gustav Mahler: The Wunderhorn Years*: "Mahler had an almost Ives-like capacity to incorporate sound-events into his music, taken, so to speak, 'from life,' though Mahler's ear was a good deal more discriminating (more traditional and orthodox, some might say) than that of his contemporary in the U.S.A. . . . There is no doubt, I think, that in a very interesting and novel way Mahler did enormously expand the scope of his music by a remarkable receptivity to sound-experiences and sound-stimuli, the context, location, and function of which were often remote from or even contrary to the sphere of 'pure' or traditional symphonic music" (pp. 169–170); and, later: "There are many different forms of musicalization, and if one of them is the capacity to discover in an instrument a musical character (or characteristic) that is dramatically opposed to its established character, then in this field, too, Mahler showed remarkable powers of clairvoyance" (p. 328). And, in Deryck Cooke's summation of Mahler's symphonic music: "Much of their quality is due, of course, to the amazing orchestration . . . [brief discursion] There is no point in trying to give an inventory of Mahler's orchestration, even if it were possible: it is his most admired feature, and it speaks for itself" (Cooke, *Mahler,* p. 14). Composers, especially, have also found much to admire in Mahler's orchestration; thus, Aaron Copland writes, in 1941: "Two facets of his musicianship were years in advance of their time. One was the curiously contrapuntal fabric of the musical texture; the other, more obvious, his strikingly original instrumentation. . . . Mahler's was the first orchestra to play *without pedal,* to borrow a phrase from piano techniques. . . . In Mahler's case, the timbre of the orchestra is, of course, entirely his own. His scores are full of orchestral *trouvailles.* The many years he spent as conductor of leading orchestral ensembles taught him how to manage with complete assurance unusual combinations of instruments, sudden unexpected juxtapositions of sonorities, or thinly scored passages of instruments playing far apart in the less likely registers—all such effects as are to be found again in the orchestral works of Schoenberg, of Honegger, or even of very recent composers like Shostakovich or the young Englishman Benjamin Britten" (*Our New Music,* pp. 32–34).

15 Bauer-Lechner, *Recollections of Gustav Mahler,* p. 131.

16 See Floros, *Gustav Mahler: The Symphonies,* pp. 25–26.

17 This seems to correspond well to Monelle's reading of this quotation (*The Sense of Music,* pp. 171 and 184–185); Monelle emphasizes also the childish crudity of Mahler's procedures and relates his use of topics to montage: "the topics seem to possess a rawness, as though they were meant to speak for themselves instead of becoming part of the composer's language" (184; cf. my discussion of montage in chapter 2, and of the autonomous dimension of musical quotation in chapter 6).

18 See, e.g., Mitchell's discussion of the introduction to the first movement of the First Symphony in *Gustav Mahler: The Wunderhorn Years,* pp. 212–217, where he details Mahler's struggles, as he conceives them, "to get this passage to sound exactly as he wanted it" (p. 217).

19 Bauer-Lechner, *Recollections,* pp. 30–31.

20 "My two symphonies contain the inner aspect of my whole life; I have written into them, with my own blood, everything that I have experienced and endured —Truth and Poetry in music" (Bauer-Lechner, *Recollections,* pp. 30, 231).

21 Regarding the Third Symphony: "It's the best and most mature of my works. With it, I shall conclude my 'Passion Trilogy'" (La Grange, *Mahler I,* p. 362).

22 Bauer-Lechner reports: "Referring to the three preceding symphonies, Mahler emphasized the close connection of the Fourth with these, to which it forms a conclusion. In their content and structure, the four of them form a perfectly self-contained tetralogy" (*Recollections,* p. 154).

23 Monelle makes a related point regarding the "subjectless utterance" of nature through folk materials, arguing for an "abdication of subjectivity" in Mahler's routine use of folklike and blandly generic material (*The Sense of Music,* pp. 173–176). Elsewhere, however, Monelle discusses the "projected subjectivity" of the German symphonic and *Lied* traditions in connection with Mahler (pp. 152–156) and delineates a variety of modes for Mahler's presentation of subjectivity (p. 178). As Monelle thus makes clear (and as my extended argument will also make clear, if somewhat differently), the rather schematic mapping of folklike to nature, with its potential for objectification, represents only a part—albeit a vital one—of Mahler's fondness for and deployment of these and other musical "found objects" (see also note 9 above).

24 Cf. Peter Franklin's observations regarding the opening movement of the Third Symphony: "Perhaps, nearly a century later, we are better able to deal with this extraordinary symphonic exposition because the juxtaposition of initially mysterious fragments of unconnected narratives, first tried in the equivalent introductory business of the Second Symphony's finale, has become a standard device of film-producers" (*Mahler: Symphony No. 3,* p. 84). See also Adorno's citation of the *Ländler* movement of the Ninth Symphony as the "first exemplary case of musical montage" (*Mahler,* p. 161), which he goes on to describe also in related pictorial terms, as "a collage picture made from deformed clichés" (p. 162).

1 Pudovkin recounts the experiment in "Types Instead of Actors," part of his highly influential *Film Technique* (published in Berlin, 1929; assembled and trans. from 1926 Russian pamphlets, now lost); see Pudovkin, *Film Technique and Film Acting*, pp. 168–169. The exact dating of the experiment is unclear, and the later proliferation of sometimes conflicting accounts of the experiment has further clouded the matter. Pudovkin claims participation, which would place the time in 1923 or later, when he joined Kuleshov's film workshop; on the other hand, Ekaterina Khokhlova suggests that the experiments took place in Spring 1921, and Ronald Levaco in 1918; the earlier dating is later corroborated by Kuleshov's own account of the experiment, given in Levaco's collection of his writings (see Kuleshov, *Selected Works*, p. 264; and *Kuleshov on Film*, pp. 7–8 and 200). In any case, related "experiments" were made over a period of some years within Kuleshov's group; in Pudovkin's *Chess Fever* (1925), e.g., publicity footage taken of the grand master Capablanca was incorporated into a romantic comedy, creating the impression that he played the pivotal role of reconciling the star-crossed lovers (see *Film Technique*, pp. 377–378).

2 Typically, this is put in terms of significant meaning being located exterior to the image, and thus to some extent independent of it, as a construct of creative juxtaposition; thus, in a fairly conventional formulation: "Montage creates a third meaning through the collision of two images. A meaning that is produced outside the image in point of fact" (Hayward, *Cinema Studies*, p. 97). For related discussions, see Levaco's introduction to *Kuleshov on Film*, pp. 7–8; and Fischer, "Film Editing," pp. 67–68.

3 See especially his 1929 essays "The Cinematographic Principle and the Ideogram," "A Dialectic Approach to Film Form," "The Filmic Fourth Dimension," and "Methods of Montage" (Eisenstein, *Film Form*, pp. 28–83). In the first of these essays, he dismisses Kuleshov's theorizing: "'Cemented together, these shots form montage. When this is done in an appropriate rhythm, *of course!* This, roughly, is what is taught by the old, old school of film-making, that sang: 'Screw by screw, Brick by brick.' Kuleshov, for example, even writes like a brick: 'If you have an idea-phrase, a particle of the story, a link in the whole dramatic chain, then that idea is to be expressed and accumulated from shot-ciphers, just like bricks.' 'The shot is an element of montage. Montage is an assembly of these elements.' This is a most pernicious make-shift analysis" (p. 36). Eisenstein cites a Russian source for the quotation from Kuleshov (*Iskusstvo Kino*, Leningrad, 1929); the passage may be found, in translation, on p. 91 of "The Art of Cinema," in *Kuleshov on Film*. Kuleshov also came to view his early theorizing as naive, mostly due to historical circumstance; see, e.g., his "The Principles of Montage" from 1935 (*Kuleshov on Film*, pp. 183–195), in which he cites Eisenstein with approval (p. 187).

4 Kuleshov is most explicit about political realities as a motivating force in his "Is Cinema an Art?" (introduction to "The Banner of Cinematography," written in 1920, reprinted in *Lev Kuleshov: Selected Works,* pp. 37–55); he later came to see his earlier arguments about montage from a more nuanced—and more balanced— perspective (see, e.g., "The Principles of Montage"). The association of montage with "art film" remains strong; see, e.g., Hayward, *Cinema Studies,* p. 96. See also Fischer's discussion of Rudolph Arnheim and his 1933 book *Film,* in "Film Editing," pp. 66 and 81n.

5 Bazin, "The Evolution of the Language of Cinema," in *What Is Cinema,* p. 25. Bazin's essay, a landmark discussion compiled from three articles written, in order of presentation, in 1952, 1955, and 1950, theorizes what he terms "image" and "reality" as governing two opposing trends of the silent era. The former trend, which depended on montage as its central technique, is best exemplified by D. W. Griffith and the Russian montage movement, while the latter, as revealed in the films of Erich von Stroheim, F. W. Murnau, and Robert Flaherty, is given to longer takes, a greater attention to lighting and framing, increased depth of focus, moving camera work, and greater attention to the setting of the scene. The French phrase for the last of these characteristics, *mise-en-scène,* has sometimes been used to identify this trend more generally, although Bazin uses it only once in his essay, in the narrow sense; while the phrase does not cover everything that goes into Bazin's concept of filmic realism, it does identify something vital to realism and scarcely acknowledged by montage theorists, and has thus provided a convenient binary opposition to montage for reductive accounts. Yet, significantly, Bazin does not discount montage entirely, but rather consigns it to a subordinate function in the sound era by identifying, in turn, its limitations, the incompatibility between many of its signal effects and spoken dialogue, and its enhanced power when used within a more realistic filmic landscape.

6 See Levaco's discussion in *Kuleshov on Film,* pp. 3–10.

7 Pudovkin, *Film Technique,* pp. 168–169.

8 The full history of his plans for the song is considerably more complicated even than this. Mahler completed the voice and piano version on 10 February 1892, and the orchestral version on 12 March 1892 (see Mitchell, *Gustav Mahler: The Wunderhorn Years,* p. 127). He then considered—and quickly rejected—the idea of using "Das himmlische Leben" as the finale of his Second Symphony, as well, although there were no directly resultant compositional consequences beyond 1) his readiness to fashion a heaven-based finale to the Second after he heard Klopstock's funeral ode at Hans von Bülow's funeral in 1894, 2) his continued preoccupation with the notion of using the song as a symphonic finale, and 3) a specific reinforcement for the general sense that the Third and Fourth Symphonies continued and then completed the general project begun by his first two symphonies. Regarding this earlier inspiration for the finale of the Second Symphony, see pp. 386–387 and 410 (n55) of Hefling, "Mahler: Symphonies 1–4"; Hefling here cor-

rects a long-standing misunderstanding perpetuated by La Grange (*Mahler I*, pp. 249–250). "Das himmlische Leben" opened the most extensive early presentation of Mahler's orchestral *Wunderhorn* songs to the public in Hamburg, 27 October 1893, with six of the songs being performed in groups of three, sung by Clementine Schuch-Prosska and Paul Bulss, respectively, in the first half of a program; the concert also included two concert overtures and two arias in the first half, and Mahler's First Symphony as the second half (see La Grange, *Mahler I*, p. 281). Aside from this event, the song would become known to the public only in its final setting, as the finale of the Fourth Symphony. A year earlier (December 1892), two orchestral *Wunderhorn* songs had been sung in Berlin, without Mahler's participation (La Grange, *Mahler I*, pp. 262–263). By summer of 1895, Mahler was thinking of using the song in his Third Symphony (La Grange, *Mahler I*, p. 809), but he cut it some time in 1896 (Mitchell, *Gustav Mahler: The Wunderhorn Years*, p. 317). He also once planned to include it as part of first published collection of *Wunderhorn* songs in 1900, where it was to come before (!) "Das irdische Leben," the last song in the set (Mitchell, *Gustav Mahler: The Wunderhorn Years*, p. 140). When he began the Fourth Symphony in 1899, it was with "Das himmlische Leben" already in mind (La Grange, *Mahler I*, pp. 581, 585, and 811). The most thoroughgoing attempt to consider the variety of contexts Mahler created for "Das himmlische Leben" may be found in Zychowicz, "Sketches and Drafts of Gustav Mahler, 1892–1901." In particular, he devotes considerable space to the song itself (chapter 4), its place in the Third Symphony and in relation to "Es sungen drei Engel" (chapter 5), and to minor changes made to the instrumental setting of the song (see especially pp. 385–389); some parallels to and divergences from specific discussions here are noted below, in passing.

9 For discussions of this ambiguity, see Bonds, "Ambivalent Elysium: Mahler's Fourth Symphony" (in *After Beethoven*, pp. 175–200) and chapter 7 (previously published as "Suffering Children: Perspectives on Innocence and Vulnerability in Mahler's Fourth Symphony"). A very different reading of the song, as wholly Nietzschean and unremittingly harsh in its satire of Christian beliefs, is offered by Elizabeth Abbate ("Myth, Symbol, and Meaning," pp. 177–188).

10 Mahler's decision to abandon his various titles for the movements of his Third Symphony came long after this movement was dropped.

11 Mahler himself admitted to Natalie Bauer-Lechner that he knew nothing of St. Ursula or her associated legends; nevertheless, he was sufficiently taken with the image of her smile in the final stanza that he claimed that the third movement of the Fourth Symphony, with its "divinely serene and deeply sad melody" that would cause Natalie to "both smile and weep," "bore the countenance of St. Ursula." Remarkably, he even found his ignorance of the saint to be valuable, claiming that "otherwise I would certainly not have been in a position, or in the mood, to make such a distinct and splendid portrait of her" (Bauer-Lechner, *Recollections*, pp. 152–153). The adroit manipulations of evocative Christian names and their associated sym-

bols in "Das himmlische Leben" come not from folkish processes of dissemination, but courtesy of Peter Sturm, an older contemporary of Arnim and Brentano (the compilers of *Des Knaben Wunderhorn*) who was obviously well versed in both the Scriptures and relevant folk idioms (see Hefling, "Mahler: Symphonies 1–4," pp. 386 and 411 n57; for further details regarding its possible provenance, see Zychowicz, *Mahler's Fourth Symphony*, pp. 37–38; and "Sketches and Drafts," pp. 106–108). Although this information about the *Wunderhorn* poem was published in 1894 (between Mahler's composition of the song and his subsequent work on the Second, Third, and Fourth Symphonies), Mahler never acknowledged the non-folk origins of the poem, either because he did not know or because he wished to preserve the illusion of a folk derivation. Mahler's musical engagement with the heavily symbolic text of the poem is considered below.

12 See Mitchell, *Gustav Mahler: The Wunderhorn Years*, pp. 138–139, regarding an early draft program for the Fourth Symphony, which includes "Das irdische Leben" as the second movement; see also Zychowicz, *Mahler's Fourth Symphony*, pp. 47–50.

13 In the poem as given in *Des Knaben Wunderhorn*, there are yet additional steps in the preparation of food (reproduced in the 1916 edition of Karl Bode, which also includes original or alternate versions of many other poems; 1:287–288).

14 The original *Wunderhorn* titles for "Das himmlische Leben" and "Das irdische Leben" were, respectively, "Der Himmel hängt voll Geigen" (Bode ed., 1:205) and "Verspätung" (1:287).

15 The divisions of the symphony given here are as given in the score. The programmatic titles given in parentheses here are Mahler's, although they changed somewhat over time and were in the end withdrawn; the most variable of these designations was that for the fourth movement (see note 36). A particularly useful account of the programmatic history of the Third Symphony may be found in Franklin, *Mahler: Symphony No. 3*.

16 This link to previous chorale-like symphonic themes, especially to Beethoven's Ninth and Brahms's First, may provide additional support for Mark Evan Bonds's somewhat unusual decision to use "Das himmlische Leben" as his Mahlerian exemplar in *After Beethoven*, rather than the perhaps more obvious finale of the Second Symphony.

17 See, however, the possibility raised by Filler that Mahler may have once thought to use "Das himmlische Leben" as the second movement ("Editorial Problems in Symphonies of Gustav Mahler" pp. 77–78); see also Zychowicz's discussion of this possibility in *Mahler's Fourth Symphony*, p. 41.

18 While the default "Petrus" here is clearly St. Peter, the penitent's identity is much less certain; while the former identity might ordinarily be taken as unambiguous, the doubt cast on that of the penitent invites us to notice, and perhaps read with greater nuance, the less obvious potential for doubt about "Petrus," as well.

19 See Floros's discussion of "My" Happy Science ("Mahler versus Nietzsche," in

Gustav Mahler: The Symphonies, pp. 91–92); Floros argues that, for Mahler, Nietzsche by himself proved inadequate. The finale of Mahler's Second Symphony, which bypasses even the last judgment traditionally mandated in Christian doctrine, in favor of infinite grace and universal redemption, may also provide a useful point of reverence here. Cf., however, Elizabeth Abbate's readings of both symphonies as fully in accord with Nietzsche ("Myth, Symbol, and Meaning," pp. 135–215); for Abbate, not only does Mahler's revision of Klopstock follow Nietzschean ideas, but also his settings of both "Es sungen drei Engel" and "Das himmlische Leben" put "forward a doctrine of heretical gaiety" (p. 177). See also McGrath, "The Metamusical Cosmos of Gustav Mahler"; he finds in the work (lying, in a sense, behind Nietzsche) an "ancient proto-tragedy" with an admixture of Wagner and Schopenhauer.

20 Also being mocked, perhaps, is the Jew who is left out of the joyful celebration, and whose perspective is represented by the Ten Commandments, which the penitent confesses to having violated; accordingly, the penitent is offered a specifically Christian redemption not available to Jews. The relevance to Mahler's own situation, a Jew who is "redeemed" through his conversion to Catholicism, is abundantly clear. While less overt here than in some *Wunderhorn* texts, the anti-Semitic thread that runs through much of German folk traditions may also be implicated in one of Mahler's most notorious folk references, to "Bruder Martin" in the First Symphony. Apparently, this song, which is identified consistently as "Bruder Martin" in the Mahler literature, also exists in a version closer in nomenclature to the "Frère Jacques" of the French version; as "Bruder Jacob," the song may be seen to mock the Jew who is left out of Christian festivities. Even "Bruder Martin" may have once had a similarly mocking context, targeting the Protestant (i.e., Martin Luther) who has renounced Catholic customs (i.e., Matins). For related discussions, see chapter 3 of Draughon, "Mahler and the Music of *Fin-de-siècle* Identity" ("'As a Jew throughout the World'"); and Draughon and Knapp, "Mahler and the Crisis of Jewish Identity."

21 Regarding heteroglossia (a plurality of voices; thus, novelistic polyphony), see Bakhtin, "Discourse in the Novel."

22 Mahler's explanation to an anonymous friend who "disapproved of the . . . 'Angels' movement on the grounds that the music was too slight after such solemnity" (reported in Bauer-Lechner, *Recollections,* p. 60) must be understood in these terms. Thus, Mahler goes on, "He didn't understand (and, incidentally, only the fewest of the few *can* grasp such a thing) how the humour here has to aim at such heights of expression where all other means fall short." As in the "forest" movement (discussed in chapter 4), Mahler presents a humorous heteroglossia, this time to be construed as the only possible gateway to joy from out of the more restrictive world of Nietzsche's poem. Cf. Franklin's account of the expressive shift between songs: "The elaborate artifice of the previous movement's song of individuated inwardness is now replaced by a public celebration—a musical

party to which everyone has been invited, from the local church choir to the village band. . . . Private agony may here be overcome in the religious practice of the social group" (Franklin, *Mahler: Symphony No. 3*, p. 70). But see also Elizabeth Abbate's virtual equation of Mahler's claim for "humor" with what she identifies as a purely cynical take on the *Wunderhorn* poem ("Myth, Symbol, and Meaning," pp. 188–189). Monelle, for his part, usefully extends the familiar trope of the Mahlerian symphonically reproduced "world" in his discussion of the juncture of these two movements (*The Sense of Music*, pp. 152–157); for Monelle, the reactive component is understood (in part) as the musical text's self-reflexity, mirroring the world by reproducing its paradoxical duality of being at once "inside" and "outside." Monelle's nuanced reading of both of these movements, and their relationship to the sixth movement, may usefully be compared to that given here and extended below; see also chapter 4.

23 Jesus is not directly represented except through narrative quotation—perhaps out of respect for the first of the Ten Commandments, which are referred to in the text.

24 Mahler's instructions in the score read: "The tone is to imitate the sound of a bell, the vowel to be struck briefly and the tone to be carried by humming the consonant <u>M</u>" (Der Ton ist dem Klang einer Glocke nachzuahmen, der Vocal kurz anzuschlagen und der Ton durch den Consonanten <u>M</u> summend auszuhalten.)

25 Zychowicz offers an intriguing symbolic explanation for the absence of violins in "Es sungen drei Engel," relating it to the original title of "Das himmlische Leben," which in *Des Knaben Wunderhorn* is given as "Der Himmel hängt voll Geigen" (Heaven is Full of Fiddles): "In the context of these two songs, if heaven is 'full of fiddles,' they would not be found in 'Es sungen drei Engel,' heaven being only a possibility in the latter" (Zychowicz, "Sketches and Drafts," p. 76). Since the "fiddles" in the *Wunderhorn* poem tend to undermine conventional notions of what heaven might be like, this seems somewhat of a stretch, although perhaps the long-standing association of the violin with the *diabolical,* which will figure into the "Freund Hein" movement of the Fourth Symphony, played a part in their absence here. See related discussions of "Der Himmel hängt voll Geigen" and of "Freund Hein" in chapter 7.

26 E.g., in his rebuke to his disciples, "Suffer the little children to come unto me, and forbid them not: for of such is the kingdom of God. Verily I say unto you, Whosoever shall not receive the kingdom of God as a little child, he shall not enter therein" (Mark 10: 14–15, King James Version).

27 See, however, Elizabeth Abbate, whose discussion of the poem details only the "John the Baptist" connection ("Myth, Symbol, and Meaning," p. 179), finding in the "we" of the poem a general indictment of human nature. Even without the traditional clarifying words "the Baptist" or any other textual reference to baptism, and even though all other names mentioned in the poem except "Herod" refer to saints, the proximity in the song between John and Herod arguably makes

"John the Baptist" the default association (see also Hefling, "Mahler: Symphonies 1–4," p. 399). Yet, surely, given the deft balancing of biblical learnedness and folk-like imprecisions throughout this manufactured folk lyric, the potential for confusion is a deliberately fostered one. Further, Mahler depends precisely on these folkish imprecisions to help establish the perspective of a child, who may be assumed to be supremely indifferent to the question of which particular John might be involved. While our reading of the song may legitimately parse the full range of possible associations, we must refrain from actually choosing absolutely among them (remembering, too, that Mahler himself confessed to not knowing precisely who Saint Ursula was, and felt it compositionally important not to enlighten himself in the matter; see note 11).

28   Without a secure link between the lamb and Jesus, who does not appear in "Das himmlische Leben," we must presume this to be St. John, especially given his proximity in the poem to both Peter and Luke, the first a fellow apostle, the second a fellow evangelist. The playful rhyming and repetition of "geduldig's" ("ein geduldig's, unschuldig's, geduldig's ein liebliches Lämmlein") is in the original *Wunderhorn* poem. While mapping the penitent's sin to the slaughtering (sacrifice?) of the lamb does hint at the network of meanings discussed in the previous paragraph, this possible interpretation has little other support and is flatly denied by the established playful tone, which can scarcely be overturned here, virtually at the end of the referential passage.

29   This sly verbal and musical resonance, in which "weinen" in one song lines up with "Wein" in the other, intersects with a network of oblique references in "Das himmlische Leben" to Jesus' sacrifice. Thus, the punning transmutation of tears into wine parallels the playful treatment of the lamb's slaughter heard just before and is reinforced in turn by the next line of the song, "die Englein, die backen das Brot." This completes the song's reference to the paired transmutations of the Eucharist, in which, following Jesus' directions when he prophesied his own death at the Last Supper, the sacrament of Communion reformulates the Jewish blessings of wine and bread by converting these elements into Jesus' blood and body.

30   Mahler himself described this funereal allusion as "Der kleine Appell," implicitly the more modest sibling of the "Der grosse Appell" ("the great calling of the roll") in the finale of the Second Symphony; see Bauer-Lechner, *Recollections,* p. 154. A facsimile page from the autograph manuscript of the Second Symphony, headed "Der grosse Apell [*sic*]," is given in Hefling, "Mahler: Symphonies 1–4," p. 388.

31   Mahler's sketches reveal that he had also at one point planned to incorporate musical detail directly referential to "Das himmlische Leben" in the first movement of the Third Symphony; see Zychowicz, *Mahler's Fourth Symphony,* pp. 43–45.

32   See Solomon, "The Ninth Symphony: A Search for Order."

33   These processes have received a great deal of attention; particularly useful discussions may be found in Solomon, "The Ninth Symphony: A Search for Order,"

and Kramer, "The Harem Threshold." Wagner was perhaps the first to note this aspect of the finale, which he chose to understand as a negotiation between music (as woman) and poet (as man); in his view, the series of "arrivals" might be broken down to the presentation of the melody, the "seduction" of the poet, who at first conforms to the contours of the melody, and the emergence of a more appropriately conceived relationship, when the melody follows the words more closely (beginning with "Seid umschlungen, Millionen!"); see Wagner, *Oper und Drama,* for a critique of the gendered aspect of Wagner's reading (see also Knapp, "On Reading Gender in Late Beethoven: *An die Freude* and *An die ferne Geliebte,*" forthcoming in *Acta musicologica*).

34 Regarding a recent separate performance of this movement, Mahler remarked in a letter to Richard Batka (Nov. 18, 1896), "Of course no one gets an inkling that this Nature includes all that is terrifying, great and also lovely. . . . I always feel it strange that when most people speak of "Nature" they think of flowers, little birds, the scent of the forest, etc. No one knows the god Dionysus, or the great Pan!" (*Gustav Mahler Briefe,* pp. 179–180; translation taken from Olsen, "Culture and the Creative Imagination," p. 196). And, according to Bauer-Lechner (*Recollections,* p. 52), Mahler concludes his account of the movement, "As you might imagine, the mood doesn't remain one of innocent, flower-like serenity, but suddenly becomes serious and oppressive. A stormy wind blows across the meadow and shakes the leaves and blossoms, which groan and whimper on their stems, as if imploring release into a higher realm."

35 Cf. Elizabeth Abbate's characterization of this opening as like "the distant rumbling toll of a deep bell," after which "the alto voice begins to toll with the bell sound" ("Myth, Symbol, and Meaning," p. 198). Mahler's later song "Um Mitternacht" (a 1901 setting of a text by Friedrich Rückert) also uses an oscillating figure as its central motive, as one of many elements it shares with "O Mensch! Gib Acht!," including vocal range and type (alto), subject matter, and pervasive use of darker timbres. In the later song, however, the textual referent for this oscillation is neither bells nor the voice of midnight, but rather the poet-singer's own heartbeat: "Um Mitternacht nahm Ich in Acht / Die Schläge meines Herzens; / Ein einz'ger Puls des Schmerzens / War angefacht um Mitternach" (At midnight I took heed of the beats of my heart; a single sorrowful pulse was aflame at midnight). This, too, resonates with the Nietzsche setting, not only in the phrase "nahm Ich in Acht," but also and more especially in its linking of internal trouble with the eternity of midnight. And, in both cases, Mahler chooses to follow the path toward consummated redemptive joy much further than the poem itself seems to suggest, as manifest in the ecstatic B major conclusion to "Um Mitternacht," and in the succeeding movements of the Third Symphony.

36 "Man" is always an alternative here, but displaces "Night" in the title in the later stages. See La Grange, *Mahler I,* pp. 798–799.

37 See Greene, *Mahler: Consciousness and Temporality,* pp. 168–170, for a somewhat different reading of the evolving dactylic chorale phrase, relating significant moments in movements 1, 5, and 6.

38 The diminution occurs sooner in Mahler's extension of the opening phrase than it does in the original folksong.

39 The song became an anthem of sorts for the *Leseverein der deutschen Studenten Wiens,* whose members (many of whom were to remain close associates of Mahler) "took to the streets in protest, singing . . . 'Wir hatten gebauet ein stattliches Haus'" in December 1878 after being closed down by the government (Franklin, *Mahler,* p. 40; Mahler is believed not to have been in Vienna at the time). See also McGrath, "Mahler and Freud: The Dream of the Stately House"; in connecting the Third Symphony to Freud, McGrath notes both the dream scenario of the work and the politicized text for the 1819 "Wir hatten gebauet ein stattliches Haus" (by August von Binzer, often called the *Burchenschaftlied* because it commemorated the dissolution by Metternich of the Deutsche Burchenschaft). McGrath finds Freud's associations with the song to have "a political dimension . . . even more significant than in the case of Mahler" (p. 48), yet as Franklin shows, a politicized reading for Mahler's use of the tune is eminently feasible and even mandated; see discussion below. The version of the song given in Example 8a is taken from Erk, *Deutscher Liederschatz;* see also Franklin, *Mahler: Symphony No. 3,* p. 82.

40 Bauer-Lechner, *Recollections,* p. 59.

41 See La Grange, *Mahler I,* pp. 808–809.

42 Cf. Moretti, *Modern Epic,* pp. 56–59. Moretti argues for an important difference between this kind of heteroglossia and the novelistic heteroglossia described by Bakhtin. After quoting Mahler's well-known use of the word "polyphony" to describe the cacophony produced by a number of mutually oblivious musical groups performing simultaneously in the same forest clearing—indeed, Mahler claimed this as the source for his own sense of polyphony—Moretti writes: "Instead of Bakhtin's dialogic polyphony, critical and intelligent, just an incredible din. Voices that talk and talk without paying any attention to one another" (p. 58). In an interpretation that will sound familiar to most Mahlerians, Moretti takes this type of heteroglossia, which he finds already operating in Goethe, as a device intended to "give the reader the impression of being truly in the presence of the world; [to] make the *text* look like the world—open, heterogeneous, incomplete" (p. 59). Yet, Moretti's distinction is often hard to enforce, at least in music, since a more "reasoned" heteroglossia has a tendency to collapse into what can scarcely be distinguished from poetic monologism; thus, in the allusive passage in Example 11a, the "dialogue" consists of four non-overlapping phrases that together may be understood as a single unified whole, a single musical idea worked out in "developing variation." This kind of collapse happens, indeed, at other key moments in the "Forest" movement of the Third Symphony (see below), and re-

lates to an important aspect, more generally, in Mahler's sometimes nervous dance around the issue of music's absoluteness, as will be discussed in the next chapter.

43 As noted, Mahler thus completes his slide through the gamut of Moretti-Bakhtin categories, moving from chaotic heteroglossia, through more rational heteroglossia, to poetic monologism.

44 See chapter 7.

45 See chapter 7.

46 Bonds (*After Beethoven*) provides by far the most extensive—and most useful—discussion of this dimension of the Fourth Symphony. Cf. also, Hefling ("Mahler: Symphonies 1–4), who notes that the third movement is "a double variation set (like the third movement of Beethoven's Ninth)" (p. 402; see also Hefling, "Variations *in nuce*").

47 But see Nowak, "Zur Deutung der Dritten und Vierten Sinfonie Gustav Mahlers," and Elizabeth Abbate, "Myth, Symbol, and Meaning," pp. 177–188.

48 The horns play a similar fatherly function near the end of the first movement; see my discussion in chapter 7. Additional ties between the third movement and "Das himmlische Leben" are cited in Hefling, "Mahler: Symphonies 1–4," p. 405. Of the latter, an anticipation of the song's phrase "Sankt Ursula selbst dazu lacht!" in mm. 69–71, in which the comforting swoops of the song are reconfigured as wrenching appoggiaturic plunges, is particularly telling, for it helps us make sense of Mahler's impressionistic description of St. Ursula's presence in the third movement as both "divinely serene and deeply sad" (see note 11).

49 See chapter 7.

50 Mahler remarked to Natalie Bauer-Lechner (*Recollections*, p. 152), "The Scherzo is so mystical, confused and uncanny that it will make your hair stand on end."

51 See Röhrich, "Himmel," pp. 717–718.

52 Thus, Adorno writes (*Mahler*, p. 56) concerning the opening of the symphony: "The bells in the first measure that very softly tinge the eighth notes in the flute have always shocked the normal listener, who feels he is being played for a fool. They really are fool's bells, which, without saying it, say: none of what you now hear is true."

53 Indeed, Mahler apparently planned even closer connections between the "Freund Hein" scherzo and "Das himmlische Leben," by incorporating thematic elements of the latter in the former; see Zychowicz, *Mahler's Fourth Symphony*, pp. 80–85.

54 This set of meanings attached to the word "fiddle," involving the notion of play (often with less than wholesome goals in mind), belongs to English usage, although it is little more than an extension of some Germanic associations, in which "to fiddle" means to play badly. Yet Elizabeth Abbate makes the association without apparent qualms: "'Der Himmel hängt voll Geigen' . . . implies a heaven full of fiddlers—irreverent dancemasters, or followers of the devil himself" ("Myth, Symbol, and Meaning," p. 178).

55 Regarding the known stages of revision to the song, see Zychowicz, *Mahler's*

Fourth Symphony, pp. 38–40 and 147–150; as he summarizes the situation: "While [Mahler] left the content of the song intact, he refined the details of the score to fit an evolving concept of the work" (40). In a literal sense, Mahler did change the piece when he reorchestrated it; even apart from setting material in different instruments or instrumental combinations, or introducing and removing doublings and other thickenings of texture, he also (for example) occasionally changed the articulation of the percussion and added a bar to extend the fermata that concludes the third and most elaborate chorale. But both main orchestral settings remain, fundamentally and fairly strictly, straightforward orchestral elaborations of his original *Lied*. Zychowicz seems to take Mahler at his word to the effect that Mahler's reorchestration was in the main to take advantage of the somewhat larger orchestra of the symphony (as reported by Bauer-Lechner; see Zychowicz, *Mahler's Fourth Symphony*, p. 147), yet also describes many instances in which he thinned out the texture (p. 148). One way to reconcile this disparity is to note *where* Mahler actually does enhance the orchestra's presence, that is, during the orchestral interludes that (in the symphony, at least) recall the opening movement; by thinning the orchestra at other times, he not only makes this central enhancement all the more telling, but also thereby helps to enforce his admonition that the orchestra should not overpower the soloist (see Zychowicz, *Mahler's Fourth Symphony*, pp. 149–150).

Notes to Chapter 3

1 *Sybil* originally aired on television in a 198-minute, two-part version, winning an Emmy for its leading actress (Sally Field) and receiving nominations for several other awards; it has since been released as a 132-minute video, which is my source for the observations that follow. Based on the controversial book by Flora Rheta Schreiber, the film version of *Sybil* was made in consultation with Dr. Cornelia Wilbur, Sybil's psychiatrist, sympathetically portrayed on screen by Joanne Woodward. The basic premise of the book, which details a case of Multiple Personality Disorder (MPD) and its successful treatment, has been both discredited and fervently defended; detractors cite the unscholarly forum, the sensationalist manner of presentation, the reported behavior of the psychiatrist (which may have encouraged the kind of abnormal behavior associated with MPD), and the suspect theoretical basis for the disorder itself. For a discussion of MPD both as a complex psychological state and as a historically situated explanation and diagnosis, see Ian Hacking, *Rewriting the Soul: Multiple Personality and the Sciences of Memory*; Hacking identifies *Sybil* as the key text in starting the movement (pp. 41–43), in part because American culture was at that historical moment able and willing to deal with the fraught topic of sexual abuse of children. On the other hand, Joan Acocella has interpreted the multiple personality movement in primarily political terms, and argued for an antifeminist basis; see her *Creating Hysteria:*

Women and Multiple Personality Disorder, especially pp. 133–149. The standard text-book on MPD is Frank Putnam's *Diagnosis and Treatment of Multiple Personality Disorder;* in tracing its history from the nineteenth century, he notes a decline in interest between 1920 and 1970, and credits *Sybil* for "reintroducing the public and mental heath professions to the syndrome of multiple personality" (p. 35). But we are here concerned primarily with the role of music within the filmed version of the story (where it is both more immediate in effect and dramatically more central than in the book), not with issues of psychological credibility related to MPD. Leonard Rosenman is given credit for the music in the film; probably, however, many of the effects discussed here, which involve preexisting music, should be credited to Ken Runyon, the film's music editor.

2 For readers of the book, the content of this scene will not shock, since it is, if anything, more oblique than the more clinical descriptions given in the book (Schreiber, *Sybil,* pp. 211–212, recalled p. 342); nevertheless, the filmed scene is clearly meant to disturb more profoundly, as it is set up to be a dramatic, revelatory climax and gives an overpowering presence to the music itself (something the book cannot do). Moreover, our knowledge of the book deepens our horror, since we know (from the book, not the film) that her mother could not abide incomplete performances of musical works: "It was heresy and a violation of her code to play the fourth movement of a symphony, for instance, without having preceded it by movements one through three" (p. 212). Knowledgeable viewers will thus realize, when hearing the opening bars of Dvořák's finale, that they are witnessing in this mercifully brief moment a mere fragment of an extended sequence of torture, within a ritual that was often repeated. Readers of the book will also note some critical differences between this scene and what Schreiber describes: it seems unlikely that her mother would speak to Sybil during the music, nor would a Dvořák symphony be a likely choice for her, since symphonic transcriptions would have been an atypical repertory for a trained pianist who apparently preferred Chopin and Beethoven. (Dvořák is not mentioned in the book; the above quotation about symphonic movements refers to phonograph records, which had by Sybil's childhood largely displaced piano transcriptions in providing home access to symphonic music.) Yet, in the context of the film these differences make eminent sense. What the mother is saying is mostly for our benefit, an economical means to convey what is going on in the scene without disturbing overmuch the central features of her tormenting behavior: her monstrous indifference to her daughter's agony, and the manner in which she embodies that indifference musically. And, although seemingly inconsistent, the choice of Dvořák's *New World* Symphony is an inspired one, not only because of its expressive profile, but also because the passage will be easily—even if subliminally—recognized as a relatively late moment within a massive work, yet with a substantial span of music still to come.

3 The most familiar example of this trope, often used parodistically, is the oblivious

spectre playing Bach's D minor Toccata and Fugue at the organ, an almost obligatory aural presence in a purportedly haunted house.

4 Hence the explanation "Vicky" provides (in the book) for the fear "Peggy Lou" exhibits for music: "Music hurts. . . . It hurts way inside because it is beautiful, and it makes both Sybil and Peggy Lou sad. They're sad because they're alone and nobody cares. When they hear music, they feel more alone than ever" (Schreiber, *Sybil,* p. 112; "Vicky" and "Peggy Lou" are among the most active of the identities coexisting within the adult Sybil). Yet, given the panic that seizes Sybil as we see her experience this kind of music—indeed, she appears to be physically brutalized by it, her appearance transformed into that of a cringing child—the operative aesthetic category for the oppressive capacity of music in the film is neither the sad nor the beautiful, but the sublime.

5 See La Grange, *Mahler I,* pp. 273, 275, and 774.

6 See Floros, *Gustav Mahler: The Symphonies,* pp. 82–107.

7 In Mahler's explanation for the song (given below), he identifies this grotesquerie as the voice of the preacher as heard by the fish.

8 For a useful summary of this mode of understanding the movement, see Carolyn Abbate, *Unsung Voices,* p. 126, in the chapter titled "Mahler's Deafness: Opera and the Scene of Narration in *Todtenfeier.*" Abbate's own provocative engagement with the program for Mahler's scherzo will be discussed below. Some who do not take Mahler's program literally nevertheless hear a more prominent dance topic in the movement than would otherwise be warranted; see, e.g., Cooke, who notes both a "quicker type of Ländler" and a "fast waltz-tempo" for the scherzo, which he terms a "futile dance of life" while arguing as well that Mahler's program "resolves itself into a symbolic description of a psychological mood-sequence" (*Mahler,* pp. 56–57).

9 Bauer-Lechner, *Recollections,* pp. 32–33. The German reads: "In der 'Fischpredigt' dagegen herrscht . . . ein etwas süßaurer Humor. Der heilige Antonius predigt den Fischen, und seine Worte verwandeln sich sofort in ihre Sprache, die ganz besoffen, taumelig (in der Klarinette) erklingt, und alles kommt daher geschwommen. Ist das ein schillerndes Gewimmel: die Aale und Karpfen und die spitzgoscheten Hechte, deren dumme Gesichter, wie sie an den steifen, unbeweglichen Hälsen im Wasser zu Antonius hinaufschauen, ich bei meinen Tönen wahrhaftig zu sehen glaubte, daß ich laut lachen mußte. . . . Und wie die Versammlung dann, da die Predigt aus ist, nach allen Seiten davon schwimmt: 'Die Predigt hat g'fallen, / Sie bleiben wie alle'—und nicht um ein Jota klüger geworden ist, obwohl der Heilige ihnen aufgespielt hat!—Die Satire auf das Menschenvolk darin werden mir aber die wenigsten verstehen"; see Bauer-Lechner, *Gustav Mahler in den Erinnerungen,* p. 28.

10 La Grange, *Mahler I,* p. 883, n53; Böcklin was a particular favorite of Mahler's (see chapter 7).

11 Böcklin himself laughingly explained that his models were not specific fish but a church congregation; see Christ, *Arnold Böcklin, 1827–1901*, p. 215.

12 Mahler's Second Symphony, completed in the summer of 1894, was premiered in its entirety in late 1895, although an incomplete performance had been essayed earlier in the year in Berlin (including the scherzo, but not the last two movements, which require vocal forces as well as instrumental). Before even this earlier performance, Mahler had conducted Bruckner's Fourth Symphony during the subscription concerts in Hamburg (February 1895), his first time conducting a Bruckner symphony (although Mahler had by then conducted both his Te Deum and Mass No. 1 in D Minor); later performances of Bruckner's Fourth by Mahler included a performance in Vienna with cuts to the second and fourth movements (January 1900) and a performance of the scherzo in Paris (June 1900). By 1900, however, he apparently thought considerably less of the work, terming it "musical junk," albeit with "divine ideas and themes" (to be sure, Mahler's view of Bruckner had long been divided along these lines). For accounts of these various performances, see La Grange, *Mahler I*, pp. 319–322, 344–345, 555, and 576.

13 Context makes this modulation somewhat less exotic. The G♭ major Trio is a ♭VI "escape" from the scherzo's B♭, so that the modulation is a reversion to the overall tonic, albeit unexpectedly abrupt.

14 Mahler also quotes "Ablösung im Sommer" in his next two symphonies, most extensively and obviously in the scherzo of the Third Symphony (see below), but also near the end of the first movement of the Fourth, where its brief appearance is, as here, absorbed into established "motion" figures (see chapter 7).

15 For a descriptive/interpretive account of Berio's adaptation, see Osmond-Smith, *Playing on Words*; see also note 40 below.

16 Carolyn Abbate, *Unsung Voices*, pp. 119–155.

17 This possible model is discussed at some length by Stephen Hefling in "Mahler's 'Todtenfeier' and the Problem of Program Music," to whom Abbate responds in her essay. Mahler's earlier title—"Todtenfeier"—for what was to become the first movement of the Second Symphony represents a more overt allusion to Mickiewicz's epic poem *Dziady* (in German, *Todtenfeier*).

18 See Wagner, *Oper und Drama*. As Dahlhaus notes, it was Wagner who first applied the term "absolute" to music in this sense, and quite pejoratively, although he later had an unacknowledged change of heart; see Dahlhaus, "The Twofold Truth in Wagner's Aesthetics: Nietzsche's Fragment 'On Music and Words.'"

19 Carolyn Abbate's emphasis provides considerably more dramatic expression than would seem to be demanded by a simple highlighting of a passage she wishes to draw attention to for the sake of discussion, since simple highlighting would have included the entire phrase (or at least the subject of the phrase, "you") and would thus have read much less like the "undisguised terror" of a composer obsessed with deafness, which is how Abbate wishes to construe Mahler (cf. the passage

without this emphasis, given below). Context, too, serves to overemphasize this element in Mahler's explanation, since Abbate, in a literary version of the Kuleshov effect, juxtaposes Mahler's note with Wagner's discussion of Beethoven's deafness, given just before. A consideration of obvious alternatives to Abbate's choice of emphasis—whether "*from such a distance that you can't hear the music they dance to!*" or "from such a distance that *you can't hear the music they dance to!*"—reveals the degree of distortion she introduces with her application of a supposedly neutral scholarly convention (Abbate, *Unsung Voices,* p. 124; we may also note, in passing, how ill-suited Mahler's second explanation is to Abbate's purposes, even though he uses the same example: "When one watches a dance from a distance, without hearing the music, the revolving motions of the partners seem absurd and pointless.").

20 Carolyn Abbate, *Unsung Voices,* p. 124, emphasis removed and original emphasis restored. The German reads: "Wenn Sie dann aus diesem wehmütigen Traum auf-wachen, und in das wirre Leben zurückmüssen, so kann es Ihnen leicht gesche-hen, daß Ihnen dieses unaufhörlich bewegte, nie ruhende, nie verständliche Ge-triebe des Lebens *grauenhaft* wird, wie das Gewoge tanzender Gestalten in einem helle erleuchteten Ballsaal, in den Sie aus dunkler Nacht hineinblicken—aus so weiter *Entfernung,* daß Sie die *Musik* hierzu *nicht* mehr hören! *Sinnlos* wird Ihnen da das Leben, und ein grauenhafter Spuk, aus dem Sie vielleicht mit einem Schrei des Ekels auffahren!"; see *Gustav Mahler Briefe,* p. 150.

21 La Grange, *Mahler I,* pp. 784–785. The German reads: "Der zweite und dritte Satz, Andante und Scherzo, sind Episoden aus dem Leben des gefallenen Helden. Das Andante enthält die Liebe. Das im Scherzo Ausgedrückte kann ich nur so ve-ranschaulichen: Wenn du aus der Ferne durch ein Fenster einem Tanze zusiehst, ohne daß du die Musik dazu hörst, so erscheint dir Drehung und Bewegung der Paare wirr und sinnlos, da dir der Rhythmus als Schlüssel fehlt. So mußt du dir denken, daß einem, der sich und sein Glück verloren hat, die Welt wie im Hohl-spiegel, verkehrt und wahnsinnig erscheint.—Mit dem furchtbaren Aufschrei der so gemarterten Seele endet das Scherzo"; see Bauer-Lechner, *Erinnerungen,* p. 40.

22 La Grange, *Mahler I,* p. 785. The German reads: "Der Geist des Unglaubens, der Verneinung hat sich seiner bemächtigt, er blickt in das Gewühl der Erscheinun-gen und verliert mit dem reinen Kindersinn den festen Halt, den allein die Liebe gibt; er verzweifelt an sich und Gott. Die Welt und das Leben wird ihm zum wirren Spuk; der Ekel vor allem Sein und Werden packt ihn mit eiserner Faust und jagt ihn bis zum Aufschrei der Verzweiflung"; see Alma Mahler, *Gustav Mah-ler: Erinnerungen und Briefe,* p. 262.

23 This "sad dream" is more in the nature of a pleasant reverie and remembrance, and becomes sad only because it no longer reflects reality; thus, Mahler writes, in the passage immediately preceding the first of these quotations: "The second and third movements are conceived as an interlude; the second, a memory! A ray of sun, clear and untroubled, from the hero's life. I am sure you have experienced

this while you were carrying to his grave someone who was near to your heart; perhaps on the way back there suddenly appeared the image of an hour of happiness long passed, which lit up your soul and which no shadow can spoil. One practically forgets what has happened! That is the second movement!" (La Grange, *Mahler I*, p. 784). Mahler's 1901 program more explicitly traces the transmutation of happy memory into sadness in the second movement: "Andante. A blissful moment in the dear departed's life and a sad recollection of his youth and lost innocence" (p. 785).

24 Mahler's reported dissatisfaction with the second movement notwithstanding (see La Grange, *Mahler I*, p. 783), the andante is thus critical to the setting for this movement.

25 In the most extensive recent explication of this movement, by Elizabeth Abbate ("Myth, Symbol, and Meaning," pp. 118–131), the more conventional reading of the "Fischpredigt" as mocking only the fish and not the preacher is extended to find a specific, private motivation for Mahler's scherzo, in which he is "striking back at those who were preventing him from practicing his art" (p. 130), so that the "'Fischpredigt' movement itself is an expression of Mahler's will to actively bring about change in his society" (p. 131). Intriguing as this reading is, it seems, oddly, to be at once too narrow an understanding of the movement's conflict and an extrapolation of a broader situation from what actually occurs in the movement, where the subjective element is depicted as powerless to effect worldly change.

26 Zenck, in "Technik und Gehalt im Scherzo von Mahlers Zweiter Symphonie," argues that some sections of Mahler's scherzo deliberately evoke a "high art" dimension when he moves beyond the original song. Thus, regarding the second broad section as she analyzes the music (mm. 190–211): "aufgreifende und stilisierende artifizielle Musik: die autonome, da ausgesprochen instrumentale Musik der Kunst-Sphäre" (taking up and stylizing music artificially: there expressing autonomous, instrumental music of the art sphere; p. 182). Zenck breaks apart the topic I am proposing into two differently alienating processes, the grotesqueries of the original song, now without its text, and the abstract musical processes that extend and develop its material. Yet, as I argue, the separation is more seamless than this, as Mahler introduces process from the beginning. Also, it is important to note that my references to a "popular" and "classical" opposition are specifically to a later development, and that Mahler's procedures are all grounded in a "high art" tradition, however characteristically they draw upon "lower" musics.

27 This is a complicated issue, of course, since many concerns, sometimes conflicting, might inform the decision of what music is chosen. Thus, for example, a particular choice might reflect the decision-makers' own tastes, a desire to entertain the movie audience, or to create a resonance between the chosen music and other elements in the film. Depending on the effect desired, filmmakers may also choose music according to its position along a projected continuum of audience familiarity.

28 A brief account of the genesis and recording of "Eleanor Rigby" may be found in Dowlding, *Beatlesongs,* pp. 133–136; purportedly, in this account, the string accompaniment was inspired by Paul McCartney's listening to Vivaldi. More likely, given his continued contributions along these lines, is that the track was entirely the work of George Martin. According to Bill Harry, Martin "said he was inspired by the work of Bernard Herrmann, particularly his scoring of *Fahrenheit 451*"; see Harry, *The Ultimate Beatles Encyclopedia,* p. 217. An account of the recording session itself (which lasted nine hours) may be found in Lewisohn, *The Complete Beatles Chronicle,* p. 196.

29 Nor was I thinking of this parallel when I first thought of "Eleanor Rigby" in connection with the scherzo; indeed most of the above descriptive account was written before I realized the overlap in subject matter.

30 Actually, the figure is a four-note chromatic descent, but creates the effect of a full chromatic tetrachord through its combination with a pedal a seventh below. Thus, as transcribed in Lennon et al., *The Beatles Complete Scores,* pp. 243–246, the figure descends twice from D to B (mm. 19–26) over a pedal E.

31 See, among others, Allanbrook, *Rhythmic Gesture in Mozart*; McClary, "Narratives of Bourgeois Subjectivity in Mozart's 'Prague' Symphony"; and Zaslaw, *Mozart's Symphonies.*

32 A particularly useful discussion of this issue, as it evolves in Wagner's formulation and through his later tacit acceptance of the legitimacy of absolute music, may be found in Dahlhaus, "The Twofold Truth in Wagner's Aesthetics."

33 Hanslick, *On the Musically Beautiful*; Hanslick did not, however, use the term "absolute music."

34 That the close identification of high musical culture and German instrumental music was the result of a deliberate strategy during the generation following Beethoven, has been persuasively argued by Sanna Pederson; see, e.g., her "A. B. Marx, Berlin Concert Life, and German National Identity," Celia Applegate has challenged this view, positing a less central role for nationalism in the elevation of music, without, however, denying the place Marx and others claimed for "serious" music within the context of a developing German nationalism, nor arguing effectively against either the gravity of the consequences nor the often pernicious tenacity of this coupling; see Applegate, "How German Is It? Nationalism and the Idea of Serious Music in the Early Nineteenth Century."

35 Mahler had once planned a somewhat longer introduction for the scherzo, for two timpanists (given and discussed in Mitchell, *Gustav Mahler: The Wunderhorn Years,* pp. 427–429), which does much to clarify the deliberateness of his procedures of derivation. Ironically, however, the degree to which this alternative focuses on motivic derivation would have undercut considerably the connection to the previous movement, so that the final version may be seen to represent an effectively balanced compromise between the two.

36 One may note, in this regard, Floros's avoidance of the designation "trio" in his dis-

cussion of this movement as articulating a five-part structure (Floros, *Gustav Mahler: The Symphonies*, pp. 63–65), and La Grange's rather confused presentation of a three-part structure (scherzo-trio-scherzo; La Grange, *Mahler I*, pp. 788–789).

37 Exceptions may be found, as for example in the scherzo of his final quartet, op. 135—which, if not actually threatening, becomes at least darkly comic in its sustained climactic eruption.

38 In his Ninth Symphony, Beethoven works an equally prominent fugal element to much different ends. The scherzo presents almost as a stylized version of Mahler's "Fischpredigt," opening with an oppressive, marchlike fugue and yielding to a song-based pastoral trio; despite this outer resemblance, however, one may more plausibly hear heroic subjectivity in the fugue, and find in the trio a vision of the future rather than an escape to the past, especially given its overt melodic derivation from the *Freudenthema* of the finale (see Solomon, "The Ninth Symphony: A Search for Order"). The position of the fugue within the finale makes a similar reading of heroic subjectivity seemingly mandatory; thus, it grows out of the "call to arms" of the Janissary episode, serves as a referential marker for both development generally and the second movement in particular (see Treitler, "History, Criticism, and Beethoven's Ninth Symphony"), and leads to the climactic variation of the *Freudenthema,* the most fully realized version of what was foreshadowed in the pastoral trio.

39 Thus, Floros terms it a "perpetuum mobile" (*Gustav Mahler: The Symphonies,* p. 63), and Cooke a "moto perpetuo" (Cooke, *Mahler,* pp. 57–58).

40 This capacity of the absolute-music topic to generate an absorbing flow of music, so that individualizing gestures might occasionally "surface" but with no lasting autonomy, seems precisely the quality Berio sought and found in Mahler's scherzo: "The third part of *Sinfonia* . . . is a tribute to Gustav Mahler (whose work seems to carry all the weight of the last two centuries of musical history) and, in particular, to the third movement of his *Second Symphony* ("Resurrection"). . . . This movement is treated as a generative source, from which are derived a great number of musical figures ranging from Bach to Schönberg, Brahms to Stravinsky, Berg to Webern, Boulez, Pousseur, myself and others. The various musical characters, constantly integrated in the flow of Mahler's discourse, are combined together and transformed as they go" (Berio, liner notes to *Sinfonia*).

41 The precise status of this intervening section is ambiguous, as it belongs fully to neither scherzo nor trio. La Grange starts the trio with the shift to C major at the beginning of the second fugal episode, a division followed by Floros, who avoids calling the second part a trio. While this division makes sense from a technical perspective, since this is the point when direct quotations from "Fischpredigt" cease, the narrative of the movement unfolds much more incrementally, with a full arrival at trio-like remove from the scherzo occurring only with the E major trumpet melody beginning at r40.

42 The nostalgia in this passage may well have had a personal dimension for Mahler,

if we accept Zychowicz's quite plausible speculation that the trio pays homage to Hans Rott's Symphony in E Major of 1880. Rott was a slightly older composer (b. 1858) known to Mahler in his student years, whose bouts with insanity and tragic death in 1882 Mahler believed to have been caused by his rejection by Brahms and the Viennese critical establishment. Since Mahler, too, had had bitter disappointments of this kind (most famously, the earlier rejection of *Das klagende Lied* by a committee on which Brahms sat, and Hans von Bülow's more recent rejection of the *Todtenfeier* movement of the Second Symphony), the movement's scenario of alienation may be mapped fairly easily to either composer's experiences of despairing rejection; or it may be read, more complexly, as Mahler recalling Rott's tragedy so as to underscore its parallels to his own circumstances, but managing Rott's (and his own) despair through aesthetic sublimation and a larger narrative of redemption. The association underscores several ironies, since Brahms and von Bülow had long since become staunch advocates of Mahler, paving his way to the directorship in Vienna; moreover, von Bülow's funeral famously provided Mahler with the inspirational source for his finale to the work whose first movement von Bülow had rejected, and it was on the basis of the Second Symphony (published before the First), with its brief homage to the rejected Rott, that Brahms proclaimed Mahler "the true revolutionary" (a comment as significant for its dismissal of Richard Strauss as for its somewhat oblique praise for Mahler). Zychowicz's discussion ("Mahler's Motives and Motivation in His 'Resurrection' Symphony") has not been published; I base my comments on the brief discussion in Palmer, "Program and Process in the Second Symphony of Gustav Mahler," p. 124n.

43 See Hefling, "Mahler's 'Todtenfeier' and the Problem of Program Music." On the general question of the relationship between the personae/subjectivities projected in Mahler's symphonies and Mahler himself, see Monelle, *The Sense of Music,* especially the discussion of "Urlicht" that concludes "Mahler and Gustav" (186–195).

44 Mahler's reaction upon seeing the Jewish quarter in New York, as reported by Alma (Alma Mahler, *Memories and Letters,* p. 162): "'I can hardly believe that these are my brothers.' . . . He shook his head in despair. With a sigh of relief we at last turned a corner and found ourselves in a well-lighted street among our own sort of people." This account is undoubtedly colored by Alma's own anti-Semitism, although the possibility that it is merely a projection of hers seems unlikely. For more on Mahler's ambivalent denial of his Jewish heritage, see Draughon and Knapp, "Mahler and the Crisis of Jewish Identity."

Notes to Chapter 4

1 Respectively, "Man lies in deepest need! Man lies in deepest pain!" and "Deep is your [man's] woe! Deep is your woe!" Significantly, the Nietzsche lines that

Mahler chooses for the Third Symphony may be read as a deepened, more intense and rarefied version of "Urlicht" in the Second. Thus, in its apparent binary opposition of pain and joy (which is highlighted in Mahler's setting, "O Mensch! Gib Acht!," as noted) stands somewhat apart from the Nietzschean construct, derived from Schopenhauer, of willed pain leading to joy. On the other hand, Mahler's setting also remains true to Nietzsche in that "pain" seems to evolve—or attempt to evolve—into joy, an effect that derives in part from Mahler's maintaining through organic musical processes a monologic poetic perspective; thus, Nietzsche's joy, as set by Mahler, has a much different aspect from the joy offered in the following movement, as discussed in chapter 2. The parallel noted here between "Urlicht" and "O Mensch! Gib Acht!" engages with only one dimension of Mahler's setting, which implicitly preserves as well the Nietzschean alliance between pain and joy. An engaging but quite different accounting of these two movements and their relationship to each other may be found in Monelle, *The Sense of Music*, pp. 152–157, 186–195.

2 Respectively, "Dear God will grant me a little light, to light my way to eternal blessed life!" and "But all joy desires eternity! / Desires deep, deep eternity."

3 For another detailing of parallels between Beethoven's Ninth and Mahler's Third, see Hefling, "Mahler: Symphonies 1–4," p. 289. For a comparison of Mahler's programs for his Second and Wagner's program for Beethoven's Ninth (paying particular attention to the parallel use of instrumental outcries), see Palmer, "Program and Process in the Second Symphony," pp. 67–73.

4 It is probably in order to maintain this pattern—and also, perhaps, to project an archaic tone—that Mahler adds "e" to the end of Tod.

5 Peter Franklin hears cynical irony in these occluded gestures of mourning: "The cuckoo's fate inspires a grotesque little minor-key dance with a dry, wry vocal line, whose caricatured weeping on the thrice-repeated word 'willow' suggests that the singer's sad face is ironically painted on, like a clown's" (Franklin, *Mahler: Symphony No. 3*, p. 60).

6. Text as given in Bode's edition; see Arnim and Brentano, *Des Knaben Wunderhorn* (1916), 2:300.

7 Regarding the latter, the score reads: "Von [the indicated phrase] kann die Gesangsstimme eventuell nach Bedürfniss des Sängers weggelassen werden."

8 This is, in fact, the only time in the song that "Kukuk" is set directly to the characteristic "cuckoo" motive, which may be rendered variously as a falling third (major or minor) or fourth; all other instances involve simple narration and are set to a simple repeated-note figure. Although the word "Kukuk" is set to repeated triplet eighth notes in its final appearance, the piano underlay reproduces all three typical settings for the cry: falling minor and major thirds in the left hand, and a falling fourth in the right hand, as part of the head motive.

9 Another interpretation, offered by Elizabeth Abbate, is that "the cuckoo is unaffectedly announcing its own death, rather like cartoon commercials for beef

products featuring a smiling or dancing steer praising the merits of eating beef" ("Myth, Symbol, and Meaning," p. 204).

10 The longer version of the poem, which Arnim and Brentano apparently shortened, is given in the 1874 edition of *Des Knaben Wunderhorn*, ed. Birlinger and Crecelius, 1:382–383.

11 The original poem concludes with a moralistic verse warning young women not to get "caught."

12 See my discussion in "A Tale of Two Symphonies"; see also Jander, "The Prophetic Conversation in Beethoven's 'Scene by the Brook.'"

13 The trio in the Second Symphony also involves a semblance of nostalgic song, but more socially oriented (and thus less absolute; see below), more generically rendered, more obviously a locus for sympathetic subjectivity (in contrast to the scherzo), and ultimately less poignant.

14 From Lenau, "Der Postillion," in *Poems and Letters of Nikolaus Lenau*, pp. 108–113 (translation emended).

15 Floros, *Gustav Mahler: The Symphonies*, p. 102; cf. discussion in Elizabeth Abatte, "Myth, Symbol, and Meaning," pp. 15–16.

16 See, however, Greene's discussion of this movement (*Mahler: Consciousness and Temporality*, pp. 188–190), in which he reads this contrast in terms of the impingement of the future rather than the past on the music that represents a human presence, opposed to the eternal present of the animals in the scherzo proper.

17 Franklin convincingly connects this distinction in temporal sense to "Schopenhauer's belief that animals 'peacefully and serenely enjoy every present moment . . . the life of the animal is a continual present . . . in contrast to the conduct of human beings which is withdrawn from the innocence of nature by the first appearance of the faculty of reason,'" concluding that "the threat that man (in Mahler's description) represents to the life of the animals is not only physical; his consciousness of mortality will destroy their world of 'eternal present.'" (Franklin, *Mahler: Symphony No. 3*, p. 64; quoting from Schopenhauer, *The World as Will and Representation*, 2:61).

18 Contributing as well to this opening up of the end of the song is Mahler's reconfiguration of the original vocal close: now absent are the cadential alternations between tonic and dominant ("und wenn der Kukuk zu Ende ist"; corresponding to r3.5–6), so that the stage is all the emptier for the tutti to come.

19 Cf. Elizabeth Abbate ("Myth, Symbol, and Meaning," pp. 15–16), who understands the horn choir to be the echo of the postilion referred to later in Lenau's poem, taken as his comrade's response from beyond the grave ("Und des Hornes heller Ton / Klang vom Berge wider, / Ob der tote Postillion / Stimmt' in seine Lieder." [And the horn's bright tone echoed from the mountains, as if the dead postilion joined in his *Lieder*.]). As an echo, however, it is oddly configured (a deeper-voiced choir that plays different music, and only sporadically—even if sometimes slightly out of synch in the manner of an echo); nor does it seem plausibly to be, more simply, his dead comrade responding in kind, particularly given

the "heller" qualifier in Lenau's lines. If Mahler is indeed following Lenau here, he seems rather to be folding both echo and fallen comrade into a deeper, more embracive response.

20 Cf. Franklin's descriptive account: "What happens *after* the two episodes is of the greatest interest. The music on both occasions becomes instinct with a kind of nervousness, shading into fear" (*Mahler: Symphony No. 3*, p. 64).

21 Cf. Greene's rather puzzling claim that "in no movement [of movements 2–5 of the Third Symphony] does a future beyond itself impinge upon it" (*Mahler: Consciousness and Temporality*, p. 166). As argued here, the sensibilities of the fourth movement, anticipated in the posthorn passages, not only impinge on the scherzo, but destroy its autonomy, in terms of both its "content" and its form.

22 Regarding the scherzo, see Floros's substitution of "rondo" for "scherzo-trio" (*Gustav Mahler: The Symphonies*, pp. 99–102) and La Grange's more conventional analysis (*Mahler I*, pp. 804–806). Concerning larger issues of musical narrative as applied to music that "misbehaves," see various writings of Susan McClary, especially "Sexual Politics in Classical Music," in *Feminine Endings*, pp. 53–79 (especially pp. 69–79, concerning Tchaikovsky's Fourth Symphony); and "The Impromptu That Trod on a Loaf."

23 Adorno introduces the term "breakthrough" on p. 6 and later discusses it along with "suspension" and "fulfillment" as "essential genres in [Mahler's] idea of form" (*Mahler*, p. 41). For a more recent application of this concept to Mahler's form, see Buhler, "'Breakthrough' as Critique of Form."

24 See Draughon, "Mahler and the Music of *Fin-de-siècle* Identity," chapter 3; see also Draughon and Knapp, "Mahler and the Crisis of Jewish Identity." Significantly, it is again knowledge of death and a true sense of mourning that distinguish humanity from forest creatures, even if in the First Symphony that knowledge is presented through the perspective of the creatures and thus "mit Parodie." See the related discussion in Olsen, "Culture and the Creative Imagination," pp. 214f.

25 Cf. Greene, *Mahler: Consciousness and Temporality*, especially pp. 185–190. Intriguingly, the temporality-challenged forest creatures evoke a sense of sympathetic estrangement from adult humanity that has something in common with many aspects of *Sybil* and Multiple Personality Disorder as it is recounted there. A threefold loss of temporal competence is part of what happens to Sybil: she (the Sybil self) loses awareness of large blocks of time when other personalities take over; she frequently regresses to the condition of a child who occupies an "eternal present" (to use a phrase Mahler derived from Schopenhauer and once intended for his Fourth Symphony); and, during these periods of regression, which recur in response to obsessive classical music, time collapses for her and she relives her childhood torture. Temporality also matters in the scherzo of the Second Symphony; there, it seems to operate on two incommensurate levels, as the "observer" cannot connect to the rhythms of living humanity, yet has a keener sense of larger temporal issues than do the living.

1 Cf. Monelle's distinction between "Mahler and Gustav" in *The Sense of Music.*

2 See, e.g., La Grange, *Mahler I,* p. 774.

3 See discussion and textual comparison in La Grange, *Mahler I,* pp. 742–743; see also Youens, "Schubert, Mahler, and the Weight of the Past."

4 See La Grange, *Mahler I,* pp. 113f, and Mitchell, *Gustav Mahler: The Wunderhorn Years,* pp. 124f.

5 For related discussions, see Draughon, "Mahler and the Music of *Fin-de-siècle* Identity," chapter 2; and Youens, "Schubert, Mahler, and the Weight of the Past."

6 See Mitchell, *Gustav Mahler: The Wunderhorn Years,* pp. 158–159, for a comprehensive chart of all versions and titles for the symphony.

7 This is precisely the harmonic shift, to VI from a major key, that will articulate heavenly arrival in the second and fourth movements of the Fourth Symphony. All three instances mix a sense of emergence into light with a sense, as well, of projected death. Perhaps this harmonic and affective configuration may be thought of as a variation of the ♭VI topic (see note 22 below), "unnaturally" brightening and expanding a conventional deceptive arrival to vi, which would generally mark an unhappy deflection of short duration. In contrast to both the conventional deceptive arrival to vi and typical applications of the ♭VI topic, however, Mahler's shift permits no easy return; in none of the cited applications does he complete the harmonic frame by returning to the referential tonic.

8 Cf. Elizabeth Abbate's explanation for Mahler's reordering of the song's musical structure for the exposition ("Myth, Symbol, and Meaning," pp. 31–36): aligning Mahler's reworking of this material with the original song text, she finds that Mahler's revision "emphatically focuses the exposition upon the way in which the walker internalizes the transcendent, as manifested in the symbolic landscape. The 'topic' of the exposition is this internalization by the walker" (p. 36). Abbate also finds text-based explanations for other of Mahler's procedures in the movement, drawing upon both the poem and Jean Paul's *Titan;* yet these explanations lead her to conclude that "the repeat of the exposition . . . makes no sense," and to dismiss altogether Mahler's repeated explanation for the conclusion of the movement (p. 36n and pp. 40–41; cf. my discussions below).

9 From Hamburg, 1893: "Die Einleitung stellt das Erwachen der Natur aus langem Winterschlafe dar"; and, from Weimar, 1894: "Die Einleitung schildert das Erwachen der Natur am frühesten Morgen." See Mitchell, *Gustav Mahler: The Wunderhorn Years,* pp. 158–159.

10 The extreme form of these false "solutions" is a particularly Beethovenian trope and virtually requires a minor-mode context. Nevertheless, some mode of problem-solving is an important driving force in most sonata-form expositions of more than modest dynamic impulse. Other examples of expositions "solving problems" include most minor-mode movements that move to the relative major and, among major-mode works, Beethoven's *Pastoral* Symphony, which aligns its

unstable main motive (C–G) with the secondary tonic (see Knapp, "A Tale of Two Symphonies"). More modestly, major-mode expositions routinely set up and solve problems as they unfold, most conventionally by moving after a period of unrest to a lyrical second-group theme, creating a sense of harmonic crisis (Tovey's "purple patch" or Mozart's turn to the minor), and then emphatically securing the secondary tonic. And, of course, many sonata-form openings "solve" their introductions only to face major repercussions later; examples include the first movements of Mozart's *Prague* Symphony (No. 38, K. 504) and Haydn's *Military* Symphony (No. 100), and the finale of Brahms's First Symphony. Solving problems within a three-key exposition often becomes a complicated affair, but smaller-scale patterns may be found, for example, in most of Brahms's symphonic three-key expositions, which generally move from minor to major in the process; see, e.g., the first movements of the First (C minor–E♭ major), Second (F♯ minor–A major), and Fourth (E minor–G major), and the finale of the Third (F minor–C major) Symphonies.

11 The repeat is given only in Mahler's penciled-in emendation to the 1899 published score, with no previous source; see Mitchell, *Gustav Mahler: The Wunderhorn Years,* p. 195.

12 Mahler complained of Schubert to Natalie Bauer-Lechner (*Recollections,* p. 147): "No elaboration, no artistically finished development of his original idea! Instead, he repeats himself so much that you could cut out half the piece without doing it any harm. For each repetition is already a lie. A work of art must evolve perpetually, like life. If it doesn't, hypocrisy and theatricality set in" (Keine Verarbeitung, keine künstlerisch vollendete Ausgestaltung seines Vorwurfs! Statt dessen wiederholt er sich, daß man ohne Schaden die Hälfte des Stückes wegstreichen könnte. Denn jede Wiederholung ist schon eine Lüge. Es muß sich ein Kunstwerk wie das Leben immer weiter entwickeln. Ist das nicht der Fall, so fängt die Unwahrheit, das Theater an; Bauer-Lechner, *Erinnerungen,* p. 158).

13 See, e.g., Mitchell's discussion of the development (*Gustav Mahler: The Wunderhorn Years,* pp. 207–208), in which he objects to programmatic concerns resulting in unsound musical choices; typically, responses along these lines implicitly find conventions of musical forms and procedures "natural" and purely musical. In a more recent form-based criticism of the First Symphony, Stephen Hefling sees its "imperfections" in terms of Mahler's relative immaturity within an ongoing narrative of developing craft, which reaches its "second maturity" in the Fourth Symphony; thus, according to Hefling, "the development section of the First emphasizes musical drama more than motivic working out. (Beethoven had managed both; Mahler would achieve a better balance beginning with his Fourth)"; and, "Although completed only months after the First Symphony, Mahler's 'Todtenfeier' movement considerably surpasses the First in both formal cogency and dramatic intensity" (see Hefling, "Mahler: Symphonies 1–4" especially pp. 378, 386, 389, and 407).

14 E.g., as in Elizabeth Abbate's reading, "Myth, Symbol, and Meaning," p. 37.

15 Elizabeth Abbate aptly calls this "the 'striving' motive" ("Myth, Symbol, and Meaning," p. 37).

16 Other models—to list only a few of the more prominent possibilities—include Haydn's *Creation*, Beethoven's *Pastoral* Symphony, and Mendelssohn's *Die erste Walpurgisnacht*.

17 The intensification of subjective energy at the recapitulation in the Ninth may help explain the fact that this moment has been read, credibly, in so many seemingly incompatible ways, ranging from McClary's "juxtaposition of desire and unspeakable violence" (*Feminine Endings*, p. 128) back to Tovey's "catastrophic return" in which "we see the heavens on fire" and feel "almost relief when it turns into the minor" ("Beethoven, Ninth Symphony in D Minor, Op. 125," p. 100).

18 As James Buhler argues in "'Breakthrough' as Critique of Form," Mahler's explanation for having two separate arrivals in D major in the finale can be understood only in this way: "At the place in question [the first arrival] the solution is merely apparent. . . . A change and breaking of the whole essence is needed before a true 'victory' can be won after such a struggle" (Mahler, as quoted in Buhler, p. 126).

19 La Grange, *Mahler I*, p. 749. Mahler's description comes from an explanatory text sent by way of Natalie Bauer-Lechner to a Viennese critic. In a slightly different accounting, Bruno Walter claims that it is Beethoven who laughs and runs away (*Gustav Mahler*, p. 110).

20 Draughon, "Mahler and the Music of *Fin-de-siècle* Identity," chapter 3; see also Draughon and Knapp, "Mahler and the Crisis of Jewish Identity."

21 Ringer finds a specific source for the dotted-note figures that Mahler uses as a refrain in this song in Gaetano Donizetti's *Don Sebastian*; see his "'Lieder eines fahrenden Gesellen,'" pp. 599–601.

22 Traditionally, this kind of shift registers as an escape, converting the previous tonic into the third of a major tonic triad. In the minor mode, the shift can be accomplished, as it is here, by activating the third degree as dominant. While this makes the minor mode more feasible as an outcome, Mahler's subsequent manipulations, alternating between major and minor modes, make it seem as if this is an attempted but unsuccessful escape. Regarding this use of the ♭VI, see McClary, "Pitches, Expression, Ideology," and Nelson, "The Fantasy of Absolute Music."

23 Draughon, "Mahler and the Music of *Fin-de-siècle* Identity," chapter 3; see also Draughon and Knapp, "Mahler and the Crisis of Jewish Identity."

24 Another credible interpretation of Mahler's procedures is that the dancelike counterpoint is a necessary complication to what would otherwise be rather tedious repetitions of a joke worn thin. But this consideration by no means invalidates the reading offered here of the *effect* of the device.

25 Mahler's use of absolute music as a topic is often aligned with situations in which, allegorically, animals represent a world unattuned to human concerns (cf. earlier discussions, in chapters 3 and 4, of "Des Antonius von Padua Fischpredigt," "Ablösung im Sommer," and the scherzos of the Second and Third Symphonies).

In discussing some of these movements, Olsen concludes, "His approach to the animal pieces provides a telling testimony to the unsettling dissonance between mortal tragedy and the brutal workings of an uncaring world. Thus Mahler turned to the animals to express his disenchantment" ("Culture and the Creative Imagination," p. 222). Yet, as argued here, the "animal pieces" are much too subtly nuanced to sustain this generalization, reflecting Mahler's almost pervasive ambivalence; significantly, none may be taken as a pure indictment of the world.

26 If it is surprising that the net modulatory result in the movement is identical to that in the song, we must remember that modulation, like addition, is commutative, so that $IV + \flat VI = \flat VI + IV = \flat II$.

27 This device for enhancing excitement, derived largely from Beethoven, later in the twentieth century became a device for artificially "juicing up" repetitions in some genres of popular music. It was already well on its way to becoming a cliché in the late nineteenth century; most relevantly for Mahler, examples abound in Bruckner. In this case, the effect is made particularly startling because it centrally involves one of the traditionally stable components of the orchestra, the timpani, and because the lift occurs only after a substantial intervening section.

28 A more subjectively rendered cry of despair, matching more closely those in his next two symphonies, launches the finale of the First; see the discussion in Olsen, "Culture and the Creative Imagination," pp. 223–226.

29 Cf. Monelle's summing up in *The Sense of Music*: "It was discovered [after high romanticism] that you can only dislodge the human subjectivity of the utterance through irony and polyvocality. . . . Mahler is engaged in a new kind of structural manufacture; he is not building temporal sequentiality but subjective multi-layeredness" (p. 229).

30 See Moretti's discussion of Mahler's heteroglossia in *Modern Epic*, pp. 58–59.

31 Monelle again (here referring specifically to "Urlicht"): "Behind the many subjects which speak through this movement, there must, presumably, be a single voice which links them all in a compassionate message. This is Cone's 'complete musical persona,' who 'is by no means identical with the composer' but 'constitutes the mind of the composition in question.' Or perhaps it is 'Gustav,' the artist's creation and reflection of himself, parallel to the 'Marcel' who narrates Proust's long novel. . . . To be sure, the symphonies are full of Gustav, with his tricky elusiveness, his dubious sincerity and his chameleon nature. Mahler is, on the whole, absent" (*The Sense of Music*, pp. 194–195; internal quotations from Edward T. Cone, *The Composer's Voice*). Cf. also Monelle's discussion on pp. 176–177 regarding the "I" in Mahler's music.

32 La Grange, *Mahler I*, p. 785.

33 Mahler's distinction between narrative and drama would seem to fall in line with Carolyn Abbate's requirement that there be a "past tense" for musical narrative to occur (*Unsung Voices*, pp. 19–29); yet, surely, Mahler's "motion and occurrence" cannot be taken literally, denoting rather a heightened *sense* of drama. Thus, not

only would Mahler's earlier movements most likely fail to qualify as narrative in Abbate's sense, but there is little practical value to the distinction between the (metaphoric) enacting of drama and the relating of narrative except as different modes of communicating a series of events.

34 But see Monelle, *The Sense of Music,* pp. 186–195.

Notes to Chapter 6

1 As discussed in chapter 3; see Alma Mahler, *Memories and Letters,* p. 162.

2 Here we may note not only the intense anti-Semitism Mahler encountered in Vienna, but also his own unorthodox cosmology, as detailed in his Second and Third Symphonies.

3 Among other sources, see esp. Lea, *Gustav Mahler: Man on the Margin;* Mahler as outsider is a much visited subject in the literature.

4 See, e.g., the responses to his conducting Beethoven's Ninth in February 1900, cited in La Grange, *Mahler I,* pp. 556–559.

5 Important support for Mahler's articulated sense for this aspect of music's autonomy—and for my larger claim that Mahler not only consciously held but also acted upon the beliefs that I argue here as implicitly revealed in his compositional behavior—may be found in Schopenhauer's writings, in which music is aligned with the *will,* the essence of all things, to be distinguished from mere representation (see Schopenhauer, *The World as Will and Representation*). As has been widely noted, Schopenhauer's writings profoundly influenced Wagner and Nietzsche, and continued to influence Mahler's intellectual circle, both directly and indirectly.

6 Regarding the belief structure of absolute music, see Knapp, *Brahms and the Challenge of the Symphony,* pp. 273–283.

7 The date of actual orchestration has not been fully clarified; see La Grange, *Mahler I,* p. 741.

8 Specifically, the movement is based on a trumpet melody that recurs throughout the larger work, transformed episodically as an emblem of the hero. Thus, borrowing the love episode would have reinforced the episodic dimension of the first three movements (part 1 of the symphony), as well as the sense that the symphony is a heroic narrative. Regarding *Der Trompeter von Säkkingen,* see La Grange, *Mahler I,* pp. 716–717.

9 While the Frankenstein story as Mary Shelley originally tells it is more one of abandonment than one of rebellion, the mythology of the monster has given at least equal stress to the latter dimension. Intriguingly when seen in terms of Mahler's predicament, Shaw's *Pygmalion* also took on a life of its own, so that his original intentions for its denouement were soon put aside in favor of a performing tradition that gave Eliza more agency and yet also gave in to the impulse to merge Shaw's play with the Cinderella story that it shadows.

10 For an excellent survey of biographical and cultural factors in this shift, however, see Schorske, "Formation and Transformation."

11 See Draughon, "Mahler and the Music of *Fin-de-siècle* Identity," chapter 3; see also Draughon and Knapp, "Mahler and the Crisis of Jewish Identity."

12 Mahler obliquely articulates this very difficulty, if inadvertently and in somewhat different terms, in a letter to Fritz Löhr written in 1895 before he decided to drop "Das himmlische Leben" from the Third Symphony. After explaining that movements 2–7 detail "my *personal* emotional life (that is, what things say to *me*)" and listing movements 2–5 without special comment, Mahler elaborates the remaining two movements under one heading, as follows: "VI. W[hat] love *tells* m[e] is a summary of my feelings in respect to *all being,* which does not transpire without *deeply painful* digressions, which, however, gradually resolve into a *blessed trust:* 'die *fröhliche* Wissenschaft.' As conclusion, dhL [Das himmlische Leben] (VII), to which I have given the definitive title: '*What the child tells me.*'" Then, after a paragraph describing the first movement, he reiterates, "Over and above all, *eternal love* moves within us—as rays come together in a focal point" (see *Selected Letters of Gustav Mahler,* no. 137). Thus, the "love" movement is the programmatic culmination of the symphony, the climax of a process that progressively merges more closely the subjectivities of "me" and each successive "teller" until, with the sixth movement, the symphony's "meta-subjectivity" is listening both inwardly and outwardly to an eternal, all-embracing love. Inevitably, Mahler refers to "Das himmlische Leben" in the manner of an afterthought, implicitly acknowledging that the song stands largely apart from the central narrative of the symphony; thus, its childly perspective refuses assimilation, enforcing instead an essential difference between it and the symphony's "me," which can now *only* listen.

13 Discussed in Adorno (*Mahler*), Bonds (*After Beethoven*), and chapter 7, as noted.

Notes to Chapter 7

1 Alma Mahler was perhaps the first to compare the Fourth to Haydn; as she reports in *Memories and Letters,* her first reaction to the piece, when playing it over with Mahler, was, "'Haydn has done that better'" (p. 24).

2 Adorno and Bonds provide the most perceptive articulations of this perspective. See Adorno, *Mahler,* pp. 53, 55, and 57; and Bonds, *After Beethoven,* pp. 175 and 199. See also Allsburg, *The Polar Express.* Mahler himself made repeated references to the child orientation of his Fourth, as usefully recounted in Floros, *Gustav Mahler: The Symphonies,* pp. 112–115, and La Grange, *Mahler II,* pp. 757–759. Moreover, a *kindlich* tone is specifically requested in the score for the soprano in the finale. Two other thoughtful—and thought-provoking—discussions of the Fourth center in very different ways on its child orientation; see Schiff, "Jewish and Musical Tradition in the Music of Mahler and Schoenberg," and Nowak, "Zur Deutung der Dritten und Vierten Sinfonie." For his part, Mitchell, in line with many others, prefers to emphasize the Fourth's "neoclassical" spirit and hidden sophistication, referring briefly to its central concept of "innocence" (see Mitchell, *Gustav Mahler: The Wunderhorn Years,* p. 344); in a later, more direct en-

gagement with Adorno's claims, Mitchell seeks to achieve a rapprochement of sorts by resolving Adorno's references to childhood into a more generally conceived "innocence" more in line with his own interpretation (Mitchell, "'Swallowing the Programme': Mahler's Fourth Symphony," p. 201). Monelle (*The Sense of Music*), following suggestive observations by Adorno, brings greater historical precision to ascribing an archaizing impulse in the symphony by placing it not as neoclassical, but as neo-Biedermeier, betokening a "Schubertian man of feeling"; his observation may be supported not only by pointing to the allusion to Schubert in the main theme (see below), but also, perhaps, by aligning the child orientation of the symphony with the cozy, home-based aesthetic of the Biedermeier era generally.

3 See his comments as reported by Bauer-Lechner in *Recollections,* pp. 178 and 183; see also his 1911 letter to Georg Göhler in *Selected Letters,* pp. 371–372.

4 Adorno's comment about the "fool's bells" of the opening may be taken along these lines, with the arch foreignness of the sound marking the entire work off within ironic quotation marks. While this is not quite the same thing as locating childly images and sophistication as two separate, antagonistic elements within the work, it also fails to account for the darker vision of childhood as considered below.

5 For an extended and quite useful discussion of this juncture in Mahler's career, see Schorske, "Formation and Transformation."

6 See Handler, *Blood Libel at Tiszaeszlar,* p. 170.

7 Regarding Hilsner, see Wolff, *Postcards from the End of the World,* pp. 102–113, esp. pp. 105–107, where Wolff draws specific connections between audience behavior, Mahler's reaction, and the ongoing Hilsner controversy; see also Wistrich, *The Jews of Vienna in the Age of Franz Joseph,* especially pp. 339–340 and 514–515. An anonymous article published in the *Deutsche Zeitung* in the year of Hilsner's conviction reads, in part, "Mahler's left hand often jerks convulsively, marking the Bohemian magic circle, digging for treasure, fluttering, snatching, strangling, thrashing the waves, *strangling babies*" (emphasis added); see Knittel, "'Ein hypermoderner Dirigent,'" p. 268, and La Grange, *Mahler I,* p. 486.

8 See Wolff, *Postcards,* pp. 110–113.

9 See Rosen, *The Classical Style,* p. 349.

10 Cf. Bonds's discussion of this opening. Although he notes the disturbing role played by the return of the opening sleigh bells in the finale, and also by their alliance later with the funereal passage late in the development of the first movement, Bonds sees the opening as essentially innocent in tone, although contrasting severely with the string theme that follows (Bonds, *After Beethoven,* pp. 186–187, 190). See also Adorno (*Mahler,* pp. 56–57), who discusses the disturbing incompatibility of the "bell opening" with the theme that succeeds it, and who, like Bonds, accepts the innocent tone of the opening at face value.

11 The focus here and below is obviously narrower than that in the related discus-

sions of chapter 2, which probe more deeply the wealth of sometimes conflicting meanings that might have been drawn from the song in its earlier projected settings; here, it is specifically the resonances between "Das himmlische Leben" and the opening movement that are at issue.

12 To be sure, Andersen's child dies of exposure rather than hunger; nevertheless, the four visions she sees before dying are obviously compatible with those offered in Mahler's Fourth Symphony, involving warmth, plentiful food, Christmas, and heaven-beckoning love.

13 Cf. Bonds's and Adorno's discussions of the finale, particularly regarding its curiously distressing images of animal death and cheerful carnivory, the perverse confusion of many emblems of Christianity, and the intrusion of a nightmarish version of sleigh bells. Bonds also cautions against overemphasizing the "darker elements" of the symphony (Bonds, *After Beethoven*, p. 199), without endorsing the general preference to hear only innocence and bliss in the finale. Perhaps the bleakest view of the symphony is offered by Adolf Nowak. If we combine his view of the finale as an unacceptably childish refuge (in line with Nietzsche's views on religion) with Adorno's understanding of the "fool's bells" from the very opening of the work as a clear statement that "none of what you now hear is true" (Adorno, *Mahler*, p. 56), we must take the returning fool's bells in the finale as an overt, devastating mockery of that refuge. However tempting Bonds's advice may be not to give too much weight to the "darker elements," it is hard to discern a viable middle path, and he himself seems only wistfully able to imagine one: "Mahler created an ending in which believers . . . can continue to hear the sleigh bells as a memory of childhood's innocence" (Bonds, *After Beethoven*, p. 199). Yet, this is no middle path: to hear the sleigh bells in this way—to be a believer—is to deny the darkness completely; on the other hand, even the slightest of doubts leads inexorably to something like Nowak's Nietzschean view, wholly incompatible with belief. See Bonds, *After Beethoven*, pp. 191–199; Adorno, *Mahler*, 56–57; and Nowak, "Zur Deutung der Dritten und Vierten Sinfonie." See also La Grange's attempt at mediation (La Grange, *Mahler I*, pp. 771–773).

14 See, e.g., Mitchell, *Gustav Mahler: The Wunderhorn Years*, pp. 187–194 and 312–318, esp. 194. Mitchell stands somewhat apart for his lengthy elaboration of the problem but refrains from attempting an explanation. Another obvious consideration is a consistency of scoring: for the Fourth Symphony, Mahler did without trombones, which are indispensable to the Third Symphony but which "Das himmlische Leben" does not use.

15 Mahler's earlier intention to reunite "Das himmlische Leben" with "Das irdische Leben," by including both in the Fourth Symphony (discussed in Mitchell, *Gustav Mahler: The Wunderhorn Years*, pp. 138–139 and 259n), would have served, ironically, to overemphasize the childlike innocence of the former through the direct opposition of the two songs, even if the latter would have centered the subject matter of the symphony more specifically around a child's starvation. A more general context for

understanding Mahler's seemingly greater allegiance to the song as opposed to its projected symphonic context is explored in chapters 2 and 6.

16 Regarding the Ninth, see Solomon, "The Ninth Symphony," and Treitler, "History, Criticism, and Beethoven's Ninth Symphony." The opening of the Fifth is no less successful in creating a need for clarity; putting aside the extreme familiarity of the opening, we may note how little is actually communicated by the first four bars beyond an anxious, crisis-ridden sense of moment, for neither key nor mode, neither meter nor tempo, is defined until after the second fermata.

17 See Rosen, *The Classical Style,* pp. 64–67 and 387–389, regarding "rhythmic transition" in general and Beethoven's use of metrical subdivisions in particular. Note that the displaced accents in m. 2 are also tokens of Beethovenian discourse, even as they also provide a hint of more negative associations with sleigh bells than simple nostalgia.

18 Oddly, Simon Rattle restores the "normal" hierarchy to this opening in his 1997 recording by playing the opening slower than the string theme that follows it. Although Rattle claims to base his approach on the counsel of Berthold Goldschmidt (1903–1997), "who could remember how Mahler actually sounded in the 1920s, when his own performing tradition was still in minds and fingers," the result seems to me more a retreat from Mahler's daring reversal than a welcome restoration (see Rattle, notes to *Mahler: Symphony No. 4,* p. 6). Cf. the exaggerated *ritardandi* with which Willem Mengelberg, who had earlier worked directly with Mahler, introduces the string theme in his 1939 recording (reissued by Phillips as a CD [416 211-2] in 1997).

19 Mahler's possible modeling of this theme on Schubert's Sonata in E♭ Major, D. 568, serves to highlight its relaxed character, largely through the expansion of Schubert's 3/4 meter to 4/4. Adorno terms this probable allusion a quotation (Adorno, *Mahler,* p. 56); see also La Grange, *Mahler I,* p. 764. David Schiff, on the other hand, claims that "the reference is to the famous Serenade from Haydn's Opus 3—a set of quartets which we no longer attribute to Haydn, but which was considered authentic in Mahler's time" (Schiff, "Jewish and Musical Tradition," p. 255). Schiff presumably means the slow movement of op. 3 no. 5, which is not nearly as close to Mahler's theme as is Schubert's, although Haydn is surely invoked in the opening themes of the symphony, if only because by the end of the nineteenth century he had come to symbolize naiveté. Another apparent reference to Schubert in the Fourth Symphony has been identified in the triplet figures of the finale (e.g., m. 128), which Miriam K. Whaples traces to Schubert's D-major Sonata (D. 850, mm. 31–32), but which Jon Finson traces instead to a folksong setting of "Der Himmel hängt voll Geigen." See Miriam Whaples, "Mahler and Schubert's A Minor Sonata D. 784," pp. 256–257; Jon W. Finson, "The Reception of Gustav Mahler's *Wunderhorn-Lieder,*" pp. 111–12; and the discussion of these identifications in Zychowicz, "Sketches and Drafts," pp. 83-86.

20 See McClary, "Pitches, Expression, Ideology," and Nelson, "The Fantasy of Ab-

solute Music," for discussions of this function of ♭VI harmonic relationships in nineteenth-century music. Here, the melodic slide upward to G, the unexpectedness of the resulting harmonic shift, the recasting of the previous harmonic root as the third of a major triad, and the deceptive nature of the arrival strongly resonate with the paradigm of ♭VI as McClary describes it. But this is by no means a straightforward application, since, as noted, B has only equivocally been offered as tonic prior to the shift to G (which might be understood, less extremely, as the relative major of E minor), and since, more generally, shifting to the lower submediant in the minor mode does not entail the chromatic inflection that helps give shifts of this kind an otherworldly quality in the major mode. Nevertheless, the thoroughgoing rearrangement of other musical elements that accompanies the shift aligns this passage much more closely to McClary's ♭VI paradigm than to, for example, a more conventional shift to the relative major.

21 While Mahler's drawing on the expressive power of deceptive resolution in the Ninth Symphony is often understood as a gesture of leave-taking, resonating with a key passage in the introduction to Beethoven's "Das Lebewohl" Sonata (Op. 81a), it may also be usefully related to Wagner's practice in *Tristan und Isolde,* not only with regard to the first harmonic arrival (a deceptive resolution to F, functioning as ♭VI/A), but also because *Tristan* played a pivotal role in developing the sense of discomfort later composers felt for straightforward V–I resolutions.

22 This sense of nostalgia functions within both the traditional "leave-taking" reading of the finale of the Ninth Symphony and Anthony Newcomb's "spiraling quest" plot archetype for the work; see Newcomb, "Narrative Archetypes and Mahler's Ninth Symphony." Newcomb argues against the narrowness of what has been, after Adorno, the traditional view of the Ninth Symphony (Adorno, *Mahler,* p. 145). While Newcomb's alternative is compelling, his argument does not extend to the larger issue of understanding the Ninth as musical autobiography, since this line of inquiry is always justified in Mahler. Thus, a reading of the Ninth as a self-reflective attempt by Mahler to merge his own life quest with more universal quests—a project similar to what Maynard Solomon argues for Beethoven's Ninth (see Solomon), if arguably more self-conscious—does not falter just because Mahler did not realize he was dying; both composers had much to reflect on in their lives when they composed their respective Ninth Symphonies. In Newcomb's plot archetype, the need to reconnect to origins may be seen to reach beyond the first movement, in technical terms querying the language of tonality and its origin in the cadence, in figurative terms embracing religious quests for meaning and preoccupations with origins (hence the hymnlike style). The link between technical matters, religion, and the idea of leave-taking—so recently addressed, and with similar means, in *Das Lied von der Erde*—is profoundly simple: the cadence, which is problematized throughout the Ninth (and also in the closing stages of *Das Lied*), is not only the origin and defining condition of tonality, but also its primary resource for achieving closure, a duality that provides Mahler with a ready symbol for mapping the circu-

lar journey between birth and death. In confronting the cadence, Mahler confronts both birth and death and the attempt to configure meaning between them, religious or otherwise.

23 See Winter, "The Bifocal Close and the Evolution of the Viennese Classical Style"; according to Winter's criteria, this movement offers a full implementation of the device, since, in the recapitulation, Mahler continues in the tonic after the close on the dominant (mm. 262–263).

24 With no explanation, Adorno terms this passage a "false recapitulation" (Adorno, *Mahler,* p. 54). Traditionally, this term has been applied to premature returns to the opening theme and key *within* (that is, not preceding) a developmental section, especially as found in Haydn.

25 It can scarcely be coincidental that the form of this opening movement resembles that in the First Symphony, not only in recalling a varied form of the opening after the exposition in order to establish a context for long-range signification, but also through its emblematic naiveté, here evoking childhood, in the First evoking the callowness of youth (see chapter 5). Notable as well is the subtle engagement, in both movements, with older formal conventions, which are problematized as much as followed through the naive manner in which they are implemented.

26 Given the provenance of the song, it is extremely unlikely that this is an intentional allusion. "The One Horse Open Sleigh," by James Pierpont (1822–1893), was published in Boston in 1857 and republished in 1859 as "Jingle Bells or The One Horse Open Sleigh." (Pierpont, an uncle of J. Pierpont Morgan and the rebellious son of the controversial Unitarian minister, poet, and abolitionist John Pierpont, went on to write patriotic songs for the Confederacy in relative obscurity.) While the quick reissue of the song with the name changed to include its "hook" indicates some early popularity, its "world-wide familiarity seems to be a twentieth-century phenomenon" (Jackson, *Popular Songs of Nineteenth-Century America,* p. 272; Jackson's collection includes a reproduction of the 1859 publication). Moreover, the tune has evolved over the years, especially the chorus: the original chorus was considerably more mobile both harmonically and melodically. Thus, for example, although the repeated-note motive on 3 ("Jingle bells") was present in the earlier version, the motive then moves up to 5 (with dominant harmonic support), and the first phrase ends on the leading tone to vi (see Example 35).

   If the resemblance might thus be better ascribed to parallel motivic representations of sleigh bells, an argument for allusion might nevertheless be made on internal evidence. Mahler's procedure, if intentionally allusive, follows precisely the strategy I have argued for many of Brahms's allusions ("Brahms and the Anxiety of Allusion" and "Utopian Agendas: Variation, Allusion, and Referential Meaning in Brahms's Symphonies"), subtly manipulating the opening, which is itself only vaguely allusive, in order to create a stronger resonance at an appropriate later moment, but nonetheless steering clear of explicit quotation. Further, the gradual

conversion of the grace-note figure to a new motive that yields precisely three repeated eighth notes at the beginning of each half bar might easily be construed as
evidence of a deliberate derivation. In any case, if one does hear an echo of the
carol in this passage, that echo is made more difficult to ignore by the coherent reinforcement it offers to the more abstractly conceived effect of Mahler's transformation. Thus, one may claim a functioning allusion here independent of either
composer intention or historical plausibility.

27 The strange effect of Mahler's orchestration here has provoked a variety of interpretations. Deryck Cooke hears the episode as untroubled, "like a boy whistling,"
while Adorno describes it as "an effect sui generis, that of a dream ocarina: such
must have been children's instruments that no one ever heard." See Cooke, *Mahler,* p. 67, and Adorno, *Mahler,* p. 53; see also the discussion in La Grange, *Mahler
I,* p. 762. Yet, despite its anticipation of the finale theme, which for many encour-
ages a more positive reading, this passage, through its combination of incompatible worlds, is profoundly disturbing.

28 Adorno terms this an "intentionally infantile, noisily cheerful field" (Adorno,
Mahler, p. 54). Cooke, on the other hand, hears this tutti as a "joyous climax,"
with the trumpet taking up the earlier flute tune (my no. 2). To be sure, Cooke's
benign reading follows inevitably from his view of the symphony as a whole, decidedly different from that offered here, as a "neo-rococo 'pastoral symphony'"
deriving from the "naive picture of heavenly bliss" offered by the finale and beginning with the "pastoral 'walk through the countryside'" of the first movement;
moreover, he does acknowledge the "nightmare climax" of the development (my
no. 6; see Cooke, *Mahler,* pp. 67–68). The trumpet theme during the preceding
tutti (my no. 5), which evolves further during the E major outburst near the end
of the third movement to anticipate the main theme of the finale, is here combined with a number of other themes, including the raucous close of the bridge
(horns, winds, and carillon), a grotesque rendering of the second-group theme
(upper winds and strings), and an insistent jingling of the triangle that gives way,
in m. 216, to an anticipation of the funereal trumpet rhythm (my no. 6) in the
bass drum. It seems too easy to take this nightmarish confusion as joy; as climax,
it is severely undermined by its ambiguous subdominant orientation (IV/G, but
more locally V/f) and its imminent collapse.

29 Mahler's own explanation for this intrusion masks only somewhat its threatening
invocation of death while implicitly supporting the foregoing "nightmare" reading of the development: "when the confusion and crowding of the troops, who
started in orderly ranks, becomes too great, a command from the captain recalls
them at once to the old formation under his flag"(Bauer-Lechner, *Recollections,*
p. 154); see related discussions of this "kleine Appell" in chapter 2 and in Zychowicz, "Sketches and Drafts," p. 89.

30 This passage thus provides a challenge to Adorno's claim that "no father figures
are admitted to its [the Fourth Symphony's] precincts," made in regard to Mah-

ler's doing without the "heavy brass" within a generally light scoring (Adorno, *Mahler*, p. 53). The horns are deployed with similar effect in the third movement (mm. 283f), shortly before the E major outburst.

31 Note that the possible confusion between the two relevant meanings of "man"—either "humanity" (including women) or "adult male"—is somewhat clarified through this interpretation. In the Third Symphony, we might argue that the former obtains, even if it is traditionally masculine attributes (strength of character, reason, and thoughtful reflection) that would seem to be relevant, and even if the instrumentation betokens masculinity. The context leaves this interpretive loophole firmly shut against those who may want to "rescue" Mahler by exempting him from the chauvinistic attitudes of his era.

32 As discussed in chapter 4, there are in effect three interacting "characters" in the forest scherzo of the Third Symphony: the creatures of the forest (whose material derives from "Ablösung im Sommer"), the postilion, and the embracing deeper spirit of the forest (the horn choir), which honors the postilion (and alarms the creatures) through its warm response to the posthorn solo. Here, the roles of intruding postilion and deeper spirit are combined, which registers striking differences between this scenario and that of the forest scherzo of the preceding symphony. Thus, the intruder (the "father figure") here acknowledges the priority of the intruded-upon and responds warmly to it, whereas in the Third Symphony the postilion does not recognize the sensibilities of the creatures, which in turn provoke no response whatever from the deeper spirit of the forest.

33 From a letter from Bruno Walter to Ludwig Schiedermair (5 December 1901), which according to La Grange was "plainly dictated by Mahler himself"(La Grange, *Mahler I*, pp. 757–758).

34 Holbein's series of woodcuts has been connected to Mahler's scherzo because of Willem Mengelberg's note on his score: "Totentanz Holbein: Der Tod führt uns" (La Grange, *Mahler I*, p. 764; La Grange erroneously gives the number of woodcuts in the series as 51).

35 As reported by Jack Diether (notes to *Levine Conducts Mahler: Symphony No. 4 in G*, RCA ARL1-0895, 1975); I have found no other reference to substantiate this claim.

36 In a letter to Gisella Tolney-Witt (February 1893), Mahler disparages playing great music at home, which is good only for calling "the great masters' works to mind—as good, as a recollection, as, say, an engraving is as a reminder of the brilliantly colourful paintings of a Raphael or a Böcklin" (*Selected Letters*, p. 149). We know, as well, that Mahler's "Fischpredigt," which forms the basis for the scherzo of his Second Symphony, was partly inspired by a Böcklin print (shown on the cover of this book and discussed in chapter 3). And later, in a letter to Alma written from Maiernigg (June 1904), Mahler mentions that he prefers spending time in "the Böcklin room" to being in his own room (Alma Mahler, *Gustav Mahler: Memories and Letters*, p. 237).

37 Thus, Rolf Andree observes that "it was not the paintings, but the themes of the paintings, leading his viewer astray into mental associations, that fascinated art-lovers. . . . His paintings exerted their influence even in reproductions"; see Andree, introduction to *Arnold Böcklin*, pp. 7–9, at pp. 7–8. Another of Böcklin's paintings proved inspirational for a composer only slightly younger than Mahler: Sergei Rachmaninoff's *Isle of the Dead* (1908) was conceived in response to a black-and-white print of Böcklin's 1880 painting—whose popular title, *Die Toteninsel*, is not, however, Böcklin's own.

38 Thus, Donald Mitchell, seconded by Constantin Floros, finds Böcklin's painting—which Mitchell terms "a Mahlerian canvas, if ever there were one"—relevant to this movement, even in the absence of a documented connection. See Mitchell, *Gustav Mahler: The Wunderhorn Years*, p. 303, and Floros, *Gustav Mahler: The Symphonies*, p. 122.

39 Thus, although Holbein entitled his set of woodcuts *Bilder des Todes*, the series is most often referred to as *Todtentanz*, as reflected in Mengelberg's note.

40 The picture in question is No. 39; the last two woodcuts, with the first two, serve to frame the set, with No. 1 depicting the Creation; No. 2, Adam and Eve in Paradise; No. 40, the Last Judgment; and No. 41, Death's coat-of-arms. The title would be rendered "Das junge Kind" (The Young Child) in modern German.

41 As noted, in only one of these is there a violin; other musical instruments pictured include a guitar (no. 3, the first in which Death appears, looking on as Adam and Eve are expelled from Paradise), trumpets and drums (No. 5, "Gebeyn aller menschen" [The bones of all men], depicting a band of skeletons), a bell (as Death summons "Der Pfarrherr" [The Clergyman]), a xylophone for both "Das Altweyb" (The Old Woman) and (less clearly) "Der Altman" (The Old Man), and a tambourine for "Die Edelfrau" (The Noble Woman). Far more prominent in the series than musical instruments is the empty (and sometimes broken) hourglass, which is nearly ubiquitous.

42 See Claudia Pohl's discussion regarding speculation that Death may have been a late addition to the self-portrait (Pohl, "Subjekt und Ideal," pp. 188–237, 228). If, indeed, the painting began as a more straightforward self-portrait, its smugness would have been nigh intolerable, especially if we imagine Böcklin's thoughtful expression as more purely a pose, stemming from his negotiating, not between an imagined painting and Death's bewitching music, but rather between two versions of his own image, the one on the canvas and the other in a mirror. Böcklin's portrayal of Death as mocking his victim through parody may be seen as an extension of one of Holbein's tropes, even if the parodic element is more subtle, since Böcklin's Death is fiddling rather than painting.

43 Cooke, *Mahler*, p. 68.

44 Nor is there a strong tradition for associating the figure with music, apart from an early reference in Theobald's "Hussitenkrieg"(1623) to a *Vöglein* ("Heintzlic") whose singing impels auditors to dance the *Todtentanz* and, more obliquely,

through the recurring tendency to merge images and attributes of Death with those of the Devil; for further discussion of Freund Hein, see Röhrich, *Lexikon der sprichwörtlichen Redensarten*, 2:409. Other, related terms in English include "Old Harry," "Old Nick," and "Old Scratch," although these generally refer more specifically to Satan.

45 Notably, although Holbein's woodcuts may also be interpreted along these lines, the mockery they project is more sinister than in Böcklin's self-portrait. The sharp division between childhood and adulthood, with puberty marking the division between the two, was undergoing scrutiny during Mahler's lifetime, most significantly by Freud, who posited the latent sexuality of children (see James R. Kincaid, *Child-Loving: The Erotic Child and Victorian Culture*, pp. 69–70 and 124–128). Thus, Mahler's attitude toward childhood, it would seem, was already veering in the direction of the old-fashioned and sentimental, although less idealized notions of childhood, revolving around the idea of original sin and children's inherent "naughtiness" have a long, persistent history, as well (see Kincaid, pp. 71–79 and 246–249). Kincaid believes, however, that the "innocent child may be a very-late-Victorian or, more likely, modern imposition . . . not . . . all that common in the nineteenth century, propaganda about 'the cult of the child' notwithstanding" (Kincaid, pp. 73–74). If he is correct in this, Mahler's attitude would not, after all, constitute a nostalgic evocation of older notions of children's innocence. Yet, belief in the innocence of children was by no means a late development, historically. The central touchstone for the idealized purity of children, which the nineteenth century rationalized through the notion of puberty and its accompanying awakening of sexuality, is Christ's rebuke to his disciples, "Suffer the little children to come unto me, and forbid them not: for of such is the kingdom of God. Verily I say unto you, Whosoever shall not receive the kingdom of God as a little child, he shall not enter therein." (Mark 10:14–15, King James Version; this passage is discussed further below).

46 Laurence Lerner, *Angels and Absences: Child Deaths in the Nineteenth Century*, p. 173. See also Kincaid's discussion of the Victorian fascination for the sick or dying child, which he relates to the desire to preserve the innocence of children in art and, especially, photographs (Kincaid, *Child-Loving*, pp. 199–200, 225–243).

47 Mahler's later preoccupation with child death, relating most famously to his *Kindertotenlieder* (1901–1904) and the death of his beloved Marie (1902–1907), has a decidedly different perspective than that revealed in the Fourth Symphony: that of an adult coming to terms with the loss of a beloved child. Friedrich Rückert wrote his 425 poems in the six months following the death of two of his six children from scarlet fever in January 1833; notably, Mahler began his setting of a handful of these poems before his own child was conceived, perhaps in belated response to the death of his younger brother Ernst at age fourteen (see Theodor Reik, *The Haunting Melody*, discussed in LaGrange, *Mahler I*, pp. 828–829). While the death of Ernst was indeed traumatic for Mahler, his was a family in

which surviving childhood, even infancy, was far from a sure thing. Most of the fourteen children born to his parents died young, many within a year of birth (including Isidor, who would have been his older brother); as Peter Franklin puts it, "Gustav seems at no stage to have had more than five surviving siblings" (Franklin, *Mahler,* p. 16). In the case of his daughter Marie, whom Mahler took credit for sustaining through a mortally endangered infancy, and whose death was indeed a painful one, Mahler's devastation extended to near identification with the dead child; in the immediate aftermath of her death, he learned of his own fatal heart condition, and later requested that he be buried in the same grave with her (Alma Mahler, *Memories and Letters,* pp. 49, 121–123, and 197).

48 Faustian associations are encouraged here by the similarity of Mahler's harmonic language with that of Liszt's *Eine Faust-Symphonie,* also in C minor, whose famous opening hinges on a manipulation of chromatically adjacent augmented triads with a similar tendency to slide downward chromatically instead of resolving directly and more conventionally to the tonic.

49 The three-note anacrusis also relates to the funereal motive in the development of the first movement, converting, à la Berlioz's treatment of the Dies Irae in the finale of his *Symphonie fantastique,* an emblem of grief into a mocking dance-motive.

50 Quantum theory was barely in its infancy at the turn of the century, and was applied to the atom by Niels Bohr only after Mahler's death (beginning in 1913). The parallel suggested here, while arguably an intriguing instance of *Zeitgeist,* is introduced only for its potential explanatory value.

51 St. Paul provides another plausible model in I Corinthians 13:9–12, where, in some of his most familiar and vivid prose, he describes three worlds, each unable to imagine the next, and each forever displacing its antecedent: the world of the child ("When I was a child, I spake as a child"), of the adult ("For now we see through a glass, darkly"), and of perfection ("but then face to face"). Despite the fact that he, too, is tracing a progression from earth to heaven, St. Paul's veneration of the adult world over that of the child is at odds with Mahler's nostalgic evocation of childhood; moreover, St. Paul's linear trajectory is fundamentally different from Mahler's more circular treatment, as discussed below. (Quotations are from the King James Version.)

52 A non-*scordatura* solo violin is heard earlier in the movement (mm. 121f), but plays, at that point, *con sordino* and in subordinate counterpoint to Freund Hein. In addition, a brief violin solo in conventional tuning appears just before the second trio (m. 199), playing an open-fifth arpeggiation of a C chord of ambiguous mode.

53 To be sure, the earlier dynamic levels are the softer, reaching *pianississississimo* in the violins, but the overall scoring at that point is both heavier and spread over a wider and generally higher register.

54 Cf. mm. 185f, which move from *pianissimo* staccato eighth notes to *fortissimo* ar-

rivals in the winds, and mm. 315f, in which the *forte* staccato eighth notes in the winds end in *pianissimo* trills.

55 Bram Dijkstra, *Idols of Perversity: Fantasies of Feminine Evil in Fin-de-Siècle Culture*, pp. 186–187. See also James Kincaid's explanation for the erotic child of the late nineteenth century, which results from the Victorian propensity to see children as "either free of any whiff of sexuality or . . . somehow saturated with it. This all-or-nothing rhetoric reflects a process of imaging the problem that makes the eroticizing of the child inevitable" (Kincaid, *Child-Loving*, p. 183).

56 Cf., however, St. Paul, writing to the Corinthians: "When I was a child, I spake as a child, I understood as a child, I thought as a child: but when I became a man, I put away childish things"(I Corinthians 13:11). St. Paul projects the Child as an imperfect adult, whose perspective can no more encompass the adult world than ours can encompass heaven (see note 51). For Paul, seemingly, perfection lies only in the future, while for Christ, the perfection we seek can be found only through reclaiming our own lost innocence.

57 Émile Zola, *Abbé Mouret's Transgression* (trans. Ernest Alfred Vizetelly), p. 96.

58 Dijkstra, *Idols of Perversity*, p. 189.

59 See Dijkstra, *Idols of Perversity*, p. 189.

60 Andersen, *The Complete Illustrated Stories*, pp. 357–359; the illustration for this story (by A. W. Bayes) shows the dead child being discussed by a small crowd of onlookers. As Andersen's tales show, perhaps more vividly than anywhere else, the idealization of children not only provides a rationale for their sufferance, according to Christ's admonition, but also leads inevitably to the perverse desire to see them suffer.

61 Andersen, *The Complete Illustrated Stories*, p. 231; cf. McClary's discussion of this story in "The Impromptu That Trod on a Loaf."

62 Zemlinsky's symphonic setting of this tale (*Die Seejungfrau*), composed shortly after Mahler's Fourth Symphony and premiered in 1905, adheres much more closely to Andersen than does the recent Walt Disney film; in the original, the sea maid is given a second chance at immortality but denied the prince. Although generally understood as an attempt to reconcile Wagnerian and Brahmsian approaches, Zemlinsky's setting, with its transcendent ending, may have been inspired by Mahler's Fourth as well, much as his later *Lyrische Symphonie* (1923) was even more clearly inspired by Mahler's *Das Lied von der Erde*. But the lines of influence probably ran in both directions, for both Zemlinsky and Mahler were engaged in fairy-tale projects at the same time: the years of Zemlinsky's opera *Es war einmal*, which Mahler helped revise for its 1900 premiere in Vienna, overlap almost precisely the years of Mahler's Fourth.

63 See, for example, Lawrence Kramer's speculations about Schumann's *Carnaval* (Kramer, "Carnaval, Cross-Dressing, and the Woman in the Mirror") and Christopher Reynolds's suggestion that Brahms composed into the finale of his First Concerto, through an interweaving of symbolic motives, a projected *ménage à trois*

involving himself, Clara, and (the memory of?) her dying husband (Reynolds, "A Choral Symphony by Brahms?," pp. 20–22).

64 William Ritter, "later one of Mahler's most devoted younger supporters," described the "Viennese themes" of the Fourth as so "'moist and persuasive, tantalizing and seductive' that they occasioned 'lewd glances in the concert hall, the salacious dribble at the corners of the mouths of some of the old men, and above all the ugly, whoring laughs of certain respectable women!'"(Franklin, *Mahler,* p. 133; see also La Grange, *Mahler I,* p. 404). Here, for once, it was not Mahler's Jewishness that was at stake, but the licentious influence of Vienna (Ritter was Swiss). The most likely backdrop for Ritter's observations is the opening soprano phrase of the finale, which sets "himmlischen Freuden" to a sensuously undulating melisma (mm. 13–14), undoubtedly meant to be more comforting than arousing. To an audience uncommitted to the nostalgic innocence Mahler intended, however, the phrase might be taken as a seductive come-on, with or without the subtle encouragement of the soloist.

Works Cited

Abbate, Carolyn. *Unsung Voices: Opera and Musical Narrative in the Nineteenth Century.* Princeton: Princeton University Press, 1991.

Abbate, Elizabeth. "Myth, Symbol, and Meaning in Mahler's Early Symphonies." Ph.D. diss., Harvard University, 1996.

Acocella, Joan. *Creating Hysteria: Women and Multiple Personality Disorder.* San Francisco: Jossey-Bass, 1999.

Adorno, Theodor W. "Mahler (Centenary Address, Vienna 1960)." In *Quasi una Fantasia: Essays on Modern Music,* translated by Rodney Livingstone. London and New York: Verso, 1998.

_____. *Mahler: A Musical Physiognomy.* Translated by Edmund Jephcott. Chicago: University of Chicago Press, 1992. Originally published as *Mahler: Eine musikalische Physiognomik* (Frankfurt am Main: Suhrkamp Verlag, 1971).

Allanbrook, Wye Jamison. *Rhythmic Gesture in Mozart: "Le nozze di Figaro" and "Don Giovanni."* Chicago: University of Chicago Press, 1983.

Allsburg, Chris van. *The Polar Express.* Boston, 1985.

Andersen, Hans Christian. *The Complete Illustrated Stories of Hans Christian Andersen.* Translated by H. W. Dulcken. London, 1983. Originally published as *Stories for the Household* (London, 1889).

Andree, Rolf. Introduction to *Arnold Böcklin.* London: Arts Council of Great Britain, 1971.

Applegate, Celia. "How German Is It? Nationalism and the Idea of Serious Music in the Early Nineteenth Century." *Nineteenth-Century Music* 21 (1998): 274–296.

Arnim, Achim, and Clemens Brentano. *Des Knaben Wunderhorn: Alte deutsche Lieder gesammelt von L. A. v. Arnim und Cl. Brentano, neu bearbeitet.* Edited by Anton Birlinger and Wilhelm Crecelius. 2 vols. Wiesbaden: Heinrich Killinger, 1874.

_____. *Des Knaben Wunderhorn.* Edited by Karl Bode. Berlin: Deutsches Verlagshaus Bong, 1916.

Bakhtin, Mikhail. "Discourse in the Novel." In *The Dialogic Imagination.* Austin: University of Texas Press, 1981.

Bauer-Lechner, Natalie. *Gustav Mahler in den Erinnerungen.* Edited by Herbert Killian and Knud Martner. Hamburg: Verlag der Musikalienhandlung Karl Dieter Wagner, 1984.

_____. *Recollections of Gustav Mahler.* Translated by Dika Newlin. Edited and annotated by Peter Franklin. Cambridge and New York: Cambridge University Press, 1980.

Bazin, André. *What Is Cinema?* Edited and translated by Hugh Gray. 2 vols. Berkeley: University of California Press, 1967–72.

Berio, Luciano. Liner notes to *Sinfonia.* Translated by John Underwood. With New Swingle Singers, Orchestre National de France, Pierre Boulez. Erato 2292-45228-2, 1986.

Bonds, Mark Evan. *After Beethoven: Imperatives of Originality in the Symphony.* Cambridge: Harvard University Press, 1996.

Buhler, James. "'Breakthrough' as Critique of Form: The Finale of Mahler's First Symphony." *Nineteenth-Century Music* 20 (1996): 125–143.

Christ, Dorothea, ed. *Arnold Böcklin, 1827–1901: Gemälde, Zeichnungen, Plastiken: Ausstellung zum 150. Geburtstag veranstaltet vom Kunstmuseum Basel und vom Basler Kunstverein 11. Juni–11. September 1977.* Basel: Kunstmuseum Basel, 1977.

Cone, Edward T. *The Composer's Voice.* Berkeley and Los Angeles: University of California Press, 1974.

Cooke, Deryck. *Gustav Mahler: An Introduction to his Music.* 2d ed. Cambridge and New York: Cambridge University Press, 1988.

Copland, Aaron. *Our New Music: Leading Composers in Europe and America.* New York: McGraw-Hill, 1941.

Dahlhaus, Carl. "The Natural World and the 'Folklike Tone.'" In *Realism in Nineteenth-Century Music,* translated by Mary Whittall. Cambridge: Cambridge University Press, 1985. Originally published as *Musikalischer Realismus: Zur Musikgeschichte des 19. Jahrhunderts* (Munich: R. Piper, 1982).

_____. *Nineteenth-Century Music.* Translated J. Bradford Robinson. Berkeley and Los Angeles: University of California Press, 1989.

_____. "The Twofold Truth in Wagner's Aesthetics: Nietzsche's Fragment 'On Music and Words.'" In *Between Romanticism and Modernism: Four Studies in the Music of the Later Nineteenth Century,* translated by Mary Whittall. Berkeley and Los Angeles: University of California Press, 1980.

Diether, Jack. Notes to *Levine Conducts Mahler: Symphony No. 4 in G.* Recording with the Chicago Symphony Orchestra, with Judith Blegen as soloist. RCA ARL1-0895, 1975.

Dijkstra, Bram. *Idols of Perversity: Fantasies of Feminine Evil in Fin-de-Siècle Culture.* New York: Oxford University Press, 1986.

Dowlding, William J. *Beatlesongs.* New York: Simon and Schuster, 1989.

Draughon, Francesca. "Mahler and the Music of *Fin-de-siècle* Identity." Ph.D. diss., University of California at Los Angeles, 2002.

Draughon, Francesca, and Raymond Knapp. "Mahler and the Crisis of Jewish Identity." *Echo* 3, no. 2, 2001. (www.echo.ucla.edu)

Eisenstein, Sergei. *Film Form: Essays in Film Theory.* Edited and translated by Jay Leyda. New York: Meridian Books, 1957.

Erk, Ludwig. *Deutscher Liederschatz.* Leipzig: C. F. Peters, n.d.

Filler, Susan M. "Editorial Problems in Symphonies of Gustav Mahler: A Study of the Sources of the Third and Tenth." Ph.D. diss., Northwestern University, 1976.

Finson, Jon W. "The Reception of Gustav Mahler's *Wunderhorn-Lieder.*" *Journal of Musicology* 5 (1987): 91–116.

Fischer, Lucy. "Film Editing." In *A Companion to Film Theory,* edited by Toby Miller and Robert Stam. Oxford: Blackwell, 1999.

Floros, Constantin. *Gustav Mahler: The Symphonies.* Translated by Vernon Wicker. Portland, Ore.: Amadeus Press, 1993.

Franklin, Peter. "'. . . His Fractures Are the Script of Truth': Adorno's Mahler." In *Mahler Studies,* edited by Stephen Hefling. Cambridge and New York: Cambridge University Press, 1997.

_____. *The Life of Mahler.* Cambridge and New York: Cambridge University Press, 1997.

_____. *Mahler: Symphony No. 3.* Cambridge and New York: Cambridge University Press, 1991.

Greene, David B. *Mahler: Consciousness and Temporality.* New York: Gordon and Breach Science Publishers, 1984.

Hacking, Ian. *Rewriting the Soul: Multiple Personality and the Sciences of Memory.* Princeton: Princeton University Press, 1995.

Hamburger, Paul. "Mahler and *Des Knaben Wunderhorn.*" In *The Mahler Companion,* edited by Donald Mitchell and Andrew Nicholson. New York and Oxford: Oxford University Press, 1999.

Handler, Andrew. *Blood Libel At Tiszaeszlar.* New York: Columbia University Press, 1980.

Hanslick, Eduard. *On the Musically Beautiful: A Contribution towards the Revision of the Aesthetics of Music.* Translated by Geoffrey Payzant. Indianapolis: Hackett, 1986.

Harry, Bill. *The Ultimate Beatles Encyclopedia.* New York: Hyperion, 1992.

Hayward, Susan. *Cinema Studies: The Key Concepts.* 2d ed. London and New York: Routledge, 2000.

Hefling, Stephen E. "Mahler: Symphonies 1–4." In *The Nineteenth-Century Symphony,* edited by D. Kern Holoman. New York: Schirmer Books, 1997.

_____. "Mahler's 'Todtenfeier' and the Problem of Program Music." *Nineteenth-Century Music* 12 (1988): 27–53.

_____. "'Variations *in nuce*': A Study of Mahler Sketches and a Comment on Sketch Studies." In *Beiträge '79–'81 der Österreichisten Gesellschaft für Musik.* Vol. 7, *Gustav Mahler Kolloquium 1979: Ein Bericht,* edited by Rudolf Klein. Kassel: Bärenreiter, 1981.

Jackson, Richard. *Popular Songs of Nineteenth-Century America: Complete Original Sheet Music for Sixty-Four Songs.* New York: Dover, 1976.

Jander, Owen. "The Prophetic Conversation in Beethoven's 'Scene by the Brook.'" *Musical Quarterly* 77 (1993): 508–559.

Kincaid, James R. *Child-Loving: The Erotic Child and Victorian Culture.* New York: Routledge, 1992.

Knapp, Raymond. "Brahms and the Anxiety of Allusion." *Journal of Musicological Research* 18 (1998): 1–30.

_____. *Brahms and the Challenge of the Symphony.* Stuyvesant, N.Y.: Pendragon Press, 1997.

_____. "On Reading Gender in Late Beethoven: *An die Freude* and *An die ferne Geliebte*" (forthcoming in *Acta musicologica*).

_____. "Suffering Children: Perspectives on Innocence and Vulnerability in Mahler's Fourth Symphony." *Nineteenth-Century Music* 22 (1999): 233–267.

_____. "A Tale of Two Symphonies: Converging Narratives of Divine Reconciliation in Beethoven's Fifth and Sixth." *Journal of the American Musicological Society* 53 (2000): 291–343.

_____. "Utopian Agendas: Variation, Allusion, and Referential Meaning in Brahms's Symphonies." In *Brahms Studies,* vol. 3, edited by David Brodbeck. Lincoln: University of Nebraska Press, 2001.

Knittel, K. M. "'Ein hypermoderner Dirigent': Mahler and Anti-Semitism in Fin-de-siècle Vienna," *Nineteenth-Century Music* 18, no. 3 (Spring 1995): 257–276.

Kramer, Lawrence. "Carnaval, Cross-Dressing, and the Woman in the Mirror." In *Musicology and Difference: Gender and Sexuality in Music Scholarship,* edited by Ruth A. Solie. Berkeley and Los Angeles: University of California Press, 1993.

_____. "The Harem Threshold: Turkish Music and Greek Love in Beethoven's 'Ode to Joy.'" *Nineteenth-Century Music* 22 (1998): 78–90.

Kuleshov, Lev. *Kuleshov on Film: Writings.* Edited and translated by Ronald Levaco. Berkeley: University of California Press, 1974.

_____. *Selected Works; Fifty Years in Films.* Edited by Ekaterina Khokhlova. Translated by Dmitri Agrachev and Nina Belenkaya. Moscow: Raduga, 1987.

La Grange, Henry-Louis de. *Mahler.* Vol. 1. Garden City, N.Y.: Doubleday, 1973.

_____. *Gustav Mahler.* Vol. 2, *The Years of Challenge (1897–1904).* Oxford: Oxford University Press, 1995. Revised, enlarged, updated, and translated from *Gustav Mahler: Chronique d'une vie* (Paris: Fayard, 1979–84).

Lea, Henry A. *Gustav Mahler: Man on the Margin.* Bonn: Bouvier, 1985.

Lenau, Nikolaus. "Der Postillion." In *Poems and Letters of Nikolaus Lenau,* edited by Winthrop H. Root. New York: Frederick Ungar, 1964.

Lennon, John, Paul McCartney, George Harrison, and Richard Starkey. *The Beatles Complete Scores.* Transcribed by Tetsuya Fujita, Yuji Hagino, Hajime Kubo, and Goro Sato. Milwaukee: Hal Leonard and Wise Publications, 1989 and 1993.

Lerner, Laurence. *Angels and Absences: Child Deaths in the Nineteenth Century.* Nashville: Vanderbilt University Press, 1997.

Lewisohn, Mark. *The Complete Beatles Chronicle.* New York: Harmony Books, 1992.

Mahler, Alma. *Gustav Mahler: Erinnerungen und Briefe.* Amsterdam: Allert de Lange, 1940.

_____. *Gustav Mahler: Memories and Letters.* Revised and edited by Donald Mitchell. Translated by Basil Creighton. London: John Murray, 1968.

Mahler, Gustav. *Gustav Mahler Briefe, Neuausgabe.* Edited by Herta Blaukopf. Vienna: Paul Zsolnay Verlag, 1982.

_____. *Gustav Mahler: Symphony No. 4 in G.* With Willem Mengelberg, Jo Vincent, and the Concertgebouw Orchestra. Phillips 416 211-2, 1997 (reissue from 1939).

_____. *Levine Conducts Mahler: Symphony No. 4 in G.* With James Levine, Judith Blegen, and the Chicago Symphony Orchestra. Notes by Jack Diether. RCA ARL1-0895, 1975.

_____. *Mahler: Des Knaben Wunderhorn.* With Christa Ludwig, Walter Berry, Leonard Bernstein, and the New York Philharmonic. Sony Classical SMK 47590, 1993.

_____. *Mahler: Kindertotenlieder, 5 Rückertlieder, and Lieder eines fahrenden Gesellen.* With Janet Baker, John Barbirolli, and the Hallé Orchestra. EMI Classics 7243 5 66981 2 3, 1999.

_____. *Mahler: The Symphonies, Volume 1 (Symphonies 1–4).* With Georg Solti and the Chicago Symphony Orchestra. Second Symphony with Isobel Buchanan, Mira Zakai and the Chicago Symphony Chorus. Third Symphony with Helga Dernesch, Women of the Chicago Symphony Chorus, and the Glen Ellyn Children's Chorus. Fourth Symphony with Kiri Te Kanawa. Decca 430 804-2, 1991.

_____. *Mahler: Symphony No. 4.* With Simon Rattle, Amanda Roocroft, and the City of Birmingham Symphony Orchestra. Notes by Simon Rattle. EMI Classics 7243 5 56563 2 2, 1997.

_____. *Selected Letters of Gustav Mahler.* Edited by Knud Martner. Translated by Eithne Wilkins, Ernst Kaiser, and Bill Hopkins. New York: Farrar, Straus, Giroux, 1979.

Mahler, Gustav, et al. *Lieder aus "Des Knaben Wunderhorn": Mahler, Brahms, Mendelssohn, Strauss, Schumann, Loewe, Schönberg, Weber, Zemlinsky.* With Thomas Hampson and Geoffrey Parsons. Teldec Classics 244 923-2 ZK, 1989.

McClary, Susan. *Feminine Endings: Music, Gender, and Sexuality.* Minnesota: University of Minnesota Press, 1991.

_____. "The Impromptu That Trod on a Loaf: How Music Tells Stories." *Narrative* 5, no. 1 (January 1997): 20–34.

_____. "Narratives of Bourgeois Subjectivity in Mozart's 'Prague' Symphony." In *Understanding Narrative,* edited by Peter Rabinowitz and James Phelan. Columbus: Ohio State University Press, 1994.

_____. "Pitches, Expression, Ideology: An Exercise in Mediation." *Enclitic* 7 (1983): 76–86.

 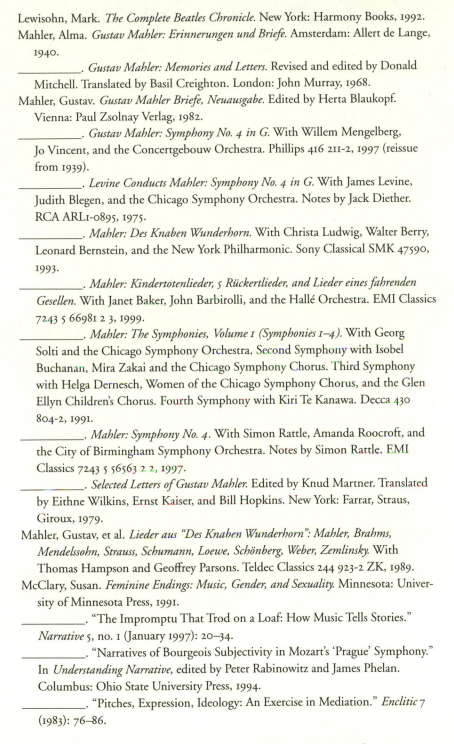

McGrath, William. "Mahler and Freud: The Dream of the Stately House." In *Beiträge '79–'81 der Österreichisten Gesellschaft für Musik.* Vol. 7, *Gustav Mahler Kolloquium 1979: Ein Bericht,* edited by Rudolf Klein. Kassel: Bärenreiter, 1981.

_____. "The Metamusical Cosmos of Gustav Mahler." In *Dionysian Art and Populist Politics in Austria.* New Haven: Yale University Press, 1974.

Mitchell, Donald. *Gustav Mahler: The Wunderhorn Years, Chronicles and Commentaries.* London: Faber and Faber, 1975.

_____. "'Swallowing the Programme': Mahler's Fourth Symphony." In *The Mahler Companion,* edited by Donald Mitchell and Andrew Nicholson. Oxford and New York: Oxford University Press, 1999.

Monelle, Raymond. *The Sense of Music: Semiotic Essays.* Princeton: Princeton University Press, 2000.

Moretti, Franco. *Modern Epic: The World-System from Goethe to García Márquez.* Translated by Quintin Hoare. London and New York: Verso, 1996. Originally published as *Opere Mondo: saggio sulla forma epica dal "Faust" a "Cent'anni di solitudine"* (Turin: Einaudi, 1994).

Nelson, Thomas K. "The Fantasy of Absolute Music." Ph.D. diss., University of Minnesota, 1998.

Newcomb, Anthony. "Narrative Archetypes and Mahler's Ninth Symphony." In *Music and Text: Critical Inquiries,* edited by Steven Paul Scher. Cambridge and New York: Cambridge University Press, 1992.

Nowak, Adolf. "Zur Deutung der Dritten und Vierten Sinfonie Gustav Mahlers." In *Gustav Mahler,* edited by Hermann Danuser. Vol. 653 of *Wege der Forschung.* Darmstadt: Wissenschaftliche Buchgesellschaft, 1992. Reprinted from *Religiöse Musik in nicht-liturgischen werken von Beethoven bis Reger,* edited by Walter Wiora, vol. 51 of *Studien zur Musikgeschichte des 19. Jahrhunderts* (Regensburg: Gustav Bosse Verlag, 1978).

Olsen, Morten Solvik. "Culture and the Creative Imagination: The Genesis of Gustav Mahler's Third Symphony." Ph.D. diss., University of Pennsylvania, 1992.

Osmond-Smith, David. *Playing on Words: A Guide to Luciano Berio's "Sinfonia."* London: Royal Music Association, 1985.

Page, Chris. "Leonard Bernstein and the Resurrection of Gustav Mahler." Ph.D. diss., University of California, Los Angeles, 2000.

Palmer, John R. "Program and Process in the Second Symphony of Gustav Mahler." Ph.D. diss., University of California, Davis, 1996.

Pederson, Sanna. "A. B. Marx, Berlin Concert Life, and German National Identity." *Nineteenth-Century Music* 18 (1994): 87–107.

Pohl, Claudia. "Subjekt und Ideal." In *A. Böcklin, 1827–1901: Ausstellung zum 150. Geburtstag veranstaltet vom Magistrat der Stadt Darmstadt: Darmstadt, Matildenhöhe, 23. Oktober bis 11 Dezember 1977,* edited by Bernd Krimmel, with Eva Huber, Claudia Pohl, and Brigitte Rechberg. [Darmstadt,] 1977.

Pudovkin, V. I. *Film Technique and Film Acting.* Translated and edited by Ivor Montagu. London: Vision Press, 1958.

Putnam, Frank. *Diagnosis and Treatment of Multiple Personality Disorder.* New York: Guilford, 1989.

Rattle, Simon. Notes to *Mahler: Symphony No. 4.* Recording of Simon Rattle conducting the City of Birmingham Symphony Orchestra, with Amanda Roocroft as soloist. EMI Classics 7243 5 56563 2 2, 1997.

Reik, Theodor. *The Haunting Melody: Psychoanalytic Experiences in Life and Music.* New York: Farrar, Straus, and Young, 1953.

Reynolds, Christopher. "A Choral Symphony by Brahms?" *Nineteenth-Century Music* 9 (1985–86): 3–25.

Ringer, Alexander. "'Lieder eines fahrenden Gesellen': Allusion und Zitat in der Musikalischen Erzählung Gustav Mahlers." In *Das musikalische Kunstwerk: Geschichte, Ästhetik, Theorie: Festschrift Carl Dahlhaus zum 60. Geburtstag,* edited by Hermann Danuser, Helga de la Motte-Haber, Silke Leopold, and Norbert Miller. Laaber: Laaber-Verlag, 1988.

Röhrich, Lutz. "Freund Hein." In *Lexikon der sprichwörtlichen Redensarten,* vol. 2. Freiburg: Verlag Herder, 1982.

_____. "Himmel." In *Lexikon der sprichwörtlichen Redensarten,* vol. 2. 3d ed. Freiburg: Verlag Herder, 1994.

Rosen, Charles. *The Classical Style: Haydn, Mozart, Beethoven.* New York: W. W. Norton, 1972.

Schiff, David. "Jewish and Musical Tradition in the Music of Mahler and Schoenberg." *Journal of the Arnold Schoenberg Institute* 9, no. 2 (November 1986): 217–231.

Schoenberg, Arnold. "Gustav Mahler (1912 and 1948)." In *Style and Idea,* edited by Leonard Stein, translated by Leo Black. London: Faber, 1975.

_____. "Gustav Mahler: In Memoriam (1912)." In *Style and Idea,* edited by Leonard Stein, translated by Leo Black. London: Faber, 1975.

Schopenhauer, Arthur. *The World as Will and Representation.* 2 vols. Translated by E. J. F. Payne. New York: Dover, 1966.

Schorske, Carl E. *Fin-de-siècle Vienna: Politics and Culture.* New York: Vintage Books, 1981.

_____. "Gustav Mahler: Formation and Transformation." In *Thinking with History: Explorations in the Passage to Modernism.* Princeton: Princeton University Press, 1998.

Schreiber, Flora Rheta. *Sybil.* New York: Warner Books, 1973.

Smith, Warren Storey. "Mahler Quotes Mahler." *Chord and Discord* 2, no. 7 (1954): 7–13.

_____. "Song Is the Basic Element of the Vast Symphonic Structures Mahler Created." *Musical America* 80 (February 1960): 10, 174.

Solomon, Maynard. "The Ninth Symphony: A Search for Order." In *Beethoven Essays.* Cambridge: Harvard University Press, 1988. Originally published as "Beethoven's Ninth Symphony: A Search for Order," *Nineteenth-Century Music* 10 (1986): 3–23.

Tibbe, Monika. *Über die Verwendung von Liedern und Liedelementen in instrumentalen Symphoniesätzen Gustav Mahlers.* Munich: Musikverlag Emil Katzbichler, 1971.

Tovey, Donald Francis. "Beethoven, Ninth Symphony in D Minor, Op. 125: Its Place in Musical Art." In *Essays in Musical Analysis: Symphonies and other Orchestral Works*. London: Oxford University Press, 1981.

Treitler, Leo. "History, Criticism, and Beethoven's Ninth Symphony." In *Music and the Historical Imagination*. Cambridge: Harvard University Press, 1989. Reprinted from *Nineteenth-Century Music* 3 (1980): 193–210.

Wagner, Richard. *Das Kunstwerk der Zukunft*. In vol. 6 of *Richard Wagner: Dichtungen und Schriften*, 10 vols., edited by Dieter Borchmeyer. Frankfurt: Insel Verlag, 1983.

_____. *Oper und Drama*. Part I. In vol. 7 of *Richard Wagner: Dichtungen und Schriften*, 10 vols, edited by Dieter Borchmeyer. Frankfurt: Insel Verlag, 1983.

Walter, Bruno. *Gustav Mahler*. Translated by James Galston. New York: Da Capo Press, 1970.

Whaples, Miriam. "Mahler and Schubert's A Minor Sonata D. 784." *Music and Letters* 65 (1984): 255–263.

Winter, Robert S. "The Bifocal Close and the Evolution of the Viennese Classical Style." *Journal of the American Musicological Society* 42 (1989): 275–337.

Wistrich, Robert S. *The Jews of Vienna in the Age of Franz Joseph*. Oxford and New York: Oxford University Press, 1989.

Wolff, Larry. *Postcards from the End of the World: Child Abuse in Freud's Vienna*. New York: Atheneum, 1988.

Youens, Susan. "Schubert, Mahler, and the Weight of the Past: *Lieder eines fahrenden Gesellen* and *Winterreise*." *Music and Letters* 67 (Winter 1986): 48–61.

Zaslaw, Neal. *Mozart's Symphonies: Context, Performance Practice, Reception*. Oxford and New York: Oxford University Press and Clarendon Press, 1989.

Zenck, Claudia. "Technik und Gehalt im Scherzo von Mahlers Zweiter Symphonie." *Melos/Neue Zeitschrift für Musik* 2 (May–June 1976): 179–184.

Zola, Émile. *Abbé Mouret's Transgression*. Translated by Ernest Alfred Vizetelly. New York: Marion, 1915. Originally published as *La faute de L'Abbé Mouret*, 1874.

Zychowicz, James L. *Mahler's Fourth Symphony*. Oxford and New York: Oxford University Press, 2000.

_____. "Mahler's Motives and Motivation in His 'Resurrection' Symphony: The Apotheosis of Hans Rott." Paper read at the Annual Meeting of the American Musicological Society, Minneapolis, Minn., November 1994.

_____. "Sketches and Drafts of Gustav Mahler, 1892–1901: The Sources of the Fourth Symphony." Ph.D. diss., University of Cincinnati, 1988.

Index

Raymond Knapp is Professor of Musicology at University of California at Los Angeles and author of *Brahms and the Challenge of the Symphony* (1997). He has a PhD. in musicology from Duke University, an MA from Radford University, and his BA from Harvard University. His articles have appeared in *Nineteenth-Century Music, The Journal of the American Musicological Society, The Journal of Musicological Research,* and *Brahms Studies,* among others.

MUSIC/CULTURE
A series from Wesleyan University Press
Edited by George Lipsitz, Susan McClary, and Robert Walser

My Music
by Susan D. Crafts, Daniel Cavicchi,
Charles Keil, and the Music in Daily
Life Project

Running with the Devil:
Power, Gender, and Madness
in Heavy Metal Music
by Robert Walser

Subcultural Sounds:
Micromusics of the West
by Mark Slobin

Upside Your Head!
Rhythm and Blues on
Central Avenue
by Johnny Otis

Dissonant Identities:
The Rock 'n' Roll Scene in
Austin, Texas
by Barry Shank

Black Noise:
Rap Music and Black Culture
in Contemporary America
by Tricia Rose

Club Cultures:
Music, Media, and
Sub-Cultural Capital
by Sarah Thornton

Music, Society, Education
by Christopher Small

Listening to Salsa:
Gender, Latin Popular Music,
and Puerto Rican Cultures
by Frances Aparicio

Any Sound You Can Imagine:
Making Music/Consuming
Technology
by Paul Théberge

Voices in Bali:
Energies and Perceptions in Vocal
Music and Dance Theater
by Edward Herbst

Popular Music in Theory
by Keith Negus

A Thousand Honey Creeks Later:
My Life in Music from Basie to
Motown—and Beyond
by Preston Love

Musicking:
The Meanings of Performing
and Listening
by Christopher Small

Music of the Common Tongue:
Survival and Celebration in
African American Music
by Christopher Small

Singing Archaeology:
Philip Glass's Akhnaten
by John Richardson

Library of Congress Cataloging-in-Publication Data

Knapp, Raymond
   Symphonic metamorphoses : subjectivity and alienation in Mahler's re-cycled songs /
by Raymond Knapp.
      p. cm.
Includes bibliographical references and index.
ISBN 0-8195-6635-7 (cloth : alk. paper) — ISBN 0-8195-6636-5 (pbk. : alk. paper)
 1. Mahler, Gustav, 1860–1911. Symphonies. 2. Maher, Gustav, 1860–1911 Songs.
3. Subjectivity in music. 4. Alienation (Philosophy) 5. Quotation in music. I. Title.

ML410.M23K63 2003
784.2'184'092—dc21   2003045094